PRINCE'S MINNEAPOLIS

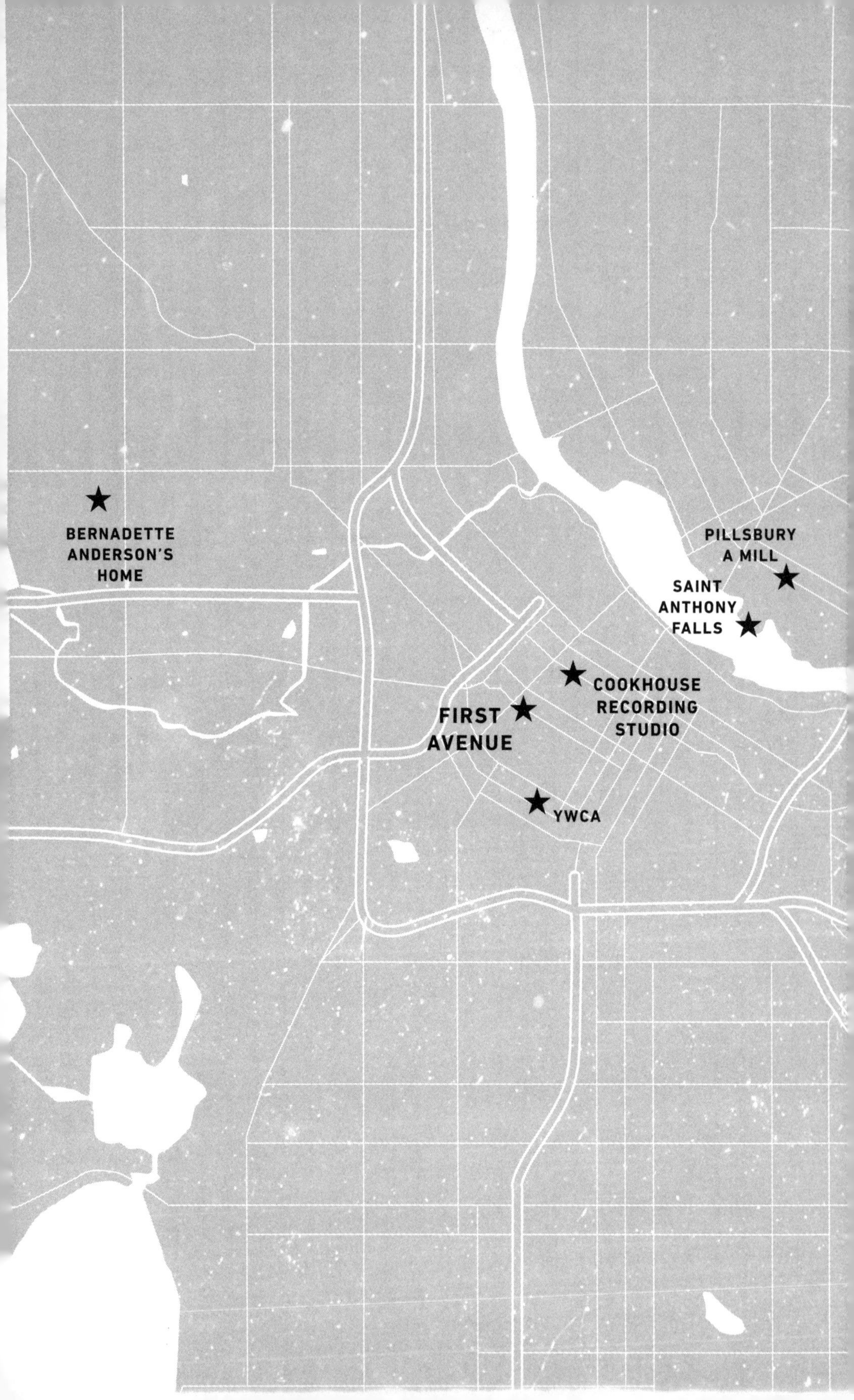
BERNADETTE ANDERSON'S HOME
PILLSBURY A MILL
SAINT ANTHONY FALLS
COOKHOUSE RECORDING STUDIO
FIRST AVENUE
YWCA

Prince's MINNEAPOLIS

A BIOGRAPHY OF SOUND & PLACE

★

Rashad Shabazz

The University of North Carolina Press
CHAPEL HILL

This book was published with the assistance of the Anniversary Fund of the University of North Carolina Press.

Manufactured in the United States of America

Designed by Lindsay Starr
Set in Quadraat Pro, Cheddar Sans Italic, and
Hello Bloomie Script by codeMantra

Cover art: *Prince Portrait* by Vectorportal.com.
Map by Panzadesign/stock.adobe.com.

Library of Congress Cataloging-in-Publication Data
Names: Shabazz, Rashad, 1976– author
Title: Prince's Minneapolis : a biography of sound and place / Rashad Shabazz.
Description: Chapel Hill : University of North Carolina Press, [2026] |
Includes bibliographical references and index.
Identifiers: LCCN 2025037604 | ISBN 9781469690940 cloth alk. paper |
ISBN 9781469690957 paperback alk. paper | ISBN 9781469683256 epub |
ISBN 9781469690964 pdf
Subjects: LCSH: Prince | Musicians—Minnesota—Minneapolis—Biography |
Popular music—Minnesota—Minneapolis—History and criticism |
African Americans—Minnesota—Minneapolis—Music—
History and criticism | LCGFT: Biographies
Classification: LCC ML420.P974 S515 2026 |
DDC 781.6409776/579 [B]—dc23/eng/20250827
LC record available at https://lccn.loc.gov/2025037604

Parts of this book were previously published in Rashad Shabazz, "Prince & Place," *Places Journal*, November 2021, https://doi.org/10.22269/211130.

For product safety concerns under the European Union's General Product Safety Regulation (EU GPSR), please contact gpsr@mare-nostrum.co.uk or write to the University of North Carolina Press and Mare Nostrum Group B.V., Mauritskade 21D, 1091 GC Amsterdam, The Netherlands.

Records can be like maps.

—Martin Keller

Music is prophecy. Its styles . . . are ahead of the rest of society because it explores much faster than material reality, the entire range of possibilities.

—Jacques Attali

Minneapolis is totally out of touch with the rest of the country.

—Terry Lewis

CONTENTS

ILLUSTRATIONS

PREFACE

'Cause I Was Your Boyfriend

My undergraduate girlfriend, Stephanie, is the reason this book exists. She reintroduced me to Prince in my late teens, and that experience not only made me a fan of his music but also interested in and curious about the city that raised him.

I first heard Prince's music in 1982 while living with my mother in San Jose, California. One day, as I rode in my mother's green Vega, "Little Red Corvette" pulsed from the radio. I was six years old and completely mesmerized by it. I loved its catchy lyrics and funky groove. It captured me. Whenever I listen to this song, it takes me back to San Jose and reminds me of the smell of the air and the look of the sky.

Two years later, Prince reentered my life with the release of *Purple Rain*, which took the music world by storm. Like many others, I was overwhelmed by the excitement of the film and the album. However, I moved away from his music after the hype died down. My musical tastes shifted toward rap by the late 1980s and early 1990s, with artists like Boogie Down Productions, A Tribe Called Quest, and Ice Cube. Prince's unique sound mix didn't fit my pre-teen musical preferences. While I still listened to him from time to time, he wasn't a top priority for me. As I entered my late teens, I went years without listening to his music and instead focused on genres like rap, R&B, alternative rock, and jazz. Prince's music was absent from my life during this time.

In the mid-1990s, my life took a turn when I enrolled at Southwest State University in Marshall, Minnesota. There, I met Stephanie, a beautiful redbone girl from the Rondo neighborhood in St. Paul. Stephanie was a true Minnesotan, born and raised in the city near Grand Avenue. We had a friendly debate about the better musician: Michael Jackson (my pick at the time) or Prince (her favorite). We spent hours proving to each other whose favorite artist was better. I believed Michael Jackson was the best at the time due to his album *Thriller*. However, Stephanie argued that Prince had more talent than Michael, which I found improbable. Who could sing and dance better than the King of Pop? *Thriller* sold over 100 million copies—case closed. For her, Prince's ability to play multiple instruments and compose music made him peerless. A stalemate ensued; I maintained my position, and so did she.

However, my views on Prince changed when Stephanie made me listen to Prince's album *Sign o' the Times*. At that time, I had never heard of the record, which was about eight or nine years old. On our next visit to her parents' home in St. Paul, Stephanie took me to a local record store where she bought a cassette of the album. She played it throughout the weekend while we hung out at Prince's former club, Glam Slam, which was renamed The Quest, and the Gay '90s in downtown Minneapolis. Although I don't recall my initial feelings toward it, I remember being amazed by how it sounded. The album was funky, rocky, and a bit futuristic. When Stephanie explained what Prince was doing on "If I Was Your Girlfriend," I was blown away. "The Ballad of Dorothy Parker" was a bit too sophisticated for my musical taste then, but I still enjoyed it. However, the final song on the album, "Adore," cemented my love for it and for Prince himself. It was the sexiest, most sultry thing I had ever heard—the talking and singing, the instrumentation, and the groove were all perfect. It was Stephanie's favorite song on the album and soon became mine.

In a matter of weeks, I found myself listening to *Sign* and his four compact discs: *The Hits/The B-Sides*, *Diamonds and Pearls*, and even *Purple Rain*. I was introduced to his early work when I listened to *1999* for the first time. Stephanie informed me that he also wrote pop songs for other artists such as Chaka Khan and The Bangles and composed the late Sinead O'Connor's hit "Nothing Compares to U." His music captivated me. I couldn't believe the diversity of his sound. Though I still loved Michael Jackson, he gradually faded from my daily playlist as more and more Prince songs took up space. It didn't take long for me to realize that Stephanie was right—Prince was truly one-of-a-kind, with no peers (with no disrespect to the King of Pop). His ability to blend forms of pop music and create something new was unparalleled.

After transferring to Minnesota State University, Mankato, during my junior year of college, Stephanie and I ended our relationship. We went our separate ways and eventually lost touch. However, my love for Prince continued to grow stronger. I found myself reading magazine articles and books about him, listening to his music whenever possible, and grabbing tickets to his shows. By the time I reached my mid-twenties, I was a dedicated Prince fan.

I always wanted to thank Stephanie for introducing me to Prince. 'Cause I was her boyfriend, I was fortunate enough to have been exposed to countless hours of Prince's music, which touched not only my life but also that of my children, loved ones, and students. Stephanie was unaware that I saw him perform live at Paisley Park in a room with only forty or fifty people. Additionally, I never mentioned to her that I had seen him perform three times and that I even chose to get married to the song "Venus De Milo" from his 1986 album, *Parade*. 'Cause I was her boyfriend, I spent years researching Prince's life, music, and the city he remained loyal to.

Thank you, Stephanie. 'Cause I was your boyfriend, Prince, and Minneapolis, came into my life and made this book possible.

Tempe, AZ

PRINCE'S MINNEAPOLIS

INTRODUCTION

This Is Not the Kind of Music That Comes from Minneapolis

January 26, 1980, was a monumental day in Prince's career. On that day, the nineteen-year-old and his mixed-race and mixed-gender band were in Los Angeles performing on Dick Clark's iconic music program, *American Bandstand*. Prince lip-synced "I Wanna Be Your Lover" off his sophomore album, *Prince*.

The young composer, who'd signed with a major recording label just two years earlier, was on the most-watched music program in the country. Millions were tuning in. Nailing the performance would grease the wheels of stardom. Falling flat would make the journey that much harder.

As Prince and his band mimicked playing the song's final notes, thunderous applause erupted from the teenage crowd, and a star was born. For many fans and critics, this performance is one of his most important because it set him on a path to superstardom; the skyrocketing of his career and the sound associated with him was, in a sense, cemented through that January performance. For me, the performance remains pivotal not for its pop-cultural significance but for what it reveals about Prince and his hometown and, by extension, about the geography of music.

Clark thought Prince was great. But he had a hard time reconciling Prince's sound with Minneapolis. Indeed, the sonic marriage in "I Wanna Be Your Lover" of funk and disco, with bright, taut guitar riffs, pulsating synthesizer chords, falsetto vocals over subtle funky bass, and an electronic drum machine pattern (done by Prince), surprised Clark. After the performance, the astonished Southern California host interviewed the shy Minneapolitan:

> Clark: Where'd you learn to do this in Minneapolis?
>
> Prince: Where?
>
> Clark: Yeah, I mean, this is not the kind of music that comes from Minneapolis, Minnesota.
>
> Prince: No.[1]

The painfully awkward interview, full of one-word answers from Prince, illustrates this point precisely. Clark couldn't understand how Prince could make such music from Minneapolis. Something in the vein of Bob Dylan—folksy, bluesy tunes—made more sense to him than the funky disco-pop Prince performed.

The exchange between Prince and Clark reveals that nothing musical happens in a placeless vacuum. However, it may sometimes seem that way for listeners used to endlessly shareable recordings. Place isn't just a background for making or transmitting music. On the contrary, space and place are "formative sounding and resounding of music."[2] And, of course, physical locations don't exist in vacuums either. They are shaped by sound as much as by social forces like racism and poverty.

This book is a geographic look at the music Prince made famous—the Minneapolis Sound. If you've never heard the term "Minneapolis Sound" before, it describes Prince's specific sound. You know it when you listen to songs like "1999," "If I Was Your Girlfriend," "Raspberry Beret," or "Purple Rain." Its signature is its unique fusion of funk, R&B, rock, synth-pop, punk, and new wave into a pop music format. This is achieved through tight guitar riffs, understated bass lines, drum machines, synthesizers instead of horns, and falsetto vocals. But the Minneapolis Sound is more than a description of Prince's music or the musical ecosystem he created. Minneapolis Sound is also a way of talking about history, music, and place. It's a way of talking about how this iconic music that filled parties and lubricated good times has a "hidden history" of violently forcing Indigenous people off the land to create a mill town. Minneapolis Sound was the soundtrack of white settlement, the mass migration of Scandinavian, German, Jewish, and Black people, as well as white Northeasterners, and the musical high cultural bona fides it enabled. Minneapolis Sound is the early twentieth-century school-based music training that forged unusually high levels of musical literacy. It's the racially segregated place where Black musicians flourished and the postindustrial city where an influential punk and indie rock scene emerged in the late 1970s and '80s. The Minneapolis Sound is all these things because all these things shaped and informed it. And if we understand its hidden history, we can hear these influences in Prince's music. The Minneapolis Sound is not lyrical but sonic. They are rooted in chord progressions, instrumentation, tempo, harmony, and rhythm; they are heard in the vocal arrangements and overall fusion of his compositions. This book uncovers that hidden history.

Prince's Minneapolis demonstrates how music shaped the creation of Minneapolis and how Minneapolis shaped music. It reveals how Prince came to play his unique mix of music and investigates how it emerged in the racially vanilla former flour milling capital of the world. It describes the emergence of Minneapolis's soundscape—born of land theft and violence; raised on mass migration, music education, and racial segregation; and evolved through sonic innovations on the Black and white sides of the color line. It details how a gifted young Black musician from the city's Near North Side, whose talents were cultivated in that same sonic milieu, mined it to create a new Minneapolis Sound and how doing so made him a superstar and the city's sound the zeitgeist of popular music.

This book is not just about Prince; it's about the music he popularized and how it came to be. Unbeknownst to many, the Minneapolis Sound did not begin with Prince. Many fans and "Prince scholars" attribute the birth of the Minneapolis Sound to tracks like "I Wanna Be Your Lover." Those songs were examples of when Minneapolis-inspired compositions entered the popular soundscape. Prince was the Minneapolis Sound's most important composer. He gave the sound color and distinction, harmony, and form. He was its high priest and the singular figure who impacted it more than anyone. But he was not its progenitor. Making Prince the inventor of the Minneapolis Sound is like making Beethoven the inventor of classical music or Mary J. Blige the creator of hip-hop soul. These artists are exquisite practitioners of their craft—arguably the best, respectively. However, the sonic traditions that formed the music they trailblazed are much older than these musical giants. The Minneapolis Sound came along before Prince's birth.

The Minneapolis Sound was born alongside the city in 1849—the year St. Anthony, which would eventually become part of Minneapolis, was founded. It reached its sonic peak in 1987 when Prince released arguably the most remarkable double album ever and a masterpiece of the Minneapolis Sound—*Sign o' the Times*. Over this period, I highlight this hidden history and the sound's birth, growth, evolution, and rise to popularity. *Prince's Minneapolis* demonstrates how the place where Prince was born and raised—Minneapolis—was instrumental in creating his sound. Prince's sound is a testament to his musical genius and unparalleled work ethic. But Prince's sound encompasses more than his talent and achievements. Listening to him, we can immerse ourselves in a soundscape nurtured by unique historical economies, migrations, racial politics, public policies, education, and social interactions.

Prince

Even with all the interviews coming out after his death, understanding Prince is like trying to hold on to air: We can feel it, but we can't grasp it. He was and will always be an enigma, full of personas and personalities we can only glimpse. No research on him will ever change that fact. Prince told stories about himself from a slanted angle—"My mother is a mixture of many things," he told *Rolling Stone* in 1983.[3] She was not. These stories make biographies of him packed with inconsistencies, contradictions, kaleidoscopes, and masks he wore often. Writing on Prince is engaging in his "kayfabe," or pretend persona.[4] Prince never lifted the curtain to let people see the real person. "I used to tease journalists early on," Prince once said.[5] Revolution guitarist Wendy Melvoin, who worked alongside Prince from 1983 to 1987, says he had "an extraordinary ability to compartmentalize his inner world," often telling her, "I'm whatever you want me to be." Even his longtime tour manager Alan Leeds said, "It was hard to determine sometimes what the real Prince was."[6]

Then how do you write about a person we can never fully grasp? Focus on the one thing he was always transparent about—his music. He told journalist Chris Heath, "There's not much I want [the public] to know about me, other than the music."[7] When a journalist from *The Guardian* asked him how he wanted to be remembered, he said one word: "Music."[8]

Prince's Minneapolis does that. I focus on how Prince created his endless mix of innovative, groundbreaking, funky sounds and the role of his hometown in their creation.

Place

Music, like all elements of life on Earth, is spatial. And to understand music, to make sense of its harmony, rhythm, melody, instrumentation, tempos, chord progressions, and sound, is to know its geography. For over a century, scholars have studied the place of music.[9] Their research has shown that how we hear, interpret, evaluate, and engage with music is marked by geography. "Music does not exist in a vacuum," argue geographers John Connell and Chris Gibson. Like race, gender, class, and sexuality, music and space create each other. In other words, "Music shapes spaces, and spaces shape music."[10]

Musicologists, journalists, and scholars have written much about what makes Prince's music unique. They have talked about his mix of genres, uses of instruments, arrangements, the colors and tones he uses in his compositions, their sparseness, and their vocal arrangements. What they haven't done is explore the place of his music. How did Minneapolis inform his sound? What was it about that "vanilla city" that enabled his musical flavors?[11] And how did the city develop them? In answering these and other questions, I show how understanding Minneapolis is essential to understanding Prince's sound.

According to Prince's childhood friend and music collaborator Terry Lewis—half of the music-producing duo Jam & Lewis—Minneapolis's being "out of touch with the rest of the country" played an essential role in fostering Prince's sound.[12] Minneapolis only had one low-wattage Black radio station, which forced Black kids like him to embrace rock music. The city didn't have music genres that dominated the soundscape, like Chicago (the blues) or L.A. (rock), creating a wide-open musical landscape for kids like Prince to create. Against the backdrop of universal music education in the city's public schools and valuing music as a cultural tool that went back to the period of Indian removal, Minneapolis indeed had a unique musical geography. *Prince's Minneapolis* shows how the city's marginality made it a gateway for musical innovation.

Tracing Hidden Histories

Decades before Prince performed on *American Bandstand*, the Minneapolis Sound began its "long fetch."[13] When it crashed "like a wave" in living rooms via *American Bandstand*, the public assumed that the young feather-haired Minneapolitan was its beginning.[14] Like the wave, he was the mysterious force that brought it ashore. This book goes back to the city's founding in 1849 to trace the influences and "hidden histories" that birthed it and to connect them to that fateful day in January 1980.[15]

Tracing hidden histories is different from historicizing them. My approach is informed by the French theorist Michel Foucault. His studies of sex, prison technologies, medicine, madness, and knowledge aimed to understand "the exercise of power."[16] Despite his writing "histories," Foucault was not a historian. He was a genealogist. Genealogy is a method of investigating the past. It seeks to understand the emergence of a phenomenon like the birth of the prison or the creation of academic disciplines.[17]

I trace the hidden history of the Minneapolis Sound from its emergence in the nineteenth century to its peak in the late 1980s. This approach allows me to follow its evolutions over extended periods and recognize how things like settler colonialism, racial segregation, the decline of the mill economy, and public education shaped the sonic landscape Prince drew on to create his sound.

Sequencing

Tracing the hidden history of the Minneapolis Sound requires thoughtful unfolding. Prince's longtime recording engineer, Susan Rogers, said sequencing an album is vital to the listening experience.[18] The same is true of books. *Prince's Minneapolis* is sequenced into four parts. Part 1 has two chapters. Chapter 1 traces the birth of the Minneapolis Sound from the city's white settlement period in the mid-nineteenth century through the development of its musical infrastructure, mass migration, and the growth of its mill economy by the end of the century. Chapter 2 works backward from chapter 1 and gives context for the city's birth. Minneapolis was born from a waterfall, the only one on the Mississippi River. This chapter shows how a Belgian priest who stumbled across it in 1680 set off a scramble for the resource-rich area that forever changed the region and created the city of Minneapolis.

Part 2 has three chapters. Spanning from the dawn of the twentieth century to the 1950s, they trace the Minneapolis Sound's growth. Chapter 3 tells how a zealot for music education, Thaddeus Philander Giddings, used his position as the superintendent of music education to create music literacy for the city's 50,000 students by making music education compulsory. Despite democratizing music education, the city's residents didn't play in the same band. With an eye on Prince's family, chapter 4 explores how anti-Black racism toward migrants fostered racial segregation in Minneapolis. Racially restrictive housing covenants baked into the housing system carved up the city along the color line in the years between the wars. Chapter 5 shows how these racially segregated landscapes created racially, geographically, and musically distinct versions of the Minneapolis Sound.

Part 3 has four chapters and spans the years between 1950 and Prince's high school graduation in 1976. Using his family as an anchor, chapter 6 traces the roles racial segregation and structural racism played in developing

Minneapolis's Black Sound—chapters 7 and 8 spotlight Prince's musical evolution by identifying the places where it happened. Chapter 7 traces this through his middle and high school years, with attention paid to his teachers and the music rooms he spent much time in. Chapter 8 traces his evolution through basements, the backroom of a community center, and local music studios. Chapter 9 explores the hidden history of indie rock, punk, and new wave development in downtown Minneapolis and its role in creating the city's most iconic musical venue, First Avenue & 7th Street Entry.

The book's final section has six chapters. They focus on the period between 1977 and 1987. These chapters show how Prince drew on the unique sonic landscape of his out-of-touch-with-the-rest-of-the-country hometown to create some of the century's most dynamic and cutting-edge pop music. In this section, I trace how the Minneapolis Sound rose to pop music prominence. Chapters 10 and 11 show how Prince mined his hometown to create a different type of sound. Chapter 12 spotlights how Prince and the Minneapolis Sound reached the peak of pop culture through the album and movie *Purple Rain*. Chapter 13 sees Prince moving in a more experimental direction to escape the trappings of his blockbuster album. The penultimate chapter shows how Prince brought the heterodox sonic geography of his hometown together to push the Minneapolis Sound to its musical apex with the release of his ninth studio album, *Sign o' the Times*. The final chapter charts the migration of the Minneapolis Sound to a southwestern suburb, where Prince built his Xanadu-like recording and performance studio, Paisley Park.

The story begins by connecting Prince's performance at a downtown venue with the city's first music festival in the nineteenth century.

PART 1

The Birth

1850–1900

Chapter 1

WHITE SETTLEMENT AND THE BIRTH OF THE MINNEAPOLIS SOUND

More than color or forms, it is sounds and their arrangements that fashion societies.

—Jacques Attali

Prince's October 1981 show at Sam's, a music venue in the heart of downtown, was a kind of coming-out party for the Minneapolis Sound. Prince performed the music he'd been making since his early teens in rooms all over the North and South Sides on the city's biggest stage. His set, with songs from his recently released *Dirty Mind* album, dazzled the hometown crowd and garnered admiration from critics. What music journalists called the Minneapolis Sound was his mix of funk, punk, R&B, and rock: the diverse sounds of the city. These sounds corresponded to racial and geographic lines that organized Minneapolis. But, despite the significance of the performance, it didn't inaugurate the Minneapolis Sound.

That beginning came in 1884 when Minneapolis hosted its first music festival. During the three-day event, some of the best US and European musicians performed before large crowds at a hall built for the occasion. Months of planning and advertising culminated in what local newspapers described as an "unparalleled success" that landed Minneapolis among the country's top musical cities.[1] The Great State Music Festival put the city's music scene on the map.

Holding this festival was a remarkable achievement. In just four decades, Minneapolis had gone from a sparsely populated outpost to a city capable of hosting a major cultural event. This was a testament to the city's quick development and the rapid growth of its music scene. Between 1850 and the end of that century, Minneapolis witnessed a musical explosion. Dozens of music halls and schools were built, the local directory listed hundreds of music teachers, and music societies were born.

Less than a century before the festival and fewer than fifty years before the city's founding, Minneapolis was an Indigenous community. The federal government and white settlers who wanted Native lands for themselves forcibly removed the Ojibwe and Sioux who'd been in the region for centuries. Minneapolis and its music scene were born on that land. White settlement was instrumental to the birth of the Minneapolis music scene. It created the conditions for the city's rise, on which its music scene was dependent. Music was part of the soundtrack of white settlement. Music, along with cannon fire, gunfire, and English, was part of the sound of white Western power that crept across the region's landscape in the seventeenth, eighteenth, and nineteenth centuries. This chapter traces the relationship between music and white settlement and shows how it laid the foundation for the Minneapolis Sound.

The Sounds of Settlement

The long fetch of the Minneapolis Sound began in August 1678. Father Louis Hennepin, a Belgian priest, and his party were traveling up the Mississippi, looking for the Northwest Passage, when they encountered two Native communities on opposite sides of the river. As Hennepin and his party sailed through, they caught the residents' attention. As it floated by, "the sound of the cannon," which boomed from the ship, "caused extraordinary alarm" among the Outtaouactz people.[2] No sound like that had ever creased the air in that region. In the 1670s, the middle west of the continent was new to white people. Most of the white population settled in the eastern colonies. Few had ventured that far west, let alone settled there. On another occasion, Hennepin and his colleagues were walking along the Mississippi banks when a soldier saw a large animal. The frightened soldier fired a shot. According to Hennepin, the "noise revealed to us a hundred twenty-five Indians of the nation of Outouagamis."[3]

The cannon blast and the gunfire weren't just loud or startling; they were unfathomable, and neither had a sonic precursor anywhere in the region. The Outtaouactz and the Outouagami knew nothing of gunpowder or the weapons of war used by white settlers. Such technology did not come to them until well into the eighteenth century. These sounds were signifiers of a historic shift: white settlement. They came in the form of guns, cannons, words spoken in English, and music. In some instances, white settlers used sound as an organizing tool to show immutable differences between them and the Native people and affirm the assumed hierarchy between them.[4]

Sound has meaning. The boom of the cannon and gunshots express power. More than their destructive capacity, the cannon and the firearm forever changed the soundscape of the region. The arrival of Hennepin and his party brought a new, alien sound that announced the appearance of a new power. The sound of the ship's cannon firing upon the Indians launched the imposition of the white settler's canon of rules and principles that would eviscerate daily life for Indigenous people through domination and destruction. Whether Hennepin knew this is beside the point. What is certain is that the reaction of the Indigenous community illustrates that those sounds mattered. In many cases, those sounds announced a period of protracted war and Indian removal, which concluded in the middle of the nineteenth century with the birth of white settlements along the Mississippi River.

Cannons and gunfire were not the only sounds of white settlement; there was also music. Music is an "audible waveband" that reflects the sounds of a society.[5] As an instrument of understanding, music confirms the world for the familiar or signals changes. It does this through chord progressions, instrumentation, harmony, tempo, rhythm, tone, beat, pitch, and scale. For thousands of years, Indigenous people in the region played music. They created a musical landscape throughout the upper Mississippi Valley using drums, tambourines, and rattles, accompanied by distinct pitches, rhythms, and harmonies. White settlements radically changed the soundscape with the sounds of war.

The Outtaouactz lived near a waterfall, the only one on the Mississippi. Hennepin was the first non-Indigenous person to see it. He wrote about it in his published account of his travels up the mighty river. When news of the waterfall got out, the federal government built its first fort in the region. Fort Snelling, which opened in 1819, was the first national footprint in the area. Its role in the transformation of the region cannot be understated. According to one historian, "Fort Snelling is perhaps the most significant landmark in the history of Minnesota and the northwest. Its establishment in 1819 at the juncture of the Minnesota and Mississippi rivers radically changed the course of events in the upper Mississippi valley . . . the establishment of the post effectively extended for the first time the authority of the young American nation over the region, paved the way for white settlement, and set in motion the transformation of the vast Indian territory into an American state."[6] St. Anthony (which would be absorbed by the later-founded Minneapolis) and St. Paul were the first settlements to spring up in its aftermath. In addition to paving the way for white settlement, Fort Snelling was also where white Western music—specifically military music—gained a foothold in the region. Music accompanied the daily activities of life at the fort. Six times every day, beginning at dawn, musicians would gather to play. Military officers summoned musicians to the fort's parade ground to perform the reveille or bugle call, which brought the company to order. The second, known as "peas on the trencher," called soldiers to breakfast. At 9 a.m., music was played to signal the changing of the guard. Six hours after breakfast, the song "Roast Beef" called them to dinner. Thirty minutes before sunset, the companies assembled for the evening dress parade. The Fifth Infantry Order Book says of the call that "troops will parade at Battalion at retreat beating . . . until further orders in full uniform."[7] Music also accompanied other military ceremonies and rituals. Musicians played for military and staff funerals. Music filled the air when high-ranking officials visited. And each rank (major, colonel, commander, general) had a soundtrack. Music was even played to discipline soldiers for offenses.[8]

In addition to playing music for daily routines, soldiers also played it for enjoyment. Fiddle players and singers performed for the families living in the fort.[9] In 1824, a piano (possibly the first in the region) was purchased by a commander's wife.[10] Soldiers even staged plays during the long, cold winter months to entertain the soldiers and their families.

The number of soldiers who could play music enabled an orchestra; more than fifty musicians were spread across ten companies. This large number of musicians enabled continuous music playing throughout the day and the formation of a band.[11]

The military music at the fort was the incubator for white Western music in the area. It expanded into the small white settlements that emerged along the Minnesota and Mississippi Rivers in the 1820s and 1830s. The settlements also brought new laws that stripped Indigenous people of their rights to their land. Businessmen from the East Coast also arrived in the region, eager to get a foothold in the new territory. Massive land theft and settler violence against the Indigenous population followed in their wake. In 1863,

Sioux were interned at Fort Snelling. Internment cleared Indigenous people from parts of the landscape to ease white settlement.

Music rode shotgun to Indian removal. Soldiers marched and organized their day to music. It floated out of the early settlers' encampments and accompanied the founding of Minneapolis. It was played on the *Yankee* steamboat that stopped at St. Anthony and Fort Snelling. Music was everywhere: in the first performance halls, society balls, Fourth of July celebrations, and political gatherings. There was music at the first "territorial temperance convention" to accompany the movement to "suppress the traffic in intoxicating drinks."[12] White settlers' brass and stringed instruments announced to the Indigenous population that a new sound, society, and moment had arrived.

Settlement created favorable conditions for the growth of a white musical culture by clearing Indigenous people from the landscape and establishing Fort Snelling, which made it possible for white settlements like St. Anthony to thrive. The musical culture expanded as the colonies grew in population and diversity. With diverse (religious, linguistic, ethnic) people flooding into the region, as industry expanded and cheap land was plentiful, music gave expression to the changes afoot. In doing so, it became the city's first public culture. Music facilitated gatherings, lubricated social interaction, and accompanied essential events. More than money, national identity, or religion, music was central to creating a sense of community in frontier Minneapolis.[13]

Music also helped define physical space.[14] Like birds that reveal their presence through song to ward off some and invite others, settler music signaled to Indians and white settlers alike the boundary lines of a new territory. Outside the noise of settlement was Indian land; within it was settler territory. And as the region of settlers expanded, music announced its presence and policed its borders.

Minneapolis, in this sense, was not unique. Sound, including music, has announced war, marked out territory, and created community for centuries. Noise and music have always been forms of power, and it would be no different in Minneapolis. It is what settlers did within the new domain that deserves attention. The settlers built their music scene through the noise of settlement. "All music, any organization of sound," observes Jacques Attali, "is a tool for creating and consolidating a community."[15] Music became a vital cultural product that settlers could identify with and rally around. Though being white brought them together, the development of music eased divisions—regional, ethnic, class, and gender. And long after the expulsion of the Dakota, Sioux, and Ojibwe to the margins, music remained an important cultural tool for creating community in Minneapolis and laid the foundation for the city's music scene.

Building the Minneapolis Music Scene

Minneapolis began as settlements on the eastern and western banks of the Mississippi River in the 1840s near St. Anthony Falls. The first of the two colonies, St. Anthony, was established on the west side. Franklin Steele, a Pennsylvanian prospector with ties to the Democratic Party, acquired the land. The State of Minnesota's establishment and St. Anthony's founding occurred in the same year—1849. Because of its location, St. Anthony became a boomtown, so much so that by 1847, human activity drowned out the sound of the waterfall.

Mills quickly took up space along the river, and as they grew, so did their need for labor, causing the economy to surge. With the national lust for wood and flour produced by mills along the river and the need to import work to fill it "will come wealth and capital to improve the inexhaustible power of our waterfall—giving employment to the surplus of labor," said the *St. Anthony Express* newspaper. The rapid growth fueled by the waterfall and the availability of cheap land opened by Indian removal midwifed the settlement's population explosion. In 1847, for example, 300 people lived in St. Anthony. Within five years, there were more than 3,000.[16]

St. Anthony's music scene sprouted from this early settlement. The first recorded music event occurred in 1851 when a Professor Bennett established a "singing school," which taught the basics of singing, like pitch, harmony, and tone. His students performed their first concert on August 21. B. E. Messer, a "teacher of good music, opened a free children's singing class in 1853. Three years later, the Tenth Infantry band of Fort Snelling performed at Edwards Hall, one of the premier venues in frontier Minneapolis. On the eastern side of the river, Minneapolis, founded at the same time as St. Anthony, was also developing a music community, with the establishment of the settlement's first singing school in 1853. Two years later, Minneapolis held its first concert in Edwards Hall.

Fort Snelling's military music culture, which contributed an assortment of "folkloric, military and marching band, patriotic and community songs" played during the first few decades, shaped the early music of St. Anthony and Minneapolis.[17] The music from the fort was also some of the first instrumental music played in the territory. Vocal music dominated the early performances. Although a piano ensemble performed in 1854 and the fort's military band played in 1856, singing schools, church and youth choirs, glee clubs, quartets, and two "negro minstrel" groups dominated during this period.[18] The singing schools were essential because they offered the simplest way to create music.

Music flourished in Minneapolis over the first half of the nineteenth century. A small but active group of music teachers and many music venues sustained this early growth. Between the city's founding in 1849 and the First World War, hundreds of music instructors taught in the dozens of venues landowners built in Minneapolis. Voice and music teachers trained children and adults in harmony, pitch, tone, posture, breath, and notation.[19]

As the city's population grew, so did music instruction. After St. Anthony and Minneapolis combined in 1872, three music schools opened—the Minneapolis Music School, the Lyman F. Brown Music School, and the Malcolm Academy. Hundreds of people attended them. In 1885, Charles Henry Morse established the Northwest Conservatory of Music, which quickly gained a reputation as the city's best provider of music education. By the end of the century, the city's directory listed more than 250 private music schools and teachers.[20]

Music education helped raise the level of musical comprehension among paying customers. Moreover, music education transformed the built environment of frontier Minneapolis. The need for space to host classes and performances led landowners to construct numerous halls during the city's first decade.[21] Though shabby and with poor acoustics, these wood buildings were incubators of the city's sound.

The surge of new construction of music spaces continued during the Civil War. As the state's population grew, many halls built just a few years earlier were obsolete by the start of the war.[22] New halls sprouted to replace them.[23]

The end of the Civil War in 1865 did not interrupt the city's musical building boom. The city's first opera house, the Pence, opened on June 21, 1867, just days before Florida, Arkansas, Alabama, North Carolina, and South Carolina rejoined the Union.[24] It was the city's first grand theater and new cultural and performance center, with a seating capacity of 1,000. (The *New York Times* referred to it as a "tiny box," while the *Minneapolis Tribune* called it "spacious.")[25]

Minneapolis continued to build rapidly in the 1870s, and music remained an important driver. With a growing population of more than 18,000 people—half foreign-born—the city needed its musical infrastructure more than ever.[26] The Academy of Music, built in 1872 at Washington and Hennepin Avenues, challenged the Pence as the most prestigious performance space, only to be outdone in 1883 when the Grand Opera House opened, after which the Academy of Music sank into disrepair. The Metropolitan Opera House was the last large theater built in the nineteenth century. It would be a mainstay for musical performances until its demolition in 1937.[27]

Like musical education, performance accompanied settlement. The first glimpse of the city's performance culture came in August 1851, when a large crowd gathered for a vocal performance at a newly established "singing school."[28] The city's premier music hall in the early 1850s, the Barber, hosted the Norwegian violinist Ole Bull and opera singer Adelina Patti.[29] Bull's popularity rose rapidly in Minneapolis for the next four decades, mainly because of the growing Norwegian population. Woodsman's Hall was the most-used space during the 1850s. The mixture of performances at Woodsman's gives insight into the city's sound: amateur military bands, singing quartets, a German violinist, and the protest music troubadours and boyband of the time, the Hutchinson Singers.[30] This family of New England transplants, "the singing Yankees," popularized protest songs about women's suffrage, labor, and, most famously, abolition in four-part harmony. These songs made them wildly popular in St. Anthony, so much so that their performances there financed their founding of the town Hutchinson, Minnesota, in 1855.[31]

Migration, Race, and the City's Sound

Large migrations in the 1870s brought significant change to the city and its sound. The arrival of Scandinavians to Minneapolis during this time had a long-lasting impact on the city's music scene. They came to Minneapolis fleeing poverty and political instability at home and quickly began contributing to the city's sound. Minneapolis's first Scandinavian performance took place on March 28, 1870. The National Scandinavian Singers performed.[32] They most likely performed at the newly built Scandinavian Hall. To support the musical efforts of Scandinavians, freshly arrived immigrants created the Norden, a Scandinavian musical society, in 1871. The Norden helped organize and showcase Scandinavian music. But more than that, music helped Scandinavians create a place in the city. Building Scandinavian Hall made Scandinavians part of the physical landscape of Minneapolis. With an active performance culture with several performance spaces, it's not surprising that Scandinavian operettas, quartets, violinists, singing groups, brass bands, and other musical forms became popular. Scandinavian music thrived in less than a decade and would only become more prominent. Music was one of the most effective ways for Scandinavians to both give voice to their cultural traditions and become part of the Minneapolis community.

The 1870s was the most diverse period of the early Minneapolis Sound. Growing immigration and the expanding railroad line were making travel to the city easier. During the decade, one could hear Russian and English operas, "Gypsy music," and Prussian music. Musicians from Italy, Switzerland, Germany, Norway, and Ireland visited the city. Minneapolis was beginning to seem more like Boston than a Northwestern frontier outpost.

International sounds notwithstanding, the most popular style during this period was blackface minstrelsy, an entertainment form that originated during the antebellum period and whose leading performers were white working-class men who darkened their faces with burnt cork. Blackface minstrelsy introduced and popularized Black popular culture in Northwestern industrial cities like Minneapolis.[33] These burlesque variety shows featured acting, dancing, singing, and comedy. Dominant in the nineteenth century, they were the first form of national popular culture in the United States. Their heyday extended from the Jacksonian period (1828) to the end of the Civil War (1865) and the early twentieth century. Even today, blackface minstrelsy remains part of popular culture through songs, theater productions, and cultural celebrations like Black Pete in the Netherlands, where the Dutch celebrate St. Nicholas's Black Companion by sporting Afro wigs, Renaissance attire, and red lipstick, as well as Halloween costumes like the ones worn by white people in the United States.[34] In some ways, minstrelsy has never left us.

Despite blackface minstrelsy's origins in the antebellum South, its performances were geared toward Northern, urban white audiences.[35] Their ubiquity in the North made them like early radio or television, where the same jokes, songs, and performances were repeated in city after city, as exemplified by the Melodeon Minstrel performance in Minneapolis in June 1856.[36]

Minstrelsy was based on racist depictions of pastoral, happy, enslaved Black people who loved nothing more than to entertain. With its grotesque mockery, minstrelsy made Blacks into racist caricatures while confirming white people's belief in their superiority. Minstrelsy was double-edged: It allowed white people to feel racially superior through farce and mockery, but it also expressed an inadmissible desire for Blackness and Black culture, even if a stereotypical and distorted version of both. It put Black music and dance front and center even as it portrayed its creators as inferior. Minstrelsy paradoxically embraced Blackness (at least culturally) while simultaneously devaluing Black lives.[37]

Such contradictions lie at the heart of racist America, and Minneapolis was no exception. Despite, if not because of the small number of Black people in cities like Minneapolis during the nineteenth century, minstrel shows were wildly popular. In 1872, "there were more minstrels than anything else that year."[38] And the premier performance space of the time, the Pence Opera House, hosted several minstrel shows. In a review of La Rue's Minstrels' June 1870 performance there, the *Minneapolis Tribune* gleefully noted that the "burnt-cork . . . troupe always draws the Opera House full."[39] A large advertisement in the *Minneapolis Tribune* announced the Shoo Fly Minstrels' three-night engagement at the Pence. In 1884, the Theater Comique hosted a minstrel show that delighted an audience of lumberjacks.

In addition to creating space where white supremacy and an attraction to Blackness comingled, minstrelsy fed the city's growing interest in musical instruments. Minstrelsy popularized the banjo and fiddle. But increasingly, orchestras emerged in cities like Minneapolis, where middle-class cultural values were ascending. In 1872, classical music lovers established the Minneapolis Symphony Concert, which debuted at the Pence. Throughout the 1870s, orchestras and musical societies were formed in Minneapolis, and local and national musicians performed in the city's venues, schools, and churches.

Great State Music Festival and Its Legacy

With abundant performance spaces and a steady stream of musicians coming to play, Minneapolis quickly became a city with a diverse and active musical community. By 1880, the city was awash with musical performances regularly advertised in the city's newspapers. In 1884, Minneapolis had a population of 67,000, a third foreign-born. That year, the city embarked on its most ambitious plan, a three-day music festival June 10–12. This "musical treat" was organized by the Minneapolis Philharmonic Association (MPA) and directed by Theodore Thomas, the most popular band conductor in the nation. Thomas's manager, Charles E. Locke, proposed the festival to the Philharmonic Association and became the event's director. Locke was a powerful manager with a stable of singers large enough to provide most of the musical entertainment for the festival, as he had done for similar events in New York, Chicago, and Cincinnati.

It was an ambitious project for such a young city to pull off in a short amount of time. A successful event meant bringing city leaders, event organizers, artists, builders, and residents together and harnessing the city's growing wealth from timber, mills, and railroads. Of primary concern was space. Though dozens of halls and performance spaces existed, none was large enough to accommodate the crowds expected for the festival.

This responsibility largely fell to the Minneapolis Philharmonic Association, which financed the festival. For business and political leaders, the festival was less about music than an opportunity to highlight this Northwestern outpost's speedy growth and fatten local businesses' coffers. But for the Minneapolis music scene, the three-day event meant national recognition, and the chance to put the city on par with its rivals in the Midwest and Northeast.

Putting together this festival was a difficult task. In less than four decades, Minneapolis had created a network of performance venues, but an event of this size and scale had yet to happen. As a result, the MPA made building a venue part of its planning. The University of Minnesota in Minneapolis needed new facilities. In collaboration with the MPA, festival organizers built a grand hall for the event that would also serve as a multipurpose space for the university. The result was the construction of the University Coliseum on the campus's east bank. With a seating capacity of 5,000, a stage that held 1,000 people, dressing rooms, an orchestral space large enough for two orchestras, and standing room for more than 500 attendees, this spacious modern amphitheater would eclipse all theaters in the state.

The event organizers also had to create transportation to get people to the theater. Railroad magnate Thomas Lowry (an MPA board member) and the MPA were boons to that effort. Four new railroad lines were laid to bring Minnesotans to the coliseum. The city's streetcar system would provide sufficient transportation infrastructure to accommodate the anticipated festival crowds.[40]

The lineup for the festival showcased Minneapolis's local talent and musical preferences. Locke, the festival director and manager of several acts performing at the festival, had directed similar festivals in Chicago and Cincinnati. Locke secured "Swedish nightingale" Christina Nilsson, one of the greatest sopranos of the time, who toured North America in the 1880s. Perhaps no constituency was as excited about Nilsson's arrival as the growing Scandinavian community in Minneapolis. For them, her visit was like having royalty in town, and they treated her arrival as such by arranging a banquet in her honor.[41]

Locke also engaged the sixty-piece Theodore Thomas Orchestra. Thomas, known as "the king of conductors," was the best-known orchestra leader in the country. While Locke secured the big acts, the MPA organized two massive choirs to showcase local talent from Minneapolis and St. Paul.[42]

The success of the festival was a boon to the city. The *Minneapolis Tribune* observed that it established "that Minneapolis is not to be, but is, perhaps one of a half dozen musical centers on the continent, where festivals of this character and magnitude can be organized and regularly maintained."[43] Indeed, the festival was the city's musical coming-out party, its notice to the world that it was a musical city. In Minneapolis, people enjoyed music and saw it as a valuable element of the city's public culture.

In the aftermath of the festival, the activity and scale of musical performance grew. There were 130 public concerts during the 1880s. The Alcazar Opera House opened in 1885. There were also more opera performances than at any other time in the city's history, thanks in no small part to the availability of venues and the growing popularity of the form. The People's Theater, built to give Minneapolis's residents access to music and theater, opened in 1887. The Northwest Conservatory of Music, the first in the region, was founded and staged its first concert that same year. The Danz Orchestra, which helped cultivate the city's tastes, remained popular even after financial problems ended its Sunday concerts at Turner Hall.[44] The music community had become so robust that in 1887, the *Minneapolis Tribune* launched a regular column that announced performances and offered biographical sketches of performers.

At this time, Minneapolis had no comprehensive music education system or adequate resources for teachers or children, which led the city's music teachers to organize the Minnesota State Music Teachers Association. Their organizing significantly impacted music education in the public school system in the early twentieth century.

In the 1890s, the music boom continued. New venues opened, like Century Hall in 1890, and staged more operas. A local Beethoven club was organized in South Minneapolis in 1892. The city's first musical prodigy, pianist Lottie Marie Edwards, began playing around town in 1892. The Danz Orchestra waned in the 1890s; after leaving Turner Hall, the band's big brass sound fell out of favor with younger music fans. Symphonies, however, remained popular. The Minneapolis Philharmonic Club was founded, led first by Willard Patton and later by Emil Oberhoffer, who headed the city's first symphony orchestra.

The Thursday Musical was the most exciting and long-lasting of the groups formed during this period. This woman-led instrumental and vocal group was radical for its time. Founded in 1892, the Thursday Musical grew from a series of concerts organized by highly respected local musician Laura Carroll Dennis. Her idea was to host "recitals that aim to reach the masses." Locals could hear classical music and operas at ten cents per ticket. But that price was too much for the working class and people experiencing poverty. Dennis sought to "educate and edify" the working masses with these concerts, an idea borrowed from her travels to London and Scotland.[45] At the time of the group's first performance in 1892, it included thirteen musicians.

By the end of the century, it had more than 500.[46] The Thursday Musical still exists, offering performances in Minneapolis.

The philosopher Jacques Attali argues that music is a barometer for understanding societies. Analyzing music in this manner allows us to see how particular sounds become popular and what is lost or gained through their emergence. "Now we must learn," Attali writes, "to judge a society more by its sounds, art, and festivals than by its statistics."[47]

Tracing the history of Minneapolis shines a light on the white settler roots of the city's music scene. By removing Indigenous peoples, settlement created favorable conditions for expanding its musical culture and various sounds, beginning with the arrival of Hennepin and the first colonists and continuing from the establishment of Fort Snelling, where music and militarism were inextricably joined, to the venues, musical societies, music education, performances, and the grand, three-day Great State Music Festival in 1884.

Chapter 2

THE WATERFALL THAT BUILT A CITY

Winding its way southward through Minnesota, the Mississippi River leaps over the sixteen-foot precipice known as the Falls of St. Anthony. The waterfall, which was responsible for the birth of Minneapolis, is the most abrupt drop in the Mississippi's entire 2,200-mile course, from its source in Minnesota's Lake Itasca to the Gulf of Mexico.

—Lucile M. Kane

The music Prince made famous in the 1980s—that unmistakable mix of funk, rock, R&B, and electronic dance music—sprang not simply from the musician's imagination but rather from a geologic event millennia ago. Prince is, without question, the most important and talented composer of the city's sound, but the city the sound is named after was born from a waterfall. That waterfall entered the popular imagination through a Belgian priest, Father Louis Hennepin. In 1680, Hennepin and his crew came upon the only waterfall on the Mississippi River. His writings about the waterfall, which he named after the Catholic saint Anthony of Padua, set off a scramble for the territory matched only by Europe's lust for Africa in the nineteenth century. The settlement that ensued gave rise to the city of Minneapolis.

In October 1930, less than a year after the start of the Great Depression, civic leaders and citizens gathered to honor Hennepin. The Catholic Church unveiled a statue dedicated to him and his impact on the city. The daylong festivity featured some of the biggest names in state politics. The mayor and local clergy attended, and even President Herbert Hoover sent his support for a ceremony that cemented in stone Hennepin's role in the city's birth. Indeed, for many, Hennepin was an indispensable cultural figure whose history was firmly tied to the city, like Thomas Jefferson to Monticello or the Beatles to Liverpool. "The memory of Father Hennepin," enthused one speaker, "must remain in Minneapolis as long as the water runs over the Falls of St. Anthony."[1]

White settlers and migrants from the Northeast, the mid-Atlantic, the South, and Western Europe came seeking fortune, work, and cheap land. Some came as property and others as refugees fleeing violence. This mix of people gave rise to the city's music scene and, eventually, the Minneapolis Sound that Prince would make world famous.

The falls were the engine that powered the region's economic development. Settlers learned to harness the water falling over the sixteen-foot cliff and turn it into industrial power. It became the force behind the mill economy that shaped the city for seventy-five years. It also gave settlers the means to transform the region physically. Towns formed. Schools and stores opened. Streets and bridges emerged. Neighborhoods were constructed. By the beginning of the twentieth century, the sparsely populated Indigenous landscape, turned military outpost and then pioneer town, had morphed into a city with a population of a quarter million people and an industrial economy rivaled only by Chicago.[2]

Indeed, the Falls of St. Anthony "built a city."[3] The sounds of that city laid the groundwork for a revolution in pop music over a century later. Prince drew on the city's unique musical history and sound to create the music he became famous for. Minneapolis was more than just a background for making music. It was a social and sonic landscape from which his music flowed.

This chapter serves as a spatial counterpart to the sonic story of chapter 1. It focuses on the city's origins during the same period. Since the location plays a crucial role in creating music, comprehending the Minneapolis Sound necessitates knowing how a waterfall built a city.

12,000 Years Before Hennepin

The people of Minneapolis have celebrated and contested Father Louis Hennepin and his "discovery" of the falls. White Minneapolitans commemorate Hennepin as a catalyst for the birth of Minnesota and as a civilizing force in

Figure 2.1. *Father Hennepin Discovering St. Anthony Falls*, by Douglas Volk, 1905. Photo courtesy of the Library of Congress.

the untamed Northwest Territory. Douglas Volk, the painter, muralist, and founding director of the Minneapolis School of Fine Art, captured this view in a turn-of-the-century oil painting (see fig. 2.1). The region's Indigenous people view Hennepin quite differently. For them, Hennepin and his colonial efforts led to deaths, land theft, and white settler control.

The Dakota and Ojibwe peoples arrived in the area at the end of the last glacial period, nearly 12,000 years ago. They were probably drawn to the region by the sound of the waterfall and the easy access to food it facilitated. Archeologists have found only a few human artifacts in the area.[4] We can imagine that Indigenous people were awed by the power and majesty of the falls. What is known for sure is that Indigenous people witnessed the slow and gradual decline of the falls' cataracts.[5] By the time Hennepin arrived, the falls had receded to a height of just sixteen feet.[6]

For centuries, the Dakota and Ojibwe created life in and through the falls and, in turn, developed a special relationship with it. They used it for spiritual purposes, hunting, and as a marker of territory among the tribes in the area. All that changed when Hennepin and his companions, Michel Accault and Antoine Auguelle, saw the waterfall. They were looking for the Northwest Passage, a sea route that links the Atlantic and Pacific Oceans, and instead stumbled upon the falls.[7] When descriptions of the falls appeared in Hennepin's journal, the secret was out.[8] Other explorers traveled to the region and wrote their own accounts.

Manifest Destiny

While popular, these narratives did not encourage settlement by themselves. They were bolstered by Manifest Destiny, the ideology that maintained that God destined white people to expand westward and acquire land.[9] Manifest Destiny transformed Northern and Western landscapes with white settlers and frontier towns. White settlers told themselves that "Indian" removal was necessary for "civilization" to march across the continent. Expropriating Indigenous people's land was excused and rationalized with the claim that profit was essential to building a nation.

A mixture of racist ideas and a series of land acts issued by the Continental Congress enabled the colonization of the Minnesota territory. Three land ordinances forever changed access to and distribution of land in the West. The first two acts, in 1784 and 1785, established the sale, surveying, and settlement of newly acquired land. The third act, also known as the Northwest Ordinance, created a legal framework in 1787 for permanent control over unsurveyed land reaching as far west as the Pacific Ocean and as far north as Alaska.[10] These acts set the stage for white expansion in the North and West by providing resources and legal protection, underpinned by an anything-goes approach to land control. In this way, the US government actively participated in a massive land grab. For example, Zebulon Pike received large amounts of land in what became the Minneapolis and St. Paul region for a mere $200.[11]

On July 9, 1817, the federal government sent Maj. Stephen H. Long and seven other crew members on a mission to St. Anthony Falls. Embarking from St. Louis, they recorded the topography of the shore to make sure it was "suitable for military purposes."[12] Nine days later, they arrived in what would later become the lower part of St. Anthony on the river's eastern shore. Long's vivid and idyllic descriptions of the natural environment capture the region before settlement. Like others before him, Long described the falls with enthusiasm and awe, proclaiming them "a beautiful cascade of fine spring water, pouring down from a projecting precipice."[13]

Long's report spurred the War Department to make the falls part of its military outpost.[14] In 1819, military leadership selected Lt. Col. Henry Leavenworth to build a fort near the falls. With the Revolutionary War only a few decades past, the fort was to be a military location to fend off foreign invasion. This strategic site atop bluffs that overlooked St. Anthony Falls, the

Minnesota River, and St. Paul allowed US troops to see potential enemies' approach from the Great Lakes. The second and most popular use of the fort was for settlement. The stone structure was "for the federal government's strategy to protect white settlement and entrepreneurial undertakings."[15]

Leavenworth got construction underway in 1820. Soon after, he was relieved of his post by Josiah Snelling. Snelling wanted a more permanent facility. After years of labor, the stone fortress emerged in 1827. The imposing structure was the first and most decisive move to gain control of the land. The War Department was so pleased with Snelling's efforts that it named the fort after him. The building of Fort Snelling provided "an island of civilization in the wilderness" of the upper Mississippi Valley and laid the foundation of mass migration.[16]

These moves set the trajectory for land disputes between white and Native peoples.[17] The federal government sold off or gave away Native lands. Treaties with the Dakota and Ojibwe peoples benefited settlers. Native people were also pushed off the land by force. Bloody conflicts with white settlers shrank the Indian population. This combination of legal maneuvers, violence, and unfavorable treaties dispossessed Indigenous people and fostered white settlement.

Steam-powered vehicles quickened the pace of settlement in the Northwest Territory. Railroads and steamboats moved people farther west and north up the Mississippi River. Technological advances married to government acts that privileged settlement strengthened settlers' grip on the region.

The building of Fort Snelling moved hundreds of people—soldiers, staff, families, Southern planters, enslaved people, and Northeastern capitalists—into St. Anthony. The falls provided a reliable power source, so the area was ripe for development. These events created the opening that would forever change the Northwest Territory. Foreshadowing what St. Anthony and Minneapolis would become economically, one of the first acts by the soldiers at Fort Snelling was to build a gristmill and sawmill to extract raw materials from the surrounding dense forest.[18]

Flour Mill Capital of the World

Frontier St. Anthony and Minneapolis initially attracted land speculators, businessmen, and hustlers looking to make money in the newly acquired territory.[19] One of those men was Franklin Steele, a Pennsylvania businessman and Fort Snelling attaché, who made the first land claims in St. Anthony. Steele was a cunning opportunist who used his military connections to grab newly opened land on which he eventually built a mill. Taking advantage of the federal land acts, Steele waited until Congress signed its lopsided treaty with Native Americans, then raced to the site and erected a shack before others, claiming rights to the land. As the story goes, other prospectors showed up early the following day, eager to access the swindled grounds, to find Steele outside his rapidly built, dilapidated residence eating breakfast. "I am in possession of this land by preemption right," he told the would-be prospectors.[20]

St. Anthony was rugged and sparsely populated when Steele arrived. By 1849, however, less than twenty years after the fort was built, St. Anthony was no longer just a military outpost. It had grown into a bustling mill town. The grist and sawmills made at Fort Snelling and Steele's first mill set the city's economic trend for eighty years. Steele was not the only "empire builder" in nineteenth-century Minneapolis.[21] John H. Stevens, Franklin Steele's assistant, built mills on the west bank to process the wheat on Steele's land. By getting into milling early and with federal recognition of the grounds, Steele and Stevens became the city's first wealthy men.[22]

The milling industry, first developed by Steele and Stevens, became the city's future. Newly arrived settlers, especially Northeasterners who had experience in the industry, played a central role in the rise of the city's mills. Following in the footsteps of towns like Lowell, Massachusetts, they poured Northeastern capital into creating mills. The abundance of wheat and thick forests in St. Anthony gave white settlers and the milling industry the natural resources needed to expand the city's prosperity rapidly. St. Anthony's economy boomed, with flour, grain, sawmills, and gristmills springing up along the river's eastern bank. Mill owners got rich from the steady supply of work brought on by industrialization and settlement facilitated by the federal land acts. European immigrants and Northeastern workers poured into the city. They were drawn to St. Anthony by the lure of millwork, plentiful land, and the prospect of getting in on the ground floor of a growing economy in a new region of the country. With Indigenous people being moved out of the region by unfair treaties, war, or disease, settlers quickly took over their lands.[23]

St. Anthony was incorporated in 1855, three years before Minnesota became a state. But it was not the only burgeoning frontier town on the river. White settlers established Minneapolis on the western side of the Mississippi River in the 1850s. Like its cross-river cousin, European immigrants and white Northeasterners settled there for mill jobs, a chance at a better life, and land acquisition. But Minneapolis grew at a slower pace. In 1855, the first suspension bridge was built, connecting the two towns and spurring industry expansion and easy travel from St. Anthony to Minneapolis. In 1872, the two settlements merged as Minneapolis.

Figure 2.2. Pillsbury A Mill, ca. 1905. Photo courtesy of the Library of Congress.

For the next half-century, Minneapolis remained a mill town. Sawmilling, flour milling, and warehousing were the three largest industries.[24] Flour milling, however, contributed most to the economy. Millers learned to turn northern wheat into some of the finest flour around. The Pillsbury flour mill was the largest (see fig. 2.2). By 1880, Minneapolis became the "flour mill capital of the world" and held that distinction well into the twentieth century.[25]

Minneapolis had become an economic powerhouse with the Civil War, creating wealth for a few elites and jobs for those looking. Eastern financers were central to the economic boom. The mills they owned were producing large amounts of valuable raw material. The birth of the Minnesota Pacific Railroad in 1862 networked the Twin Cities—Minneapolis and St. Paul—into the growing railroad expansion, which profoundly impacted the economic future of Minneapolis. Before the railroad, the Mississippi River was the primary avenue for importing and exporting products. The materials produced in the mills could be exported to places like Chicago. Products from other cities could also be imported, creating a diverse commercial sector for the growing population. The war had pushed people out of Southern regions and into expanding territories like Minnesota. And Minneapolis was on the rise, with large numbers of Western Europeans entering.

Peopling Minneapolis

No other single social force transformed the area like immigration. Immigrants came in bunches. First were deep-pocketed Easterners looking to accumulate capital. Then came New Englanders, who were integral to the city's economy. Migrants from Maine, for example, brought lumbering techniques. Those from Massachusetts mill towns like Lowell brought their knowledge of milling. The best-known milling family—Pillsbury—was from New Hampshire. Western Europeans escaping poverty and political instability came next. Jews fleeing European antisemitism arrived in Minneapolis in the late nineteenth century.

Contrary to its image as a homogenous city, St. Anthony received a diverse mix of migrants between its founding and the end of the nineteenth century. Each group contributed to the city's growth, politics, and culture. This book does not discuss every immigrant group but instead focuses on a few of the large and significant ones that shaped the city's early history and which would help lay the groundwork for the city's music scene.

Germans were among the most significant European groups who immigrated to the United States. From 1880 to the turn of the century, Minnesota received more Germans than any other racial or ethnic group.

Germans, however, were not the largest immigrant group; that distinction belonged to Scandinavians. Whereas there were some 60,000 Germans in Minnesota, Scandinavians numbered more than 100,000 by 1880.[26] Scandinavians left the most significant mark on the city's culture of any ethnic group. They shaped Minneapolis's left-leaning politics, religious culture, public education, and cuisine. Scandinavians also had a considerable impact on Minneapolis's music.

Swedes began migrating to the United States in 1845—an estimated 1.25 million arrived by the beginning of the twentieth century—and more settled in Minnesota than any other state.[27] Another wave of migration brought more Swedes to the region by the 1880s, and the city's first Scandinavian district saw growth. Minnesota also attracted more Norwegians than any other state in the country. The Norwegian presence in Minneapolis is perhaps best reflected in their impact on civic and social life. Norwegians controlled several banks, churches, and fifteen of the city's one hundred newspapers and periodicals; they also were proprietors of numerous hotels, general stores, and doctors' offices.

Jews were the only Europeans who arrived as refugees from violent persecution. After first immigrating to the Eastern and Southern states, they settled in the Twin Cities when the upper Mississippi Valley opened.[28] Because St. Paul was the first big city in Minnesota, most Jewish people migrated there. However, Jewish migration to Minneapolis grew after the Civil War, reaching 5,000 by the century's close.

Black Migration

Black migration to Minnesota started seventy-five years before Prince's paternal grandparents fled Louisiana and landed in South Minneapolis in the mid-1920s. When Black people began migrating to the territory in the 1850s, Minnesota was about to become a state. Black migration raised questions of civil rights, white supremacy, slave versus free states, and voting rights. So, even though their numbers were low, Black migration was a major political issue for Minneapolis and the entire state.

Comedian Chris Rock once joked that only two Black people lived in Minnesota: Prince and Hall of Fame baseball player Kirby Puckett. There is some truth to this. Well into the twentieth century, Minnesota had a small Black population. The confining effects of slavery, which kept Black people chained to Southern plantations, and Northern racism, which made working in the region difficult, are some reasons that kept the Black population small. That said, Black people were not absent in the Minnesota territory. At the end of the eighteenth century, when the British controlled the fur trade in the region, the best-known fur trader was a Black man named George Bonga. Fluent in French, English, and Chippewa, Bonga became a licensed trader and likely acted as an interpreter at Fort Snelling in 1837.[29]

Enslaved people were also present in the state's early days. Slavery has a history in the Minnesota territory that dates to the state's founding.[30] Southern planters were lured to St. Anthony by advertisers who targeted them, promising relief from the Southern heat and luxurious stays at a hotel near St. Anthony Falls. Some were even encouraged to purchase land plundered from Indians. Armed with the Supreme Court's ruling that allowed enslavers to bring enslaved people to free states, Southern planters had "bondsmen" accompany them on their Northern excursions.[31] Between 1849 and the end of the Civil War in 1865, Minnesota was "free territory," but it did not criminally charge Southern enslavers who traveled to the region with enslaved people. Southern planter money was sought after in Minneapolis. The city obfuscated its tie to slavery with terminology like "servant," which is what hotel owners and even city newspapers called an enslaved person.[32]

Between 1820 and 1830, several enslaved people lived at Fort Snelling.[33] The best-known resident of Fort Snelling was Dred Scott. Scott was the plaintiff in the infamous 1857 Supreme Court ruling that the US Constitution did not extend American citizenship to Black people, and that they thus could not enjoy the rights and privileges granted to white Americans. The court also ruled that the Missouri Compromise, which prohibited slavery in the former Louisiana Territory above the 36°30′ latitude line, was unconstitutional. Scott's enslaver, Dr. John Emerson, an army surgeon, brought Scott to Fort Snelling in 1836. Scott married Harriet Robinson, who'd been brought there by her enslaver, Maj. Lawrence Taliaferro, during the same period.[34] Robinson, now Scott, was sold to Emerson. Harriett, Dred, and their daughter, born on a steamboat just north of the Mason-Dixon Line, lived in the basement of Fort Snelling, tasting bits of freedom afforded in the nonslave territory.

With the Supreme Court's ruling protecting them from prosecution, enslavers continued to visit St. Anthony with human cargo in tow. The only successful case of a visiting enslaved person achieving freedom was that of Eliza Winston. Colonel R. Christmas, a wealthy Mississippi planter on vacation, brought her to the region. A plan was set in motion by the wife of a Black barber and three white abolitionists to liberate Winston. One of the abolitionists obtained a writ of habeas corpus, and a trial was held to free Winston. The lawyer defending Christmas used the *Dred Scott* ruling as a justification for invalidating the writ. In contradiction to and defiance of the *Scott* decision and backed by Minnesota's free-state status, the judge ruled in favor of Winston. Eliza was swiftly spirited out of Minnesota using Underground Railroad routes once conducted by Harriet Tubman.[35]

The *Dred Scott* ruling informed the state's debate about whether to extend the right to vote to Black people. In 1860, as the state created its constitution, the question of Black suffrage was front and center. Different versions of the constitution drafted by Democrats and Republicans amounted to a struggle between "white supremacy" and "Negro suffrage."[36] The final decision, however, came eight years later, when voters mandated Black voting rights by decree, just two years before the Fifteenth Amendment enfranchised all Black people.

Though the state opposed slavery and leaned left of center politically, partly because of the growing Scandinavian population, anti-Black racism was a reality in early Minneapolis and throughout Minnesota. Nevertheless, the end of the Civil War pushed some Blacks out of the South and into the Northwest. Blacks settled in St. Anthony and Minneapolis but in minimal numbers.[37] In 1863, the Black population in St. Anthony and Minneapolis was seventy-eight. After the Civil War, Black migration increased. Following

St. Anthony and Minneapolis's merger in 1872, Blacks moved to the west side of the river, most likely because of employment opportunities there.

Over time, a steady stream of Black people moved to South Minneapolis, near the growing Scandinavian neighborhood.[38] Between 1880 and 1930, the Black population grew from 362 to 4,276.[39] Like Europeans, Blacks relocated to Minneapolis for jobs and political freedom. In some cases, Black and European migrants took similar routes into the city.[40] But unlike Europeans, Jewish migrants aside, Blacks came to Minneapolis as refugees, fleeing the violent racism of the Southern states. Minnesota's liberalism and the state's willingness to enfranchise Black men signaled to many Black people they would receive fair treatment. (Women did not win the right to vote until the passing of the Nineteenth Amendment in 1919.)

Prince's family was part of this migration to the North. His paternal great-grandparents, Dina Ann and Handy Jenkins, were born into slavery in Georgia. Their only child, Carrie Jenkins, was Prince's grandmother. After registering to vote in 1870, Handy and Dina Ann migrated to Webster Parish in Louisiana.[41] Carrie married Clarence Allan Nelson, one of eleven children born to Emma Hardy and Edward Nelson. Carrie and Clarence had five children, one of whom was John L. Nelson, Prince's father.[42] In the 1930s, Carrie Ikner, who had remarried, left her second husband and migrated to the growing Black section of South Minneapolis. In the 1950s, John L. Nelson lived there with his wife Matty and their son Prince.[43]

As the historian Lucille Kane observes, "Minneapolis has good reason to remember the Falls of St. Anthony, for much of its history is intertwined with them."[44] The falls spurred the building of Minneapolis and, therefore, its music scene. The kinds of music played in the city, where it was played, and who played it resulted from the transformations that began near St. Anthony Falls. Indian removal, the development of a mill economy, and mass migration to Minneapolis were all facilitated by a waterfall created millennia ago.

In just under half a century, Minneapolis radically changed. In 1850, its population was a little more than 1,100. By 1900, more than 200,000 people lived in the city, one-third of that population foreign-born.[45] Although music was central to the city's public culture, the ability to play and read music was not. These skills were primarily confined to the city's elite, a consequence of a private music education system that privileged individual paid training over public music education. But all that changed when the board of education hired a committed young teacher and evangelist for music education.

As we shift from the long-term historical origins of Minneapolis and its sound to more recent history, the story turns to how one man's approach fostered musical literacy for the masses, laying the foundation for the birth of a Minneapolis musical culture that decades later would influence and be radically changed by a gifted young man from the city's Black community.

PART 2

The Growth

1900–1950

Chapter 3

MUSICAL CITY

Minneapolis is a musical city. Music clubs and societies, recitals, chamber concerts, operas, orchestral seasons—all indicate the high favor in which the people hold this queen of arts.

—Thaddeus P. Giddings

Before Prince and his sound put Minneapolis on the musical map, Thaddeus P. Giddings, a young, driven music educator, laid the groundwork. The most telling news about his impact on music education in the city's public schools came on May 2, 1915, in the Sunday edition of the *Minneapolis Tribune*. "Fifty Thousand Minneapolis Children Are Studying Music" lauded music education in the city's public schools and praised the efforts of the supervisor of music education, Thaddeus P. Giddings, whose unorthodox approach extended music education to every child. The article informed readers that Minneapolis had one of the country's most ambitious and comprehensive programs. "To those who are in touch with what the public schools are doing these days," wrote Blanche R. MacDonald, "there [*sic*] must have some conception of the fact that there has been such a marvelous development in public school music as no other city can boast." MacDonald was correct; no musical education program—not in New York, Boston, Chicago, or St. Louis—was equal to what was offered in Minneapolis public schools.[1] All public school students, more than 50,000 at the time, received daily music training. No musical education has occurred on that scale since. Making music education compulsory for all schoolchildren meant that Minneapolis "had no richer asset for the future cultural growth and happiness of its people than the musical education that is now afforded in its schools."[2]

Mass music education in the early twentieth century opened the doors to music production more than any other factor in the history of Minneapolis. By giving generations of children the tools to read and play music, the public school, in effect, changed the course of the Minneapolis Sound by democratizing musical literacy and, thus, music-making. The rapid growth of the city's music scene in the late nineteenth and early twentieth centuries was mainly among the economically mobile middle class, as was the case for many cities in the Western world. The bourgeoisie also exerted control over it. Indeed, the economic elite shaped how music was talked about, where it was played, and what was played. Many halls and performance spaces built in the mid-nineteenth century were open to the public, but the middle class owned them and could afford to attend them. Moreover, taking music lessons or attending music school required money, which disadvantaged the working-class population. Unsurprisingly, money determined the kinds of music performed, which helps to explain why opera, a sign of class mobility and social refinement, came to Minneapolis.

Minneapolis democratized music education in a revolutionary way, and Giddings, the nation's most sought-after music teacher and evangelist for music education, radically changed music literacy in Minneapolis for generations. Economic troubles at the turn of the century—a series of strikes by workers, the decline of the once-robust mill industry, the bottoming out of lumbering and agriculture, and the First World War—sent the economy into a tailspin, leaving few resources for "frivolous" things like music education. But Minneapolis, against the backdrop of an unevenly developed music scene and financial pressures, made music education an asset.

Sounding Minneapolis at the Turn of the Century

The start of the twentieth century strengthened the city's passion for music as the "queen of the arts," as evidenced by how often the word "music" appeared in Minneapolis newspapers. Between 1900 and 1906, the *Minneapolis Journal*, the *Minneapolis Tribune*, and the *Minneapolis Morning Tribune* had more than 6,400 mentions of "music."[3] They included advertisements for musical instruments and teachers offering lessons or announcing upcoming performances. Some were feature stories about the quality of the music in Minneapolis and its importance to the city's culture. In May 1906, a *Minneapolis Tribune* article argued that the public library's music section was underperforming.[4]

Although "music" was ubiquitous in the city's papers, "music education" was not. During the same period, the words appeared only nine times.[5] In a city where music was fundamental to local culture, with dozens of venues built to satisfy the public's appetite for it, as well as a music library, the lack of attention to public music education in the local press seems odd.

This disparity between Minneapolis's love of music and its lack of attention to music education may reflect the city's rapid growth. In less than a half century, Minneapolis went from an outpost to an industrial center of the Northwest. For some, the city's rapid growth was a testament to its industrious, entrepreneurial citizens' ingenuity and hard work. But speedy growth is a double-edged sword: When things come quickly, blind spots and carelessness abound. The commercial music scene benefited from the city's rapid development, but that growth did not expand access to music education. Part of the reason for this was that the middle and upper classes exerted control over the city's music scene. They owned many venues, were musically literate, and comfortable playing instruments, which bent much of the city's music to their tastes. Some working-class people learned to play instruments, of course. In the brothels that lined the river near the mills and serviced the hard-working and hard-drinking mill employees, piano players and singers provided live music to accompany the erotic economy of sex work. Middle-class residents, however, began importing pianos and melodeons in the 1850s. By the 1870s, when the Great State Music Festival occurred, orchestral music in Minneapolis had been slowly germinating.

Economic shifts further marginalized the working class and poor people from the city's music scene. The decline stemmed from technological shifts, self-inflicted wounds, and a softening agricultural market. The most significant factor in the city's economic decline was the 1908 collapse of the Pillsbury-Washburn milling company, the largest milling firm in the world.[6] The mill's failure was financially catastrophic because Pillsbury-Washburn was integral to the city's economy. In addition to employing hundreds of workers who turned wheat into flour, Pillsbury-Washburn also generated the capital to build hydroelectric plants near St. Anthony Falls. In the end, a new milling company, Pillsbury Flour Mills, emerged from the wreckage of Pillsbury-Washburn.[7]

Music and Education

Economic decline and the middle and upper classes' dominance of music education and performance threatened the vitality of Minneapolis's music scene. The public school system responded by hiring Thaddeus P. Giddings to revamp music education in the city's public schools. Giddings saw music education not as peripheral to children's learning but as fundamental to their development. Informed by the motto of his music teacher hero, Karl Gehrkens, whose motto was "Music for every child and every child for music," Giddings developed a practical system of sight-reading and playing instruments that revolutionized school music teaching.[8]

Giddings was hired three years after Pillsbury-Washburn began liquidating assets, a period of crisis in the lumber and agriculture industries. Amid the downturn, he was charged with reforming an anemic music education system. In the face of these obstacles, Giddings used the school system's resources to create the nation's most comprehensive school music program. Over his half-century career, he tested his ideas about music education with the city's schoolchildren and, in the process, created arguably the most musically literate population in the nation's history, forever changing the course of music in the city.

Giddings's first major assignment was as music supervisor for the Moline, Illinois, school district. Like Minneapolis, Moline was an upstart semi-industrial town on the Mississippi River. The position required him to teach in elementary and high schools, a challenge for which he "felt awfully green."[9] In his elementary and high school classes, he nonetheless developed the principal elements of what became known as the "Giddings system."[10] His pedagogy comprised four elements: guidebooks for teachers not skilled in music education; group instruction in sight reading; teaching children to sing in a "soft, clear, distinct tone," focusing on pronunciation and breath; and abandoning rote learning. In his 1894 report to the Moline school district, Giddings wrote that "rote work is not part of our system." Instead, he favored "individual work" with students, which he argued was "ideal."

Giddings's mix of scaling up classroom music education, sight-reading, emphasis on vocal tone, and individual work allowed school districts with tight budgets to make music part of their curriculum. His system altered students' relationship with music by instilling musical literacy, which removed the mystery of how music worked. Literacy also democratized music-making by ensuring that no one segment of society monopolized it.

As the most innovative and sought-after music supervisor in the country, Giddings received many offers. In June 1910, Giddings assumed the position of superintendent of music education for the Minneapolis public school system. He soon discovered that the city's schoolchildren were musically illiterate. How was this possible? Minneapolis was a musical city. It had a robust concert scene, active musical societies, an abundance of performance spaces, a press that promoted music, hundreds of music teachers, and several music schools.

There were other problems, too. The textbooks were insufficient. Children would have to unlearn outdated rote methods. High schools didn't have much of a musical community. There were few, if any, clubs, no regular performances, no orchestra, and no full-time music teachers. With its sixty-eight grade schools, the district's size made it impossible for Giddings to visit classrooms and work with the teachers on methods. Moreover, the written music education examinations teachers were required to take were useless. Giddings also discovered that the music program lacked community support. Again, it was a head-scratching reality for a city like Minneapolis.[11]

"Music has been taught in the country for many years," Giddings lamented, "yet the number of people who can read music, even in these favored cities, is very small. . . . Why is this?" he asked.[12]

The class bias of music education was one reason few people in Minneapolis could read music. The speed of the city's development was another factor. Minneapolis was in a rush to become the cultural and economic center of the Northwest Territory. This negatively affected the development of the city's music scene. "Men and cities that mature slowly," argued journalist and labor activist Charles Rumford Walker, "have different personalities from those who grow up fast or skip stages to an early success."[13] Minneapolis's wealthy elites were eager to establish the city as a music center. But instead of cultivating homegrown talent, musicians were imported. Although music societies and teachers attempted to develop the local scene, their efforts didn't reach most residents.

Ever the optimist and profoundly convinced of the merits of his system, Giddings began, in the spring of 1911, "to establish Minneapolis as the lead of the large cities in teaching its students to become musically literate."[14] His first hurdle was to convince the school board that learning to read music was worthwhile. In his 1911 annual report, he explained to the board that music, although essential, was being taught incorrectly. "If the pupil cannot read music after leaving eighth grade," he argued, "the music system is a failure." Giddings contended that ineffective methods of teaching music by previous supervisors, a lack of material to teach the children, and insufficient class time devoted to music education had created the musically illiterate student population he inherited. Solving these problems would make Minneapolis the first big city school district to teach its children to read music and raise the musical literacy of the entire city, one child at a time.

Giddings began by ordering new music instruction books for grades one through eight, providing abundant material for sight-reading. He also convinced the Minneapolis Board of Education that his schedule must be rethought. Rather than keep office hours, he argued that his time would be better spent visiting the district's 900 classrooms. In his 1910–11 report to the board, he discussed why being in the school was a must for supervisors and outlined a plan to accomplish this:

> Music, to be successfully taught in the schools needs more supervision than any other branch for several reasons. First, it is the one for which teachers are least prepared. The training they get in normal schools is a farce and few of them have learned enough in the grade schools to help them any. Only those who have studied it privately are at all well equipped to teach it in the schools. Having had so poor a chance to learn music it is not fair to discriminate against those who cannot do the work in this branch. The only thing to be done . . . is to provide enough supervision to help teach the children and to teach the teachers.[15]

Giddings knew that private and public music education was unequal. But he refused to allow those inequalities to stand in the way of teaching music. To help close the gap, Giddings asked the board for five assistants to help him cover all the classes so he could train teachers to teach music to children. Furthermore, rather than assessing teachers through a test he considered worthless, the assistants would help teachers learn music. Giddings understood that hiring specialized music teachers was costly and ineffective because students would be less inclined to learn from a teacher who was not their primary one. Therefore, these assistants worked with teachers who showed musical aptitude or had had private training. It was better, argued Giddings, to have teachers who could teach and learn music than it was to have musicians who couldn't teach.[16]

Within a year, Giddings saw results. So much so that he began building a high school music program, and he required all ninth-grade students to take a chorus class. Guided by his axiom "We learn to do by doing," Giddings created orchestra and glee clubs for academic credit.[17] In 1913–14, he offered music and harmony courses in high school. With the assistance of E. Ruth Anderson, a concert violinist and teacher, Giddings began offering instrument lessons to grade school and high school students at the cost of five cents per student per lesson. The classes were so popular that within three years, Giddings needed Anderson to work full time to teach the growing number of students who wanted to learn instruments.[18]

Within five years of being hired, Giddings had significantly changed the Minneapolis public school system's music program. With the publication of his book *Course in Music*, which described "what to do and how to do it from the first day of kindergarten to the end of eighth grade," Giddings sought to increase students' musical literacy by making them read music notation rather than practice drills.[19] The students' ability to sight-read significantly improved their mastery of tone, timing, rhythm, and harmony. Minneapolis had done in five years something no other metropolitan district in the nation could claim: It had made its students musically literate. Music was being taught at seventy-five elementary schools and six high schools. The district bought hundreds of records and dozens of phonographs so children could hear the music they were learning to sing and play. Every school had an orchestra, a girls' and boys' glee club, and choruses. Minneapolis was the only city in the nation to require music instruction—nearly two hours of classroom time a week—for all its public school students.[20]

By May 1915, when Blanche R. MacDonald penned the story in the *Minneapolis Tribune* on the "all-around music education" the district's 50,000 children were receiving, the crisis in music education had been averted. Hiring Giddings and the school board's investment in the music program made children stewards of the city's music scene who could use their training to evolve the city's sound.[21] They were the city's most significant musical assets.

When the United States entered World War I in 1917, Minneapolis's economic woes worsened, and despite its popularity, music education faced belt-tightening. For Giddings, it was "music as usual." Patriotic songs were part of the way music was taught during wartime.[22] But the program did not fade. It continued to grow, as did the Minneapolis music scene. In the sixty-seven years between the city's founding and the start of the Great War, Minneapolis turned itself into a musical city with an abundance of performance space, numerous choral and musical societies, several music schools, and the most robust public school music program the country had ever seen. Even against the backdrop of profound social and economic changes, the Civil War, middle-class control of music, economic decline, and the onset of a world war, Minneapolis laid the foundations for a thriving music scene. And as Black migrants entered the city between the First and Second World Wars, they forever changed the sound of Minneapolis. Fleeing white supremacy in the South, they brought new harmonies, rhythms, tempos, and unique chord structures that evolved the city's sound and brought to the surface fault lines that would plague the Minneapolis music scene and its sound for decades.

Among these new arrivals were two families from rural Louisiana: the Shaws and the Nelsons. Mattie Shaw, the daughter of Franklin and Lucile, and John Nelson, the son of Carrie and Clarence, were active participants in the Black music scene in racially segregated North Minneapolis. They performed at several North Side clubs in the late 1940s and early '50s. Mattie and John met and fell in love in that musical community. In 1958, they had their first child together. John, the self-described jazzman, named him after the band he played in: Prince Rogers Nelson.

Chapter 4

SEGREGATING MINNEAPOLIS

Why cannot a measure be passed by the city council of Minneapolis, setting aside a certain district of the city within which negroes may purchase land for homes, which shall prohibit their purchasing lots in any other portion of the city?

—*Minneapolis Morning Tribune*, 1912

During the early 1970s, Prince began performing a unique combination of funk, rock, and R&B on Minneapolis's North and South Sides, which were predominantly Black. The music played in these venues was not solely based on the musical preferences of these communities. Instead, like early Minneapolis, the sounds flowing from those spaces were created in response to violent and discriminatory public policies. This musical tradition dates to the dawn of the twentieth century, with one of its earliest expressions occurring in 1910.

That year, white Minneapolitans in the affluent Lake Harriet neighborhood formed a group to keep Rev. W. S. Malone, a Black resident, from purchasing land in the community. Opposing the creation of a "dark town in their mists," the concerned citizens of Zenith Avenue used intimidation and payoffs to keep the neighborhood white.[1] Two years later, white residents in South Minneapolis, "fearing an increase in the negro population in their neighborhood," did the same.[2] In June 1912, white residents of what is now called the Bancroft neighborhood destroyed the home that Thomas H. Green, a Black man, was building on land he had purchased there. Undeterred, Green, with the aid of other Black residents, resumed construction, despite offers to buy the lot for more than its value.[3] In 1920, white residents in South Minneapolis formed yet another group to protest "against the presence of the Negroes or persons of Negroes [*sic*] blood."[4]

Black migration to Minneapolis met with white opposition—not the smiles or at worst indifference that greeted European migrants in the nineteenth century. Payoffs, mob violence, and most important, contract law and deed restrictions built into the city's housing system were the tools used by white Minneapolitans to create racially segregated neighborhoods. Their dark twin was Black Minneapolis. South Minneapolis and the Near North Side (near downtown) are Black communities engineered through exclusion, organized by opposition. They were the landing place for thousands of Black people escaping Southern terrorism with dreams of full citizenship and a chance at dignity. They were the places where dreams were realized, differed, and augmented. Most important for this story, they were the places Prince's family called home.

With an eye on Prince's family, this chapter explores Black migration to Minneapolis and uncovers how white violence against Black residents and racially restrictive housing covenants baked into the housing system racially segregated Minneapolis in the years between and after the world wars. This geographic order not only segregated Minneapolis but also created a musical apartheid that ordered the city's sound for decades.

Southern Stories

In 1945, Minnesota Governor Edward J. Thye created the Interracial Commission in the wake of race riots in Chicago, Washington, and St. Louis that left hundreds of Black people dead and cost millions of dollars in damage. This nationalized the growth of the Ku Klux Klan, which had found a foothold in Minnesota. Between 1945 and 1949, the commission issued three reports—*The Negro Worker in Minnesota* (1945), *The Negro and His Home in Minnesota* (1947), and *The Negro Worker's Progress in Minnesota* (1949).[5] They were essentially fact-finding missions; the governor wanted to understand the nature of anti-Black racism in Minnesota in the hope of preventing riots and the "serious social disorders" they'd create.[6] The third report on housing was a detailed and clear-eyed look at the link between racism and housing. It showed the obstacles Black residents faced when trying to find housing in Minnesota.

"We find, sadly," the report observed, "that 60 percent of our white people favor segregation."[7] Widespread racism, mixed with Black people's lack of political and economic power—findings outlined in the other Interracial Commission reports—drastically reduced the options for housing, making segregation normal and enduring. Why did white Minneapolitans feel such hostility toward Black people, who, up to that point, only made up a tiny portion of the city's population?

Two related historical events hardened white Minneapolitans against Black migration. The first was the dismantling of Reconstruction (1865–77), the period after the Civil War when Union forces remained in the South to rebuild Confederate cities devastated by the war and protect newly freed Black people. The Reconstruction period was the South's first taste of multiracial democracy. Black communities were born, as were Black social and fraternal organizations like the Freedmen's Bureau. Black men elected seven Black representatives to Congress in states like South Carolina, Louisiana, and Mississippi, where Black people outnumbered white people, giving them political power that just a few years prior seemed unimaginable.

However, this short-lived experiment ended when federal troops pulled out of the South in 1877. When the troops left, the South lurched "back towards slavery," stripping Black people of the right to vote and instituting segregation in every area of Southern life.[8] To justify white supremacy and segregation, Southern white people perpetuated an ideology of Black people, particularly Black men, as violent and predatory. This racial defamation portrayed Black men as a sexual threat to Southern white womanhood. These purported characteristics of Black people proved them unfit for freedom. According to Southern segregationists, only a system of racial exclusion (backed by violence) could protect the white social order (and white women) from Black criminality.

This characterization of racial equality as uncivilized and Black freedom as a national problem (the "Negro question") traveled with Black people as they tried to escape Jim Crow by moving North. Northern newspapers ran stories that portrayed Black migration as a problem that cities should address by segregating Black people from white. When Black people arrived in Northern cities, the image of them as predatory and prone to crime followed, augmenting existing anti-Black sentiment. The racist ideology of Black threat and inferiority created grave problems for Black people who moved to Minneapolis between the First and Second World Wars, including for Prince's family.[9]

Black Migration and Prince's Family

Prince's family came to Minneapolis during the most intense years of housing discrimination and racial segregation in the city's history. The story of his maternal relatives, the Shaws, and his father's family, the Nelsons, in Minneapolis began not long after former President Theodore Roosevelt attacked the incumbent, Woodrow Wilson, during the 1916 presidential campaign for failing to prepare the country for war against the German Empire. The so-called Great War energized the most significant internal migration of people in the nation's history—the Great Black Migration.

By 1970, nearly 6 million Black people had fled the former slave states and settled in the North.[10] New York, Chicago, Detroit, Newark, Los Angeles, and Oakland absorbed the greatest number; smaller cities like Seattle, Phoenix, St. Paul, and Minneapolis received the rest. The migration occurred in two stages, the first stage between 1915 and 1940 and the second between 1950 and 1970. Prince's family left the South during the first phase. His maternal grandparents, Franklin Shaw and his fiancée Lucille Barnell left after Congress passed the Selective Service Act in May 1917, which required all nondisabled men to register for the military draft.

Franklin was born in 1896 in Arcadia, Bienville Parish, Louisiana, to Eliza and Preston Shaw, who were married in 1882, five years after the 1877 compromise that ended Reconstruction. "Pres," as he was called, was one of ten children; Lucille, born in 1899 in Ruston, Lincoln Parish, Louisiana, to Sam and Katy Barnell (or Bonnell), was one of six.

Franklin and Lucile Shaw left Louisiana sometime in 1919, when the United States entered its third year in the First World War and Chicago experienced its first race riot. They took the Southwest-to-Midwest train line—a standard method of transportation for Black migrants. Trains had the single most significant impact on where migrants landed. Ironically, the rail lines that took them out of the South were established in the nineteenth century to transport products of enslaved labor to the North, like cotton and tobacco.[11] Black migration was tied to large industrial centers like New York, Chicago, St. Louis, and Detroit. Despite joining the Union in the middle of the nineteenth century, Minnesota sent products to the South and received products from it. The state was also a vacation site for wealthy Southern planters, who arrived with their human cargo to escape the summer heat and bask in the cool waters of St. Anthony.

Lucille Bonnell and Franklin Shaw landed first in Polk County, Iowa, and married in Des Moines. From there, the Shaws took the Far West trains to Minneapolis. They arrived sometime in the mid–1920s, as Franklin's name appears in the city directory from 1927 to 1930. The Shaws show up in the

1930 census, living at 821 Dupont Avenue in the Jewish and Black Near North Side.[12] On November 11, 1933, the two welcomed into the world twin baby girls, Edna Mae and Mattie Del, Prince's mother.[13]

Records show that the Shaws lived at various places on the Near North Side. They even lived in the city's first housing projects, the Summer Field homes. The North Side was a landing place for immigrants in Minneapolis; Jewish migrants began moving to the area in the 1870s, and before them Germans and Scandinavians. Black people started moving there after 1900. Within ten years, Black people replaced Jews, who left the area for more affluent parts of the city.[14] For a while—between the 1910s and mid-1940s—Blacks and Jews lived together, forming a racially and ethnically diverse community. The Shaws were part of an uptick in Minneapolis's Black population, which, from 1910 to 1930, grew from 2,592 to 4,176, a 40 percent increase.[15] Although African Americans' numbers were small, their double-digit gains in population increased into the 1970s.[16]

Prince's paternal grandparents were also from Louisiana. His grandmother, Carrie Nelson (Jenkins), born either in 1875 or 1883, was originally from Alabama but moved to Cotton Valley, Webster Parish, in the northwest part of the state, where she met her husband, Clarence Allen Nelson, who was born 1882 in Webster Parish. According to the 1900 census, the two married in 1898. Around the turn of the century, the couple moved to New Orleans. They lived at 2108 Palmer Avenue until their divorce, shortly after John's birth in 1915. In 1920, Carrie married Charles Inker and lived with him on a farm in Webster Parish, with seventeen-year-old Gertrude, fifteen-year-old Olivia, ten-year-old Rudy, five-year-old James, and three-year-old John.[17]

Carrie left Louisiana in the late 1920s after the death of her second husband. Her name appears on the 1930 Minneapolis census.[18] The Nelsons came to Minneapolis in stages, a common way of migrating; often, one family member moved north, and once they got established, other family members followed. In 1930, Carrie lived with her mother in the thriving Black community of the Central District.[19]

John, Carrie's youngest son, arrived in Minneapolis in the early 1930s. In 1940, he and his wife Vivian moved to 2929 Fifth Avenue with their daughter Sharron. Their second daughter, Noreen, was born about a year after Sharron. John worked as a doorman at a downtown hotel.[20]

Welcome to Minneapolis

The Shaws and the Nelsons encountered a confusing and contradictory terrain in Minneapolis. The city's hustle and bustle, tall buildings, streetcars, parallel and perpendicular walkways, and industrial economy took some getting used to. Neither family had lived in a place like this Northwestern city. The larger landmass forced them to travel greater distances for goods and services, and using public transportation was a new experience. They also had more access to consumer products and unfamiliar ethnic foods in the Scandinavian eateries and grocery stores near their South Minneapolis home.

Race was different in their new city, too. Minneapolis was not the South, meaning that Black people were not subject to the social rules of white supremacy. No restrictions existed on using public facilities like water fountains, swimming pools, schools, or libraries, and lynching was rare. (Three Black men, however, were lynched in Duluth in 1920.) But Minneapolis had its racial codes, too. And Prince's family, like all Black people, learned them quickly.

The Shaws and Nelsons migrated to Minneapolis during the most significant and intense period of racial division in the United States. In cities across the country, white residents enforced racial lines in housing, restricting Black people to specific areas to "prohibit their purchasing lots in any other portion of the city."[21] Along Bloomington Avenue and Fortieth Street, in what is now called Bancroft, Thomas H. Green purchased a lot in 1912 to build a home for his family. Within days of his starting to build, white residents alerted Green that they "did not desire negroes in the neighborhood."[22] (Ten other Black families already lived within a four-block radius.) Green was even offered money to vacate. After he refused the money and resisted racist intimidation, white residents "made a midnight sally against his property."[23] They threw his wood and other building materials into the swamp, knocked the structure he'd built off its foundation, and even used his tools to tear apart tar paper for his roof. After a local Boy Scout troop helped Green gather his materials from the nearby swamp, he assembled Black community members to protect his property from further molestation. Green told white residents he would accept $175 to defray material and labor costs. However, this would risk the well-being of the Black families already living in the area by setting a precedent that payoffs were acceptable.[24]

What happened to the Green family had roots dating back to the beginning of the century. The earliest reported case is that of Rev. W. S. Malone. In the fall of 1909, Malone, a minister at the African Methodist Episcopal Church in North Minneapolis, bought a home in the Lake Harriet section of Minneapolis from Maria A. Canfield. She sold him the house for $2,600, of which Malone gave her $1,600 at the point of sale.[25] Within days of the deal, more than 100 white people, mostly Lake Harriet residents but also from nearby neighborhoods, gathered at a house across the street from Malone's home.[26] First, they tried to persuade Malone not to move in. When that didn't work, they broke the house's windows and threatened to burn it down. Malone and Maria Canfield sought protection from the police, who said they couldn't help them. Malone pleaded with the police that he was qualified to own the home. "I'll show you my credentials," the minister told them. "I bought it with my own money, and I'll live out there if I want to." But the pressure proved too much for Malone. White residents paid him to give up the house weeks after purchase.[27]

In 1920, white residents protested the presence of Black people in the city's Thirteenth Ward. Citing real estate depreciation as the reason for their opposition to Black residents, the white people formed a committee to study the impact of Black residents on housing and "check the number of residents of colored blood and ascertain who sold the property to them."[28]

Prince's grandparents certainly knew of the most egregious example of white violence against Black homebuyers. Following the playbook of previous white groups attempting to keep Blacks out, several hundred residents gathered near Forty-Sixth Street and Columbus Avenue in front of the Lee family's bungalow to terrorize them into submission. They threw black paint on the house. They even poisoned the family dog. Then, in July, hundreds, carrying rocks and making verbal threats, surrounded the house, then stoned it.[29] A brigade of police officers arrived to subdue the crowd. The incident lasted for several days, forcing the Lees to seek protection from other Black World War I veterans and Arthur Lee's coworkers at the post office. Minneapolis's mayor offered little help in the matter, claiming he had no power to stop the violence. The police made no arrests. Even with the help of the local National Association for the Advancement of Colored People (NAACP), which organized protection and battled for the family's right to be in the home, the Lees, like other Black residents, eventually sold the house and moved away.[30]

Covenants of Order

By 1930, most Black people lived in Black sections of Minneapolis on the North and South Sides. They lived there because of the intimidation and terrorism they encountered when they tried to buy houses in white-majority areas. But housing segregation was also enforced through racially restrictive covenants, legally binding contracts written into the deeds of homes.

This de jure segregation effectively kept white neighborhoods white. Racial covenants came into being in the late nineteenth century. They restricted the purchase, lease, and occupancy of housing along race lines, with language like "no Jews," "no Mongolians," "no Mexicans," and always "no Negroes." The earliest examples are from California in 1886. By 1904, restrictive covenants spread to the South, and by the 1910s, they appeared in the Midwest and Northeast. Minneapolis's first recorded covenant was in 1910 for a house in South Minneapolis. The deed read, "The said party of the second part hereby agrees that the premises hereby conveyed shall not at any time be conveyed, mortgaged, or leased to any person or persons of Chinese, Japanese, Moorish, Turkish, Negroes [*sic*], Mongolian or African blood or descent. Said restrictions and covenants shall run with the land and any breach of any or either thereof shall work a forfeiture of title, which may be enforced by re-entry."[31] Between 1910 and the mid-1950s, restrictive covenants were ubiquitous. They kept Black people out of white neighborhoods like Lake Calhoun and blocked their movement into Lake Harriet and other parts of the city.[32] Not willing to get their hands dirty in the business of mob violence, wealthy, powerful men in Minneapolis used racial covenants instead. Some of the first to use them systematically were real estate developers, like Samuel Thorpe of the Thorpe Brothers company.[33] After purchasing farmland, he divided it into rectangle-shaped lots to be sold. Thorpe then wrote restrictive covenants into the deeds.[34] In 1912, Thorpe developed a community called Nokomis Terrace, which became the city's first fully covenanted neighborhood. Another developer, Edmund G. Walton, purchased a large swath of land along West River Road and went as far as to publicize his racial covenants in a local newspaper.[35]

The thousands of covenants that blanketed the city pushed the rapidly increasing Black population into areas that didn't have covenants. When Prince's grandparents arrived sometime in the late 1920s, racial covenants controlled where they lived. Racial covenants did not restrict the house the Shaws rented on Dupont Avenue; the same was true for the house Carrie Nelson Inker and her family lived in on the South Side. In 1910, the Shaws' neighborhood had only a 5–10 percent Black population; by 1920, that percentage had doubled. By 1930, nearly a quarter of the residents were Black; by the 1940s, Blacks constituted almost half the population.[36] On Du Pont Avenue, where the Shaw family resided, all of the residents on the entire 800 block were Black people.

The Nelsons settled in the growing Black South Side neighborhood between Thirty-Eighth and Forty-Eighth Streets, along Nicollet Avenue to the west and Chicago Avenue to the east. This area was the center of Black life in South Minneapolis, with Fourth Avenue South as its business district. It had more than twenty Black-owned shops and the offices of the *Minneapolis Spokesman*, the city's leading Black newspaper.

Despite the ubiquity of racism, Black residents didn't accept segregation; they actively opposed it and created institutions to defend themselves and their communities. Black women played vital roles as community organizers. The NAACP opened its Minneapolis chapter in 1920. Lena Olive Smith, the state's first Black woman lawyer, spearheaded the chapter's efforts against housing discrimination. (Smith was the attorney for the Lee family.) The discrimination she witnessed against Black homebuyers compelled her to abandon her career in real estate and enter Northwestern College of Law in St. Paul. After joining the NAACP in 1920, a year before graduating from law school, Smith pushed back against the city's racially restrictive housing practices. She sued landlords and home sellers accused of discrimination and sued local hotels that wouldn't serve Blacks. And she took up cases of police brutality against Black residents. Smith also helped found the Minneapolis Urban League, which fought housing discrimination.[37]

Nellie Stone Johnson was another influential advocate. Born in Lakeville, Minnesota, a township twenty miles south of downtown Minneapolis, she moved to the city when she was seventeen, around the same time the Shaws arrived, in 1923. After taking a job as an elevator operator in the Minneapolis Athletic Club, Nellie entered the world of activism. She helped organize the Local 665 Restaurant and Hotel Workers Union in 1934. Johnson was also a founding member of the Minnesota Farmer-Labor Party. This unique Upper Midwest organization merged the rural Farmer's Party and the urban Labor Party under the Democratic Party banner. Over her fifty years in community action, Johnson organized workers, participated in civil rights work, and collaborated with several women's groups.[38] The Phyllis Wheatley Settlement House was among the most prominent women's groups. Lena Olive Smith and Nellie Stone Johnson were members.

The Wheatley House grew out of Black women's club organizing at the turn of the century.[39] The women created clubs for women and girls to provide services, build community, and confront racism. As the Black population of Minneapolis grew, Black club women, frustrated by the lack of housing options for Black women, worked with middle-class white women to create the Phyllis Wheatley House in 1924. The Wheatley House was one of the day's most important civic and social agencies. In addition to supporting Black women in finding housing, the Wheatley accommodated Black people barred from staying at downtown hotels. Its guest list includes luminaries like the co-founder of the NAACP, W. E. B. Du Bois; poet Langston Hughes; civil rights activist and educator Mary McLeod Bethune; and singer Ethel Waters. The Wheatley House also helped Black students who could not stay in the University of Minnesota dorms to find housing.[40]

"What Happens to a Dream Deferred?"

Both the Shaws and the Nelsons rented their homes in Minneapolis. On average, Black Minneapolitans paid higher rents, even for older houses lacking central heat and in disrepair.[41] This legacy fed into the new advancement in housing that started during the New Deal era of the 1930s.

The federal government created the Home Owners Loan Corporation (HOLC), Freddie Mac, and Fannie Mae to help Americans purchase homes and stimulate the economy during the Great Depression. Freddie and Fannie guaranteed the loans banks made to consumers. So, if a bank failed, the federal government would step in and insure the loan. The HOLC was a regulatory agency whose sole purpose was to advise banks on where they should and should not make home loans. These agencies and programs revolutionized homeownership. Before 1930, purchasing a home required at least 50 percent of the housing price up front, which only the wealthy could afford. However, with the federal government backing the loans, banks could charge low interest rates over more extended periods (thirty years) and require 2–3 percent of the housing cost upfront. If this sounds familiar, it's because this is how most people purchase homes today. Lowering the bar for entrance made homes a consumer item and opened homeownership to millions of people.

Black people were systematically excluded from these opportunities. The HOLC created thousands of color-coded maps of large, midsize, and small cities and towns nationwide that banks used to approve and restrict loans. These maps visually represented the racial geography created by restrictive covenants.

On the HOLC maps, white areas were in green; blue designated predominantly white places with some people of color; yellow meant hazardous and signified growing numbers of ethnic minorities, poor people, and Black people; red meant Black people were present in large numbers. Banks refused to make loans in the Black areas. The HOLC described the site where the Nelson family lived along Fourth Avenue:

> Running north and south along 4th Avenue South was once a very substantial and desirable area for homes about 40 years ago. A gradual infiltration of negroes and Asiatics has occurred on 4th Avenue South, beginning at approximately Franklin Avenue moving south to approximately 38th Street . . . The street car line extends out to the 48th Street and although the colored people have not moved much beyond 38th Street, development of 4th Avenue, south of 38th Street, have [*sic*] been

> very slow because of the continued colored trend southerly and the fact that the street car runs into the loop in Minneapolis through the heavily populated colored section. Fifth Avenue on the east and Clinton on the west of 4th Avenue are affected by a large colored population on the Avenue. Because of the influence of the class of people on 4th Avenue extending over and into C-8, its desirability for residential purposes is seriously affected.[42]

The HOLC described Dupont Avenue North, where the Shaws lived:

> About 40 years old; there were many fine homes in this area occupied by Germans, Irish, French and Scandinavian families. Today the buildings are badly in need of rehabilitation. On the west between Lyndale and Humboldt Avenues from Plymouth to the southern boundary of this area, most of the population today is of the poorer class of Jew and colored people. Various industries have sprung up in this neighborhood and particularly on the easterly half of this area adjacent to the business district there are some duplexes and apartment houses of the older class in poor physical condition. Most of the buildings range from 15 to 50 years; it is very difficult to place the valuation; and it is a most undesirable location for residential purposes.[43]

The "gradual infiltration of negroes" in the South and the "poorer classes of Jew and colored people" in the North reduced the possibility for many Black residents to get home loans. In addition, the HOLC also systematically kept Blacks out of developing suburbs on the outskirts of town.

As the Second World War raged in Europe, farmland on the edges of American cities like New York, Chicago, Phoenix, and Minneapolis was bought by developers, split into lots, and sold to returning GIs in search of housing. The suburbanization of the United States was one of the most significant events in the history of housing. It not only transformed the nation's landscape, giving rise to expressways like the Cross Bronx Expressway in New York or the BART (Bay Area Rapid Transit), which carried suburbanites to and from their downtown jobs. Suburbanization also racialized housing for generations, creating vast geographic gulfs between Black and white people. I-494 and I-35 West shuttled white people from Minneapolis to suburban Edina, Richfield, and St. Louis Park. And as white Minneapolitans moved, so too did restrictive covenants, affecting new housing developments and securing their whiteness for decades.[44]

Carving up the city's landscapes along racial lines created a racist geography while also fostering economic inequality. Most Americans build wealth through property appreciation over time, such as purchasing a home in 1935 for $20,000 and selling it in 1970 for three times that value. Racially restrictive covenants constituted a state-sanctioned welfare program that enabled white people to create wealth through housing appreciation while excluding Black people, who were relegated to rental housing.

"Does It Dry Up Like a Raisin in the Sun?"

Racial covenants kept Prince's grandparents from owning their homes. While the red lines on real estate maps delimited loans in those areas, unstable employment also made buying a home difficult. Franklin Shaw's employment as a porter supported the family, but the wages were insufficient to save for a home. Widowed and living with family, Carrie Nelson Inker couldn't afford a home. Prince's grandparents faced the same employment/homeownership challenges as many Black Minneapolitans.

In the years between the First and Second World Wars, 60 percent of Blacks could not find work in Minneapolis; the jobs they could find were at the bottom of the pay scale. The Minneapolis Urban League reported in 1926 that more than 80 percent of Black men worked as porters on trains, security guards, janitors, and other low-wage jobs, their wages falling below the Bureau of Labor Statistics national average of $2,262.47 to $1,172.[45] Franklin Shaw worked as a porter in the 1930s for one of the four railroads that hired Black people. Still, his inability to move up in the organization because of white worker resentment undermined his ability to save enough money to buy a home, a fact that afflicted men like him for decades.[46]

Many things stood in the way of Black people getting stable employment—white workers' refusal to work alongside Blacks, white customers who didn't want to interact with them, and employers who did not want to hire them. Perhaps one of the more insidious obstacles was labor unions. In an industrial city like Minneapolis, labor unions held considerable sway over jobs, which took decades of organizing, culminating in a wildcat strike in 1934 that broke the back of the city's antiunion forces. Yet despite this historic collective effort on behalf of the working man, those same unions locked Blacks out. "Gradually as the white workers organized," says the governor's report on Black employment, "they carried in the unions their former prejudices."[47] Blacksmiths, bartenders, hotel workers, milk drivers, bricklayers, machinists, and electrical workers unions blocked Blacks from membership, robbing them of the opportunity to work decent jobs with protections and benefits.[48]

John Nelson was the only family member who had evaded the city's discriminatory employment system. In 1940, he worked a job that reflected the city's racial hierarchy: doorman at the Andrew Hotel in downtown Minneapolis. Now, with two daughters, the Nelsons needed more income. Like my great-grandmother, Jane Toliver, who was able to find employment in a Chicago factory while men were abroad fighting in the Second World War, John Nelson landed a wartime job with a Minneapolis military supplier, the Honeywell Corporation. The increased pay was a boon for the Nelsons, allowing them to purchase a house in 1944 on Fifth Avenue, just a block from his sister. In 1942 and 1944, the Nelsons welcomed two more children, Lenora and John Jr.[49]

The Nelsons' ability to purchase a home in the highly restrictive area deserves more context: Between 1946 and 1952, just shy of 10,000 homes and duplexes were built in Minneapolis. Only 20 were purchased by Black people—John and Vivian among them.[50] This life-altering event affected the family for decades and played an important role in Prince's life.

"Or Does It Explode?"[51]

After the Second World War ended and soldiers returned home, Black (and women) workers worried about keeping their jobs. (My great-grandmother lost hers.) John Nelson, however, remained employed by Honeywell. But the Nelsons found themselves confronted by another set of racial problems: suburbanization and racially restrictive housing covenants, which prevented them from purchasing a home in Edina, Brooklyn Park, St. Louis Park, and other areas. With the war's end, suburbanization accelerated. Suburbanization also created a logistical problem for white suburbanites, who faced lengthy commutes to the city for work, entertainment, and shopping. Seeing the headwinds of the crisis, the federal government rectified them with sweeping legislation.

In 1956, President Dwight D. Eisenhower signed the Federal Highway Act, which created 41,000 miles of new highways connecting cities nationwide and faster routes to and from the suburbs. The Highway Act was one of the most significant investments in public infrastructure in the country's history. However, for Black people and working-class white people in places like Minneapolis, the Federal Highway Act negatively affected their communities by placing them in the crosshairs of construction.

In 1957, Minneapolis held public hearings on the proposed route of I-35 West through the city. The initial proposal was for it to run along Ninth Street south to Seventeenth Street south along Lyndale Avenue, in a white and wealthy neighborhood.[52] After the hearings, the route was relocated to the growing Black section of South Minneapolis.[53] Minneapolis's Black community was not the only one to experience this; highways were routed through Black neighborhoods in Chicago, New Orleans, Oakland, Los Angeles, Detroit, St. Paul, and many other cities, creating dividing lines between Black and white communities, tearing Black neighborhoods apart, and displacing their residents.

In Minneapolis, I-35 West went through the Nelsons' South Minneapolis neighborhood. The eight-lane roadway sliced the thriving Black area in half and created a barrier between the Black business district to the west and the adjacent white community. The Central District had become a haven for Black people.[54] Besides being a business district, the neighborhood also had a vibrant cultural life centered on Thirty-Eighth Street. Black venues offering blues, jazz, and rock 'n' roll attracted budding musicians like John Nelson, who played in Central District establishments. He met Mattie Shaw, a young singer in the Billie Holiday mold. John had assembled a band, the Prince Rogers Trio, and Mattie became the vocalist. Although Mattie was married and had a son, she and Nelson fell in love. John ended his relationship with his wife Vivian in October 1956 and finalized their divorce a year later. Mattie divorced her husband Alfred Jackson.

Eager to begin their lives together, Mattie and John married in August 1957.[55] They took their vows five months after the new I-35 West highway public hearing. As they began their life together, the federal government planned to route I-35 West through their South Minneapolis neighborhood, where they had met, lived, and performed.

Mattie and John's first child, Prince Rogers Nelson, was born June 7, 1958, at Mount Sinai Hospital in Minneapolis. Their first home was on Fifth Avenue South, a few blocks from the hospital and facing the site where the federal government located the new highway. The Nelsons lived there for less than a year.

No records indicate whether the Nelsons knew about the impending highway. It seems likely that they, like most neighborhood residents, didn't know about the highway, and that their leaving the community not long after Prince was born and before the highway construction began was a coincidence. Although a public notice stated that residents could comment on the highway project, the news was buried in the *Minneapolis Tribune*'s want ads section. Not surprisingly, many Black residents were shocked to discover that their neighborhood was in the project's path. Some didn't know until the bulldozers appeared in 1960.

Thousands of working-class Black residents were displaced, some by eminent domain, while others sold their homes. Robert Williams, director of the Minneapolis Urban League, observed that highway construction would crowd Black people in areas where they already lived "unless housing barriers are relaxed."[56] When I-35 West opened in 1967, Williams's prediction seemed prophetic; those forced to move had their housing options stymied by racial covenants or threats of white violence.

There were efforts to mitigate the lack of housing options for Black Minneapolitans. One example was to create a public market where Black people could buy homes. The best-known were the Tilsenbilt Homes. The sixty-three-lot development was the brainchild of Urban League President and Black realtor Archie Givens Sr., who recruited Edward Tilsen, a Jewish homebuilder, to construct the houses.[57] Built between 1954 and 1956, the Tilsenbilt Homes were the nation's first federally backed housing development open to all races. Tilsen hired Black people to construct the modest 1,000-square-foot bungalows along Third and Fifth Avenues. Black people bought 90 percent of the homes, with 10 percent bought by white people.[58]

The Nelsons only lived in their South Minneapolis house until the end of 1960. Because of John's job and the home he and Vivian owned, the Nelsons were able to use that equity to purchase a house at 915 Logan Avenue North for $12,000. The sale closed on New Year's Day.[59] Their new home was near Mattie's family and not far from John's Honeywell job. It also avoided the pathway of I-35 West.

When the Nelsons moved to their new neighborhood, the concentration of Black residents had risen to nearly 32 percent. No doubt, restrictive covenants and the threat of mob violence toward Black homebuyers eventually made the neighborhood become predominantly Black. These same forces pushed the Nelsons into the area. Prince's first memories—"my mother's eye" and "my father's piano"—came from that house.[60] Prince's sister Tyka was born there in 1960.

Hurdling job discrimination and becoming one of the handful of Black homeowners put the Nelsons on firm financial footing. Five years later, they moved to Eighth Avenue North in the heart of the Near North Side. They purchased their new house while renting out the one on Logan Avenue. This home was "where it happened" musically for Prince. He began playing piano and writing songs there.[61] The Nelsons' Eighth Avenue North home didn't have restrictive covenants or white neighbors protesting their presence. John's job at Honeywell and his regular gigs in the Central District with his Prince Rogers Trio made him the money to purchase the new home. Lyndale Avenue was the cultural and business center of the Black Near North Side community. Lined with Black-owned shops and music venues, it was the Harlem of the Upper Midwest.

Whites, including Jewish people, were leaving the Near North Side for better housing options in whiter, wealthier parts of the city and suburbs like Brooklyn Park and Edina. Between 1953 and 1961, Minneapolis's suburban population grew by 114 percent.[62] The city's segregated geography was all too evident. When Prince was in the first grade, his closest friend and favorite make-believe girlfriend was Laura Winnick, a white girl who lived near him. "No one could play-act better than Laura," he recalled.[63] While playing house one day, Laura gave him three kisses, pretending one was before work, the second after he came home after work, and one more before bed—as a married couple might. "We weren't the first interracial couple in Minneapolis," Prince said, "but we were no doubt the youngest."[64] Not long after that encounter, Laura and her parents joined the exodus of white Minneapolitans, leaving the city for what Prince described as "a way better neighborhood."[65] Race didn't create opposition in the make-believe world he and Laura played in. Those kisses "were everything" to the first grader, maybe not only because of his feelings for her but also because she helped open something in him. But as he grew up, he saw that his child's world of make-believe and the real one were at odds.

Segregating Minneapolis had effects beyond housing and wealth creation; it also affected schools. School segregation was a direct consequence of housing segregation—neighborhoods feed local schools. Though not legally enforced, like housing discrimination, de facto racial segregation of education is nonetheless harmful. Most Black children attended their neighborhood schools in South and North Minneapolis. Warrington School, for example, was 85 percent Black by 1960.[66] Black schools were overcrowded, underfunded, had higher incompletion rates, and stressed vocational training over liberal education. Black teachers were few.[67] Like many Black parents in the 1960s, the Nelsons did what they could to help their children get a better education, which for Prince and Tyka meant being bused to schools outside their neighborhood. The half-hearted effort to create better opportunities for cross-racial interaction was entirely put on the shoulders of Black parents like the Nelsons. The city only assumed the cost of busing the children. In his song "The Sacrifice of Victor," Prince recalled his experience:

> In 1967 in a bus marked public schools
> Rode me and a group of unsuspecting political tools
> Our parents wondered what it was like 2 have another color
>   near
> So they put their babies together 2 eliminate the fear.[68]

Prince and Tyka were among eight Black children bused to schools outside their neighborhoods. Prince was bused to Kenwood Elementary School at

2013 Penn Avenue South. Both Nelson children had bad experiences, enduring bullying, racist taunting, and name-calling. The experiment lasted only (or perhaps less than) a year. Prince returned to his neighborhood school, John Jay Elementary, for fifth grade, followed by Lincoln Junior High and Central High, a more racially diverse school on the South Side. He liked Central's music program and often could be found in the fourth-floor music rooms filled with instruments from Thaddeus P. Giddings's tenure as Minneapolis's public school music director.[69] Prince graduated in 1976, just one year before releasing his debut album, *For You*.

In 1967, the year Prince was bused to Kenwood Elementary, his Near North Side neighborhood erupted in days of protest that ended with federal troops brought in to quell the unrest—for the second time in as many years. Like so many other protests during this period, it began with the police. During the "long hot summer" of 1967, a fight started between two Black girls at a popular downtown event, the Aquatennial Torchlight Parade. A police officer threw one of the girls to the ground. When a young man complained about the police officer's treatment of the girl, the police struck him, too. Word of the police violence got back to residents on the Near North Side, and several gathered the next day at a local community center called the Way.[70] Prince played ball at the center and even had an early performance there. Later that night, Black residents gathered on Plymouth Avenue to protest the police response.

Soon, officers responded to the protest. Tensions escalated. An officer struck a pregnant protester in the belly, and she subsequently miscarried. Fights broke out between residents and police over what the former saw as a typically heavy-handed response to a minor incident. Protesters hurled rocks at the police officers, set fires, and threw Molotov cocktails. More police arrived to suppress the protest, and more residents joined the fighting. Minneapolis Mayor Arthur Naftalin called the National Guard to quell the protest. After four days of clashes, more than thirty people were arrested, many more were injured, and Plymouth Avenue—still smoking from buildings set ablaze—had become the latest example of what happens when housing and school segregation, displacement, and employment discrimination defer dreams of full citizenship.[71]

Chapter 5

MUSICAL APARTHEID

It was terrible, just awful . . . you go down Hennepin Avenue, and there wasn't a black face anywhere.

—Dick Mayers

The color line organized Minneapolis's housing, schools, and employment, which locked Black people out of opportunities white people received as a birthright. Segregation birthed racially and geographically separate scenes: a white downtown one along Hennepin Avenue and Black ones along the Near North Side on Lyndale Avenue and in South Minneapolis. This partition had contradictory effects. Black musicians created a rich and innovative music community blending jazz, blues, and early rock 'n' roll on the Near North Side and South Minneapolis. But they struggled to access higher pay along Hennepin Avenue and downtown. White musicians, influenced by Black sounds, missed opportunities to evolve musically alongside the creative sounds of Black musicians, whose inventive rhythm, chord changes, and harmonies offered a new musical language.

Minneapolis's musical apartheid had immense implications for the development of the city's sound and the soundscape of the various artists, venues, and music that defined an era.

Crescent City Sound

The turn of the twentieth century and national influences profoundly and permanently changed the Minneapolis music scene. New Orleans became the epicenter of music in the United States. The Crescent City sound—jazz—shaped the direction of music in every part of the country, shifting from the classical and European sounds of the nineteenth century to blues-inflected Black music equipped with new harmonic patterns, chord progressions, rhythms, tempos, and color. Prince's father, John Nelson, came to Minneapolis when jazz was in its early stages. The music's first superstar, Louis Armstrong, brought his sound to Minneapolis, paving the way for other New Orleans musicians who would migrate there. When John settled in Minneapolis, the color line partitioned Minneapolis's music scene. It remained in place until John's youngest son, Prince, synthesized Black and white styles in the late 1970s.

John Nelson, who had experienced the Great Black Migration from the South to Northern cities, was part of the jazz migration of the early part of the century. This migration brought jazz and the blues to Northern and Western cities like Los Angeles, New York, Chicago, St. Louis, and Minneapolis.[1] Jazz came to Minneapolis during the First World War, first in the form of ragtime, a style characterized by syncopated rhythms that was popular from the 1890s to the 1910s.

By 1899, ragtime had come up the Mississippi River to Minneapolis.[2] It was first played on riverboat steamers like the *Henrietta*, which ran between Minnehaha Falls in Minneapolis and Red Wing, Minnesota. The first known instance of its being played was a performance by Phinney's United States Band on the *Henrietta* in 1899.[3] The expansion of sheet music and the increasing availability of pianos helped boost its popularity.

Although cornetist Buddy Bolden is considered the first musician to play jazz, he never recorded, and his career was cut short by mental illness. Born in New Orleans, Louis Armstrong became jazz's first superstar.[4] His unique ability to play with power, soaring to the highest notes, distinguished him from all the musicians who came before and influenced everyone who came after. Before becoming a bandleader, he played in the group of fellow New Orleanian Joe "King" Oliver. When Oliver left the Crescent City for Chicago in 1918, Armstrong took a job on the *Sidney* steamer between New Orleans and Minneapolis as a member of Fate Marable's orchestra. That summer, he first saw the Twin Cities and played his horn in Minneapolis. A year later, he was likely aboard the *Sidney* and kept returning until he moved to Chicago in August 1922, following Joe Oliver.[5]

Though Armstrong didn't stay in Minneapolis, he laid the groundwork for the migration of other Crescent City musicians, like Boyd Atkins. Atkins played alongside Armstrong on the *Sidney* riverboat between 1918 and 1922, after which he settled in Minneapolis. Boyd became well-known in the city, playing at Black venues like the Cotton Club in North Minneapolis and

El Patio on the city's outskirts.[6] Another musical migrant was Warrenton, North Carolina–born saxophonist Tela Burt, who came to the town in 1912 and played on the riverboats. Still, gigs were few and far between because the larger boats had their bands and would "come up here and play and go back to New Orleans," said Burt.[7]

Perhaps the most famous musical migrant from the Crescent City to Minneapolis was saxophonist Lester "Prez" Young. Prez's brief but creative musical life is among the most significant in the history of jazz. Young was born in Woodville, Mississippi (also the birthplace of Confederate President Jefferson Davis), but raised in Algiers, on opposite bank of the Mississippi River from New Orleans's French Quarter.[8] Lester was raised mainly by his father, musician, taskmaster, and Tuskegee graduate, Willis "Billy" Young. In the early 1920s, Billy formed a band called the New Orleans Strutters and traveled the country on the Black minstrel show circuit, playing ragtime and jazz for primarily white audiences.[9] After years on the road and returning to New Orleans in the winter to be confronted with Jim Crow, Billy Young moved his family to Minneapolis in 1926. The icy city was a reprieve from the South. Billy's children could even attend school and receive daily music training, no less, a feat difficult in the South. It was in Minneapolis that Billy's oldest son, Lester, developed musically. Lester got his first alto saxophone when he was an adolescent. His father's band gave up minstrelsy in favor of a large orchestra sound like Cab Calloway's, which found favor in Minneapolis, playing at the Southside Ballroom in the city's growing Black southern section. When his family members left Minneapolis for Little Rock, Arkansas, Lester, reluctant to deal with Southern white supremacy again, made Minneapolis his home, bringing his new bride he'd met on tour in Albuquerque, New Mexico. He also fathered a daughter with a white woman in the city, which kept him coming back until he died in 1959.[10]

Locating White Minneapolis's Sound

As jazz migrated north, it transformed the new technologies of the phonograph and then radio for white Americans. The end of the First World War and, in 1920, the outlawing of alcohol were the headwinds of the "Jazz Age," as St. Paul author F. Scott Fitzgerald famously called the era in his novels *This Side of Paradise* and *The Great Gatsby*. Fitzgerald was in a unique place to witness the migration of jazz. St. Paul was Minnesota's first jazz city. Fitzgerald was among many in the Twin Cities to hear the syncopated rhythms echoing from the St. Paul port. Many white Americans who lived along the Mississippi River discovered jazz this way. Cornetist Bix Beiderbecke recalls hearing jazz aboard a steamer in his hometown of Davenport,

Iowa, likely during the war years. Minneapolitan Roy Robinson first heard it on a steamer in St. Paul in 1914. "I knew what ragtime was . . . this wasn't ragtime. This was jazz," he said.[11]

White people embraced jazz, but they lived in the racially segregated world they created at the turn of the century. That fact doesn't negate the value of white contributions to jazz. But those contributions took place in a warped world of racial segregation, which made it a "crime for cats of any color to get together to blow," according to Louis Armstrong.[12] Racial differences were grounded in place, with a white jazz world arising on the white side of the color line. The bizarre reality of white artists influenced by Black musicians, playing in white-only bands to white crowds, was still tethered to the predominant nineteenth-century musical entertainment: minstrelsy.

Over the first third of the twentieth century, blackface minstrelsy remained part of Minneapolis's cultural entertainment.[13] In 1903, Minneapolis songwriter Walter Bellam wrote a minstrel song titled "Mammy's Little Coal Black Coon." The Pence Opera House was a hot spot for minstrelsy, often with a symphony orchestra providing the backing music for the blackface performances. The State Theater, located downtown on Hennepin Avenue, also hosted minstrel shows. Minneapolis-based Northwestern Press published *The Five Star Minstrel Book*, which claimed to offer "everything needed for the production of a successful minstrel" show.[14]

However, the rise of jazz and radio and the growing opposition of Black people eventually eroded the popularity of minstrelsy. A 1915 editorial in the *Appeal*, a Black newspaper, forcefully stated, "The *Appeal* has always opposed minstrel shows and has recently called attention to the misrepresentations of the colored people, often given in public schools and churches by white people."[15]

The decline of blackface minstrelsy marked the end of the first and most prolific period of "black" music performed for white audiences. Although white performers in blackface created this music through a tangled web of mockery, desire, envy, and rejection, the genre nonetheless transformed Black cultural production into a consumable form.[16] Minstrelsy was extremely popular in the segregated community of white Minneapolis. Perhaps ironically, the enthusiasm of the city's white people for minstrelsy initiated a chain reaction that tethered race, geography, and sound for nearly seventy years.

Despite all the talk of jazz providing a social space for different musicians and music lovers to come together across (most specifically) racial lines, jazz was born and raised under segregation.[17] In Minneapolis, jazz lived in four distinct places: the Black Near North and South Sides, white downtown, and Uptown. As we saw in chapter 4, North and South Minneapolis were created by mob violence, contract law, and deed restriction. The rest of the city was white, and downtown and Uptown (west of downtown) were locations for white social and cultural life.

The years after the Great War were a boozy time in white Minneapolis. Hard-drinking mill workers and lumberjacks whose best days were behind them watched their industries shrink as the federal government outlawed the beer, wine, and liquor with which they ended their long days. But alcohol didn't disappear; it just moved to clandestine areas. These workers followed the new geography of booze to underground drinking holes and gambling spots facilitated by local gangsters like Kid Cann, who controlled nightclubs along Hennepin Avenue downtown and Lyndale on the Near North Side.[18] Jazz was the soundtrack to this network of secret clubs, lubricating late-night dances, card playing, sex work, and double-fisted, end-of-day drinking.

Jazz came ashore in the mid-1910s, moving from the steamers into St. Paul and Minneapolis. Downtown served as its staging ground. Brick buildings replaced boats as the physical infrastructure of music. These new establishments housed white jazz music in the years between the First and Second World Wars. Located along a seven-mile strip between Washington Avenue (known locally as "the Avenue") and Ninth Street along Hennepin, they were the spine of the downtown music scene.

Venues along the Avenue fell into two categories: theaters and strip clubs. The Palace Theater, the Minnesota Theater, and the Orpheum were pillars on the Avenue, offering Midwestern posh and old-world charm. Jazz wasn't on the menu at theaters, though white bandleader Paul Whiteman and his jazz orchestra played at the Minnesota Theater in 1928. But vaudeville was finding a home along the Avenue. This nineteenth-century entertainment form blended music and comedy, reaching its apex during the First World War. But it fell out of favor with the children of the Jazz Age, who wanted the sonic excitement of swing. The Orpheum stepped in to fill the void by bringing in well-known jazz musicians like Count Basie, Cab Calloway, Benny Goodman, Tommy Dorsey, Billy Eckstine, Stan Getz, and bebop architect Dizzy Gillespie, who performed there on Stan Kenton's tour during the 1950s.[19] Local acts like the North Minneapolis High School Swing Band also got on the Orpheum stage.[20]

Strip clubs, which often changed hands and names, were essential venues for music, even though it was not the main attraction. They found a home on Hennepin partly because of the city's enforcement actions against bordellos, which, by the 1930s, put them out of business. Strip clubs emerged to fill the void. Why they gathered along the Avenue is a bit of a mystery. Jazz and swing gatherings in the 1920s may have created room for strip clubs that used musicians to play for the dancers. Whatever the case, by the middle of the 1920s, several strip clubs lined Hennepin Avenue with musicians playing to accompany the seductive movements of the dancers, as the pianist and jazz's first composer Jelly Roll Morton did in the bordellos of New Orleans's Storyville district. The oldest club was Augie's on Lower Hennepin, which is still operating. Known for its divey atmosphere and scantily clad women, Augie's provided local and national musicians a place to play swing music and Dixieland. Even the New Orleans Rhythm Kings, an influential jazz band in the 1920s, played there. Sound mixed with seduction helped the club endure and, equally important, gave musicians a steady gig.[21]

There was also a network of hotels, restaurants, and speakeasies that offered jazz on the Avenue, like the Golden Pheasant Chinese restaurant on Seventh, the Flame Room in the Nicollet Hotel, the Arcadia and Trianon on Fifth Street and Nicollet, the Radisson Hotel between Seventh and Eighth, the Nankin Café on Seventh, Dayton's department store and tearoom, and Denny's, in the basement of Hudson's Jewelry. A few doors down from the Palace Theater was the Paradise. On Eighth Street was an upstairs speakeasy called the Gallery. And on the 500 block was the Camels Club, which was investigated for gambling in 1938 as the city sought to root out illegal activity.[22]

Working seven days a week was not uncommon for musicians on the Avenue, which demonstrates how central the street was to the city's sound. Local entrepreneurs like Herman Mitch opened Casablanca in the 1930s, which featured the great jazz drummer Gene Krupa. The Original Minneapolis Jazz Band played at the divey and all-male Saddle Bar. Cheap drinks drew musicians on break and those on a budget to the Brass Rail despite not having strippers. There was also Duffy's, Hoop-D-Doo off Nicollet, and the Moose Club, which hosted strippers, comedians, and musicians.[23]

While Hennepin Avenue was the spine of the downtown scene, its extremities also housed music. Tela Burt was among the few Black musicians regularly playing downtown from the 1920s to the 1940s. "I'd have two or three gigs every weekend," he recalled. Burt played at places like the Lamington Hotel, where all the musicians were white, and his big band played at the Palms on Nicollet Avenue.[24] The most prominent and best-known site for jazz or "jazzy" sounds was the Marigold Ballroom on Nicollet between Thirteenth Street and Grant. Ablaze with a sign that read, "Never grow old dancing at Marigold's," the ballroom was a staple of jazz and swing for nearly two decades. The Marigold was packed with dancers on weekends, so much so that the streetcar made unscheduled stops there. It opened in 1919 as the Marigold Gardens and underwent extensive redevelopment, becoming the

Marigold Ballroom in 1926.[25] Marigold set the trend followed by later downtown music venues like First Avenue & 7th Street Entry—booking national white bands, local white bands, nationally recognized Black acts like Cab Calloway, and keeping local Black musicians at bay.

Locating Black Minneapolis's Sound

While downtown boomed for white musicians, Black musicians were primarily kept out. Singer Dick Mayes said, "You never saw black bands" downtown. One venue consistently brought Black musicians downtown, the now-demolished Minneapolis Auditorium. Located on the southern tip of downtown at 1301 Second Avenue South, the Minneapolis Auditorium was an all-purpose theater that hosted circuses, rodeos, and some of jazz's finest artists. They performed there as part of the Jazz at the Philharmonic tours created by producer Norman Granz, which ran from the mid-1940s until the 1980s. As early as 1946, jazz legends like Sarah Vaughn, Coleman Hawkins, Dexter Gordon, Dizzy Gillespie, and Charlie "Bird" Parker graced the stage.

Besides the Auditorium, the color line kept local Black artists out of downtown. Prince was one of the first to play at the Orpheum, after the release of his second album, *Prince*, in 1979.[26] So, Black sounds emanated from the northern and southern parts of the city. The Near North Side was essential in cultivating the city's Black music. Jazz was central to the Near North sound. As early as 1926, when the Shaw and Nelson families arrived, the Near North Side had a mix of nightclubs and restaurants that presented jazz. Some of these clubs were called "black and tans" because they served customers interested in mixed-race socializing.

Black and tans were a product of Minneapolis's racial geography and a direct challenge to it. Their existence shouldn't surprise us. Creating separate racial worlds does more than place people in different locations based on race; it also generates fascination, interest, and desire for the racial other. The popularity of minstrel shows in the nineteenth and early twentieth centuries is just one example. The rise of the blues and jazz swelled white interest in Black music and culture. This interest continued with rock 'n' roll, rhythm and blues, rap music, and hip-hop culture. White Americans have always been swept up in the "tidal rhythm" of Black music and culture, and the black and tans provided a space to do it.[27] White people could live in the white world during the day, compliant with the demands of segregation, and at night leave that world behind—if only for a few hours—and enter these mixed-race landscapes where they could dance to Black rhythms, drink with Black people, and maybe have sensual encounters with Black women or men only to return to their white lives by morning.

Jazz was the soundtrack at the black and tans, and Black jazz clubs showcased the city's best, most innovative musicians. Lester Young developed his style in black and tans, even his habit of playing his tenor sax above his head and cocked to the left. "Prez" played at three well-known black and tans—the Kit Kat, Cotton Club, and the Nest. For Black musicians like Young and locals like Rook Ganz, Harold "Poppy" Booker, Adolphus Alsbrook, Walter Ruseu, Phil Pugh, and Boyd Akins, the black and tans were a boon because they paid well, a direct result of having white patrons.[28]

Interracial fascination and good music midwifed the black and tans and fattened the pockets of gangsters like Kid Cann, born Isadore Blumenfeld.[29] Cann, who also went by the alias Harry Bloom, owned at least one black and tan, the Cotton Club, named after the famous Harlem venue. Black management was critical, if only for appearances, because the clubs were in Black areas. Enter Ben Wilson, known as "the mayor of the North Side." More than just a manager, Wilson was known as a "plug"—someone who could get illegal goods for customers willing to pay for reliable, discreet service. Wilson's line in the underground trade and his ability to attract the best musicians made places like the Cotton Club and other black and tans wildly popular.[30] It also made them targets for the city, which pushed to close these mixed venues.

As early as 1921, city police, with the aid of the morals squad charged with prosecuting illegal alcohol sales and distribution, turned their sights on black and tans.[31] Within a decade, state officials were cracking down on them. The squad set up stings to arrest patrons, and even Ben Wilson was indicted and eventually jailed on federal charges that ranged from having liquor to "obscene acts" performed at one of his clubs. Kid Cann left the city as a result of the heat.[32] This was all part of Mayor William A. Anderson's campaign to "clean out questionable places on the North Side," which was code language for the black and tans.[33] Anderson was so intent on enforcement against the black and tans that he revoked the dance permit of one of the best-known venues, the Apex Club.[34]

The Kit Kat Club, located on the top floor of the Kistler Building, a three-story structure built in the nineteenth century at the corner of Lyndale Avenue and Olson Memorial Highway, was the most iconic and turbulent venue in the city's history. Some of the most significant figures in the 1930s swing era, including Benny Goodman, Gene Krupa, Fats Waller, Cab Calloway, and later Dizzy Gillespie, played there, along with famous Minneapolis musicians.

For much of its existence, the Kistler Building served several industrial and social purposes, as a meeting place for local clubs like the Elks and as a warehouse for building materials and grains to be shipped from the vast prairies to the South. The community surrounding the building shifted in the twentieth century. European immigrants, primarily Irish and Scandinavian, gave way to Jews and a slow but steady trickle of Black Southerners who, like their Jewish brethren, came to Minneapolis as refugees.

As the community changed, so did the way the building was used. In the 1920s, the Black population in the area was on the rise, and Jewish neighbors were leaving. But Black people were not moving into the neighborhood on their own accord; they were being pushed there by mob law and the restrictive covenants built into housing deeds. Segregation made the neighborhood around the Kistler Building Black, which, in 1926, resulted in the Elks leaving the top floor and the Kit Kat Club taking over.[35]

Known for late-night jam sessions that brought musicians from all over the city, the Kit Kat was the Black Near North Side music center. Its reputation as a place to jam also brought white people who wanted to listen. The mix of illegal booze, jazz, and white women in a club with Black male musicians brought the city's "purity squad" of Prohibition agents. But it wasn't the illicit liquor that was the genuine concern. It was the potential for Black men and white women to meet, mingle, and have sex that concerned them. During the frequent police raids, white women were arrested on prostitution charges and Black men as johns.

The raids forced the Kit Kat to close. It reopened in 1930 as the Apex Club. The morals squads kept up their aggression, and patrons were jailed. That didn't keep the crowds away. The interracial establishment flourished as the hot horns of Black jazz blew late into the cold Minneapolis nights.[36] By 1936, the Apex was renamed the Clef Club. Under this moniker, the square, squat Kistler Building became a venerated cultural site. Local talents like Ira Pettiford, Lester Young, Rook Ganz, and others played with greats at all-night jam sessions. "Man, we used to jive in those days," said Pettiford. Those late-night sessions also educated Pettiford. "That's how I learned to play," which helped him to work with Benny Carter, Earl Hines, and Dizzy Gillespie.[37] But in 1942, after police arrested eighty-nine patrons on suspicion of gambling and prostitution, and their names appeared in the *Minneapolis Tribune*, the Clef Club closed.[38]

By the mid-twentieth century, the once-revered Kistler Building had acquired an undesirable reputation. Moreover, the growing redevelopment of Black areas under the banner of urban renewal (famously called "Negro removal" by James Baldwin) slated the building for destruction.[39] Despite being an important cultural site where some of the best musicians in the country played, it fell to the wrecking ball in 1957. The federal government eventually gobbled up the land, and an expressway was pushed through, as would be the case in Black communities nationwide.

North Side music didn't end with the closure of the Clef Club. There was the El Grotto, which morphed into Howard's Steak House in the 1950s, and the Sportsman's Club, both on Olson Memorial Highway. Musicians played the 639 Club at 639 North Avenue, Musicians Rest on 141 Hyland Avenue, Peggie's Rhumboogie on North Lyndale Avenue, and many more—like the Ebony, the Gin Mill, the Nest, the Spot, the Hub, and the Chicken Shake—that came and went.[40]

The Phyllis Wheatley Settlement House, the city's first Black social service organization, held musical events. When the Wheatley House was founded in 1924, leading activist W. Gertrude Brown thought that Black art and creativity would help it gain wider (whiter) public support. So a music department was created at the Wheatley as a "goodwill messenger."[41] Its glee club and quartets performed for numerous churches and civic organizations. The Wheatley House program helped the organization spread its message and provided a place for music to grow and thrive. Local and national acts excluded from white establishments performed at the Wheatley House, especially after the organization moved to a new location with a large gymnasium and a balcony.[42]

Between the First and Second World Wars, the Near North Side hosted an impressive collection of spaces for Black music, which attracted jazz luminaries from the 1930s to the 1950s. North Minneapolis wasn't the only Black music center. Though not as extensive as the Near North Side's offerings, the South Side had an active music scene. One of the more popular locations was the Eagles Club, housed in a square, three-story building built between 1923 and 1924 called the Labor Temple.[43] The Eagles fraternal organization used the space to hold meetings and events, so it was constructed with a large hall on the third floor. Its dining hall, spacious balcony, and seating capacity of 2,500 helped make the Labor Temple the headquarters of South Minneapolis music until the late 1950s. Groups rented it out regularly to hold dances like the National Negro Jitterbug Dance Contest, and bands like Rook Ganz's provided the music. One of John Nelson's early public performances was at the Labor Temple. At an August 1947 dance, the Prince Rogers Trio featuring John on piano, played alongside the Bruce Dybvig Orchestra. National acts also played the Eagles Club. In 1942, the arranger and bandleader Fletcher Henderson brought his fourteen-piece band there. Legendary jazz singer Dinah Washington; the nation's most significant composer, Duke Ellington; and the father of rhythm and blues, Ray Charles, played the Eagles during the 1950s.[44]

The Eagles Club was part of a network of Black clubs that catered to Black people and musicians called the "Chitlin' Circuit." Many Black musicians played the circuit's venues throughout the twentieth century. The circuit was indispensable to Black musicians, from Billie Holiday to Lionel Hampton to Jimi Hendrix. Not only did Black musicians find steady work in them, but they also developed their styles there. For example, Hendrix learned tricks like playing his guitar behind his back and with his teeth—moves that blew the socks off white rock fans—on the Chitlin Circuit.

The Nacirema Club ("American" spelled backward) was also part of the circuit.[45] This social club, located on Thirty-Eighth Street near Fourth Avenue South, operated between 1955 and 1987 with a membership that hovered around 600. The Nacirema hosted Christmas parties, fashion shows, and, on the weekends, musicians.[46] It served two generations of musicians, with jazz players ruling in the 1950s and early 1960s. From the mid-1960s on, jazz faded and rhythm and blues and soul took over.

Musical apartheid during the jazz era in Minneapolis set the music scene on a trajectory that shaped it for the remainder of the century. The Black and white worlds created through segregation and implanted in the city's geography were sonically distinct. However, some white musicians and music lovers played and hung out in Black venues like the Cotton Club or the Eagles Club; racial division defined music in Minneapolis for nearly eighty years.

For one young musician growing up on the Near North Side, Minneapolis's musical apartheid was an opportunity for innovation. His compositions rewrote the city's fractured sound, and he did it by breaking down the sonic walls. For years, this young man and a band of renegade musicians tinkered with this new sound in spaces all over Black Minneapolis. Drawing on the innovative Black style called funk, these young people gave birth to a new, distinctive, and utterly Minneapolis sound. The rest of the nation would get its first taste of this sound when the leader of this band of renegades, Prince, performed on *American Bandstand* in 1980.

PART 3

The Evolution

1950–1976

Chapter 6

THAT DISTINCTIVELY DIRTY MINNEAPOLIS FUNK

Morris knew it was Prince when the sultry song laced with his signature falsetto sprang from the radio his coworker Tyrel played while making it through the day at the car rental counter at Montgomery Ward. "That's my boy," Morris yelled. "We played together." To which a dubious Tyrel responded, "Sure you did, Morris." The voice, the groove, "that distinctively dirty Minneapolis funk," oozed all over the first single, "Soft and Wet," off Prince's 1977 debut album, *For You*.[1]

Morris Day was the drummer for Prince's band during junior high and high school. The band was one of several born during the growth of rhythm and blues and funk between the mid-1960s and early 1970s. Between Prince's birth and the year he finished junior high school (1958–72), Black Minneapolis had become an unlikely hotbed of R&B and funk. Though Black people made up only 5 percent of the city's population, musically, they punched above their weight. They cultivated these new sounds through a collage of bands, venues, a Black-owned record label, a few record stores, and a short-lived but influential low-wattage AM radio station, KUXL, which floated sweaty crooners and funky rhythms on the Near North and South Sides. Growing up on the Near North and South Sides, Prince was exposed to and sonically shaped by these sounds. Their development changed the music scene in vanilla Minneapolis and laid the groundwork for the hybrid sounds Prince and the city would be known for.

Genesis

The rise of rhythm and blues and funk in Minneapolis grew out of the apartheid system put in place in the first half of the twentieth century. The network of Black clubs, bars, and music venues created during this period left remnants of the new sounds that emerged in the late 1950s and throughout the 1960s.[2] By the mid-1950s, Minneapolis, with a population of half a million, had a Black and white jazz landscape with different venues housing music in the city's racially segregated geography. The new musical environment taking shape overlapped and evolved as Prince came of age. In addition to being the most gifted performer to come out of the city, Prince is the throughline that connects the decline of jazz, the rise of new music, and its growth in the city's Black communities. In this chapter, we'll see how R&B, soul, and funk grew and thrived in Minneapolis alongside a kid genius from the city's North Side.

Prince Rogers Nelson, son of Mattie and John, grew up in a musical household. When Prince was just a few years old, Mattie noticed her little boy could bang out rhythms on pots and pans, and he curiously eyed the large object—John's piano—perched in the living room. Prince knew at an early age that he liked its sound, but stern John made clear that it was off limits.

When Prince was born in 1958, mid-twentieth-century America's expectations that women set aside their ambitions and personal wants to raise children bore down hard on Mattie, who became responsible for rearing Prince and Tyka. Being the primary caretaker ended her musical career.[3] Mattie was the vocalist for John's band, the Prince Rogers Trio, but after Prince was born, she left the group to rear their children; she suggested John do the same. According to Prince's longtime "scribe," journalist Neal Karlen, the image of John in the semiautobiographical film about Prince, *Purple Rain*, drew from Prince's observations of his home life. The movie depicted his father as a "frustrated jazz man" whose professional aspirations were dashed by the demands of family life.[4] "Never get married," John's fictional character told his son, The Kid (played by Prince), in the film's most dramatic scene. This scene in the movie is based on a real-life incident that ignited the conflict between Prince's parents.[5] John saw Mattie and Prince as obstacles to his musical career, which led to his aloofness, anger, bullying, and hostility toward the family.[6] In interviews with Karlen in the 1980s, Prince recalled, "See, my father didn't have the talent to be the Fabulous Prince Rogers," referring to the moniker the Louisiana-born musician adopted in the 1950s. According to Prince, John blamed Mattie, "who helped ruin his life," and their son, whose "first breath" represented the end of "the Fabulous Prince Rogers."[7]

With Mattie doing the child-rearing, John threw himself into music. He worked at the Honeywell Corporation molding plastic during the day and played at strip clubs like Augie's along Hennepin Avenue at night.[8] Occasionally, he played out-of-town gigs on the weekends.[9] Despite the negative impact of John's musical ambitions on Mattie and the family, he nevertheless was a "legend in his mind," according to Prince.[10] He refused to relinquish his pretense as a jazz musician, even though he couldn't make a living playing jazz or his compositions at the strip clubs.[11] The resentment this produced in Mattie, combined with the demanding work of single parenting and John's physical abuse of her and Prince, unleashed toxic rage.[12] When Prince was seven, Mattie and John's marriage fractured beyond repair. John left the home and moved into a one-bedroom apartment on the Near North Side.[13] John had become estranged from two families, leaving a gulf between him and his children, especially Prince.[14]

The kind of music the self-described jazzman played made his departure from that family even more head-scratching. John's brand of music was on the edge of jazz. It was "spectral" and experimental. It leaned toward Thelonious Monk and Sun Ra.[15] Prince's childhood friend and frontman for the funk band the Time, Morris Day, said John's music was "avant-garde, spacey jazz," but if you listened closely, "you'd catch a groove."[16] Prince's former fiancée, Susannah Melvoin (twin sister of Revolution guitarist Wendy), said John's music was "written in his mind . . . sometimes you'd have no idea what he was playing." But Susannah also recognized that "there was a mad genius" in him.[17] Prince respected John's experimental sound, which he reproduced in the 1980s. With some mixed feelings, he even gave his father songwriting credits on "Around the World in a Day," "Scandalous," and "Computer Blue" from *Purple Rain*.[18]

John Nelson was a self-taught musician who learned to play piano while working as a doorman at the Andrews Hotel. He cut his musical teeth in Black clubs on the North and South Sides. Sometime in the mid-1950s, he formed the Prince Rogers Trio, a name inspired by his interest in musical royalty, Duke Ellington, and the family dog, Prince.[19] The band found work performing at places like the Phyllis Wheatley House on the Near North Side and the Labor Temple on the South Side.[20] The trio's mix of jazz standards and original compositions set them apart from other groups, as did their avant-garde leanings and fondness for minor keys.[21]

Like many musicians, John's music career ended not by his hand. Perhaps he suspected this would be the case when he bestowed the band's name on his and Mattie's new baby boy. "I named him Prince because I wanted him to do everything that I really intended to do," John admitted.[22] The son would outpace his father in ways no one could imagine. In that sense, Prince was correct; his birth did mean the death of his father's musical career, not just because of the resentment John harbored against his family but also because John's son represented the sonic transformations wafting from the Plymouth Avenue record store and blaring from the city's Black musical geography. This Oedipal struggle burrowed deep into the marrow of their relationship. John fueled his son's desire to surpass his father. Prince was a sign of changing times and new sounds. Indeed, he was a twentieth-century musical version of the cannon fire that exploded in the eighteenth-century Minnesota soundscape. Every year of his son's maturation, John's chances of being the Fabulous Prince Rogers became less attainable. Jazz's popularity in the early 1960s was threatened by rhythm and blues and soul music despite the brilliant innovation of Miles Davis, John Coltrane, Art Blakey, and others. This sobering reality forced John to find peace with the twilight of his creative career and with his banal job at Honeywell.

The new sound that deposed John and elevated Prince emerged alongside the civil rights movement. This second Reconstruction was sparked by the abduction, torture, and murder of a young Black Chicagoan, Emmett Till, after he allegedly whistled at a white woman in a store in the summer of 1955 while visiting family in Money, Mississippi. The Montgomery, Alabama, bus boycott erupted the same year after Rosa Parks refused to comply with segregation laws and give up her seat to a white man. Dr. Martin Luther King Jr., an Atlanta-born minister, emerged as the movement's spokesman. Rhythm and blues, a danceable, vocally driven music, and funk, a vampy sound that put its accent on the first beat of a musical measure, became the soundtracks of this movement and filled the ears of kids like Prince.

But these new sounds didn't emerge in a vacuum; they developed from roots in decades-old music.

Rhythm and Blues

Rhythm and blues (R&B) came to Minneapolis in the late 1950s, finding space along the Near North Side's Plymouth Avenue.[23] Many musical and social antecedents are responsible for its birth. Sonically, the genre is indebted to blues and gospel music, but echoes of other kinds of Black music—like work songs, string and jug band music, Black vaudeville, boogie-woogie, and even minstrelsy—can be heard in it.[24]

Rhythm and blues is Black music created in Black Southern communities during the 1940s. Its roots reach back to the recording of Mamie Smith's "Crazy Blues" in 1920, when white record companies discovered there was an audience for Black music after her single sold 750,000 units.[25] Some of the early innovators of R&B were Nat "King" Cole, who found a sweet spot between R&B and jazz; bandleader Johnny Otis, who was responsible for establishing the tenor saxophone as part of rhythm and blues bands; and Dinah Washington, who blended the blues and jazz.[26] We might also add the likes of Billie Holiday, Ella Fitzgerald, the Drifters, John Lee Hooker, the Cadillacs, the Five Keys, the Flamingos, and many regional groups as artists who influenced the development of R&B.[27]

But if R&B has a standout pioneer, it's Ray Charles. After losing his sight as a child to glaucoma, Charles, born in 1930 in Albany, Georgia, studied at the Colored Department of the Florida School for the Deaf and Blind from 1937 to 1945.[28] School is where his musical ambitions grew.[29] Young Ray learned to read braille, including for music notation, under the tutelage of his music teacher, Mrs. Lawrence. He rapidly excelled and was as comfortable playing Bach, Beethoven, and Mozart as he was with boogie-woogie. This training helped him innovate a new form, R&B, combining jazz, blues, and gospel while playing with and arranging for Quincy Jones, Dizzy Gillespie, and Cole Porter. His 1954 breakout hit, "I Got a Woman," adapted from "It Must Be Jesus" by the Southern Tones, shot him into the musical stratosphere and carved out a new space where the secular and the carnal would meet through a twelve-bar blues structure, complex vocal arrangements, and the intense emotion and rich harmonies of gospel music.[30] Although he was not the first to bring these elements together—Dinah Washington and Big Maybelle blazed this path before Charles—his experiment pushed R&B in new directions. Charles used this style to dominate the pop charts throughout the 1950s. In 1959, he reached number six on the Billboard chart with "What I Say," the most erotically charged blues/gospel combination of his career. But some Black folks didn't appreciate Ray's mashup, and the backlash was swift. They saw his innovation as blasphemous. As blues singer Big Bill Broonzy said, "He's mixin' the blues with spirituals. That's wrong."[31]

Ray Charles's new sound resonated with Black migrants leaving the South during the second phase of the Great Migration. As in previous decades, steady Black in-migration was changing urban sounds. Between 1950 and 1970, Minneapolis's Black population increased by an astonishing 436 percent even though the statewide population, at just 1.2 percent, was "small enough to be ignored."[32] These migrants, like previous generations, radically altered the sounds of Minneapolis, bringing with them Southern-born styles like gutbucket (an early type of jazz practiced by early New Orleans and Chicago musicians), the twelve-bar blues format, and gospel vocal arrangements.

Willie Walker, a Mississippi-born gospel singer, visited Minnesota three times in 1959 and decided to stay "because I liked the place." Walker was a seasoned singer, having spent eleven years singing in the Redemption Harmonizers gospel group. While he was doing his laundry on a summer day in 1960, another teenager named Timothy Eason approached him and said, "You really do look like you can sing." Walker said he could, and they started to harmonize in the laundromat. Eason grabbed a few friends from the neighborhood, and by the end of the day, the boys had formed a group.[33] Music critic Andrea Swensson's seminal research on the Minneapolis Sound in her book *Got to Be Something Here* (2017) established the link between the national growth of R&B and Black Minneapolis, tracing the influence of early migrants who used their Southern gospel and blues musical training to create R&B in their new city.

Sonny Knight, like Walker, also found himself thrust into the city's burgeoning R&B scene postmigration. The soul singer left the stifling Mississippi heat for cool Minneapolis in 1955. Gospel singer James Martin, who also managed two well-known Minneapolis-based singing groups—the Avengers and the Exciters—left his native South Carolina and arrived in Minneapolis the same year as Knight. Perhaps the migrant from this period who had the greatest impact was the Florida-born Maurice McKinnies. The singer, guitarist, and organist, who landed in Minneapolis in 1960, carried the city's R&B community on his sharply dressed shoulders for nearly a decade until he departed for the Bay Area in the 1970s. Three years after McKinnies arrived, another Memphis-born musician appeared: "harmonica ace" Mojo Buford, who became a member of the Minneapolis-based Chi-4.[34]

Walker, Knight, and two other friends, Jimmy Crittenden and Joe Dibiaso, formed a singing group, the Valdons. With the help of local promoter Dick Shapiro, the Valdons quickly found an audience among the Jewish population that remained on the North Side.[35] The group performed at birthday parties, graduations, bar mitzvahs, and synagogues. Their music relied on repeated chords centered on vocal harmony, a far cry from the big band sounds of jazz. Unlike their parents, who listened to Cab Calloway, Duke Ellington, and the Dizzy Gillespie orchestra, Walker and his groupmates listened to "the Isley Brothers . . . The Drifters, Platters," and other rising R&B acts like those coming out of Detroit.[36]

Ray Charles, whose touring pianist would teach Prince music in middle school, influenced the Valdons and many other Black R&B acts. By the early 1960s, Charles had a string of hits and was touring the nation. He performed at the Minneapolis Auditorium in 1963 and then the Minneapolis Convention Hall in 1966. Charles's music was pushing R&B into the mainstream. A survey of Minneapolis teens in 1966 cited the genre as one of their favorites. The Isley Brothers scored high among local teens. Their 1969 hit, "It's Your Thing," was one of the most popular R&B songs in the city.

In addition to chains like Musicland, small shops that served Black Minneapolis were also vital to the growth of R&B. Dee's Record Shop on Hennepin (which became Musicland) was a must-stop. Prince, who began playing music when he was eight or nine, would ride his bike to the store and buy the latest hit records; he would transcribe the lyrics and sing along.[37]

Despite the growing popularity of R&B, it didn't get much radio play in Minneapolis because local stations catered to white listeners, playing only Top 100 hits and just a handful of Black artists. KDWB, which began broadcasting in 1959, was the center of pop radio and played white artists exclusively.[38] Even top national performers like Sam Cooke, the Supremes, the Four Tops, and the Marvelettes didn't get airplay in Minneapolis.

Black music wasn't absent from radio, however. One of the places where it lived was on a former religious station that became an R&B haven. In 1964, Universal Broadcasting Company, based in Shreveport, Louisiana, purchased KUXL. Universal's president, Marvin Kosofsky, saw "ethnic programming" as an essential market. "Out of the first sixty-five to seventy-five top markets in this country," noted Kosofsky, Minneapolis "is the only one that doesn't have a rhythm-and-blues-station."[39]

Within weeks of Universal's purchase of KUXL, the station hosted a two-hour rhythm and blues show broadcast on Saturday and Sunday, hosted by the only Black radio disc jockey in town, Rio Pardo.[40] In July 1965, Tina Turner visited the station to promote her show with then-husband Ike at the Minneapolis Auditorium. Other R&B acts, like the Four Tops, the Impressions, and the Temptations, also visited the station.[41] Even though the low-wattage KUXL, located in an old motel on Plymouth Avenue, had a limited reach, it gave Black Minneapolitans access to Motown and Stax records and interviews with well-known Black artists. In short, KUXL connected Minneapolis to the rising sounds of Blackness.

The music on the KUXL airwaves was a boon to the Minneapolis R&B scene. It gave Black teenagers like Walker, Knight, Crittenden, Dibiaso, and Prince access to Black music, helping to spur the growth of a local R&B scene. The station played a significant role in making Minneapolis the "funkytown" that the Minneapolis-based Lipps Inc. sang about in their 1980 hit of the same name. In addition to connecting Black kids to new music made in other cities, KUXL inspired Minneapolitans to grow their local sound.

One man ran KUXL: a Chicago-born DJ and musician named Jack Harris. For the six years the station was in operation (1964–70), Harris, in his on-air persona Old Daddy Soul, filled listeners' ears with the best R&B and soul music. He also used his show to promote performances at local Black venues, places like downtown's only club specializing in Black music, King Solomon's Mines.

Minneapolis's first downtown, Black-centered music venue was in the Foshay Towers. This lavish office building was a marvel of architectural innovation when erected in 1928. It was adorned with Vermont marble walls and ceilings, French-inspired interior design, terrazzo floors, and mahogany-trimmed hallways. At thirty-two stories, with fifty-mile views from its peak, it was the tallest building in the city for decades. Musically, King Solomon's Mines was a sign of its time; it replaced a jazz club in the mid-1960s as R&B was climbing the national charts. Dean Constantine, a well-dressed, handsome, "white-dance instructor-turned-bar-owner," ran the club.[42] Named after the 1950s film that reproduced racist stereotypes of Africa and Africans, the venue was decked out in safari-inspired décor.[43]

Andrea Swensson's research on the Mines provides a picture of the percolating Black music scene in the mid-to-late 1960s, the years Prince was coming of age. In that period, the Mines was a hotbed of gutbucket sweaty grooves from local R&B groups like Gene William and the Backsliders, Gwen Matthews, and a St. Paul–based group from that city's oldest Black neighborhood (Rondo). The Amazers' five Black members, Napoleon Crayton, John Price, Billy Barnes, Joe Moore, Charles Singleton, and their white drummer, Bill Lordan, sported slick suits and pompadour hair. They were considered "the number-one group in the Twin-Cities," according to their manager, James Martin. In 1967, soul superstar Curtis Mayfield invited them to record on his label, Thomas Records.[44] Their single, "It's You for Me," is a ballad filled with flawless harmony and falsetto vocals that reach for the sky.

Another group that appeared at King Solomon's Mines and influenced the local scene was Maurice McKinnies and the Champions. McKinnies, a Pensacola, Florida–born singer and guitarist, moved to Minneapolis in the early 1960s to connect with family members who'd migrated there. He was the city's first R&B, soul-man superstar, and its first incarnation of funk. His husky yet velvety voice and electric stage presence made him a favorite at the Mines. They also brought him to the attention of Jack Harris at KUXL. After seeing McKinnies perform, Harris, who had become the station manager, launched Black and Proud Records, Minneapolis's first Black-owned label.

Maurice McKinnies and the Champions' records were the first on the new label, with "Sock-a-poo-poo '69" the its inaugural recording.

Despite providing downtown with the funkiest music the area had ever heard, the politics of apartheid did to King Solomon's Mines what it did to the Apex Club in the 1930s. The city had become concerned about the rising popularity of the club and the fact it was attracting white women. *Minneapolis Star* reporter Jim Klobuchar wrote that "the joint was fully integrated, the dancers being largely white women and Negro men."[45] "While applauding the Negro's resolute rise in American Society," Klobuchar continued, "I had to acknowledge that these latest attainments do not leave the white honkies much beyond ice hockey, a few moldering country clubs, and the press agent work for Sammy Davis Jr." Black popular culture was becoming national popular culture, which made white Americans uneasy. As Swensson observes, the "generalized anxiety about black artists' increasing relevance in a largely white world, made places like King Solomon's Mines more open to criticism."[46] The increasing prevalence of Black culture opened the door for the city to portray any disturbance as a justification for closing the Mines. As the best place in town to hear Black music, the Mines attracted a diverse swath of Black life, from hustlers to teachers and entrepreneurs. One patron said, "Everybody came down to Dean's place."[47] When, for example, street fights between Black patrons happened outside the club, and a woman was arrested for weed possession, it not only made the news but gave the city a reason to be punitive.[48] In 1968, the Mines was threatened with revocation of its liquor license for underage drinking. Police license inspector Harvey Everson called the mixed-race club "the worst run place in the city."[49]

Dean Constantine organized patrons and musicians to fight the attempt to revoke the club's liquor license. They showed up at a city council meeting to defend the Mines' importance to the city's music scene and circulated a petition to support it. These efforts resulted in a minor victory; rather than revoking the Mines' liquor license, the city council suspended it for two months. The lighter punishment and the gallant fight only put off the inevitable. King Solomon's Mines closed its doors after a year and a half in operation.[50] In February 1969, Constantine sold the club to Bill Roslansky and Stu Swartz. They opened a new place where the "entertainment policy will consist of rock music by local bands."[51]

The "Funk" in Funkytown

"Black Bands Abound, But Not in Downtown," headlined a 1969 *Minneapolis Tribune* article. What staff writer Allan Holbert called the "definite, if unwritten segregation policy that keeps black bands out of the Downtown clubs" maintained the decades-old apartheid system that used any incident to disrupt interracial interactions and keep Black people and their music on the North and South Sides of town.[52] Club owners participated in it, too. As a result, Black people created their own circuit of venues. The Cozy Bar on North Plymouth Avenue was one of just two Black-owned bars in the city. James T. "Jimmy" Fuller opened the bar in the late 1960s after running a joint called the Regal Tavern a few years earlier.[53] Black patrons supported the Cozy because it played the music they liked. And white patrons came, too. "White people can always come up here and be welcomed," Fuller told the *Tribune*.[54] The construction of Interstate 94 in the 1970s forced the bar's closure, but after the federal government compensated Fuller, he opened Riverview Supper Club on West River Road.[55]

Black music also found homes at Club Malibu on East Lake Street, the Jet-a-Way on Second Avenue South, the Key Bank on Nicollet Avenue, the Taste Show Lounge on North Fifth Street, and the Blue Note on Eleventh Avenue North, where "every musician, every jazz musician, every musician of a certain age, every black musician got their start," said Maurice Jacox of Willie and the Bumblebees (the city's first interracial R&B group).[56] This hole-in-the-wall club was a testing ground or finishing school where those who wanted to play could pick up tricks and get advice.

No person better documented the sounds of R&B in Minneapolis than the Pittsburgh transplant photographer Charles Chamblis. From 1970 to the late 1980s, Chamblis compiled a treasure trove of Black life in Minneapolis, from the mundane to the marvelous. As R&B took off, Chamblis fixed his camera on the people and places where the sound was rising. He photographed the Riverview Supper Club, the Taste Show Lounge, and performers like Maurice McKinnies, the Valdons, and Flyte Tyme.[57]

The venues also incubated another new form of music from the South dubbed "funk." Between 1965 and 1972, Minneapolis sprouted a local funk scene that operated through the network of Black clubs on the South and Near North Sides. Funk was born the same way Buddy Bolden, King Oliver, and Louis Armstrong gave life to jazz, by using previous musical genres to create a new one. A child of jazz, blues, and rhythm and blues, funk broke away from complex chord changes favoring slower tempos than jazz, and using simpler, repetitive harmonic patterns or "vamps." Rather than accenting the fourth beat, the accent was put on the first when the hi-hat cymbal and snare drum hit simultaneously. The effect on listeners and dancers was hypnotic.

James Brown was the progenitor and creative genius of this sonic revolution. From the early 1960s to the end of the 1970s, Brown was the biggest star in the galaxy of pop music. No one could touch the "Godfather of Soul."

His music was impeccable, rhythmic, complex, and highly danceable; his live shows, where he led the band through dance, were polyrhythmic and musically precise. Brown was the first to marry jazz and funk. His album *At the Apollo*, recorded live at the legendary Harlem theater in 1962, topped the charts.[58] His 1965 single, "Papa's Got a Brand New Bag, Part 1," was a milestone in funk and a pop hit. According to Brown,

> The song started out as a vamp we did during a stage show. There was a little instrumental riff and I hollered: "Papa's got a brand new bag of his own!" . . . It's hard to describe what I was going for; the song has a gospel feel, but it was put together out of jazz licks . . . I had discovered that my strength was not in the horns, it was in rhythm. I was hearing everything, even the guitars, they were drums. I had found out how to make it happen . . . Later on they said it was the beginning of funk. I just thought it was where my music was going. The title told it all: I had a brand new bag.[59]

Following their leader's cue, his band, the Famous Flames, used horns, bass, guitar, and drums percussively to play different rhythms on tracks like "Cold Sweat, Part 1," and "Say It Loud (I'm Black and I'm Proud)." This revolutionary sound was infused with the politics of Black liberation. "Say It Loud" was an anthem for a generation of Black people shaking off the chains of Jim Crow and embracing self-love.

Brown's musical revolution helped push musicians like John Nelson to the margins. But for young people like Prince, it was a revelation. KUXL was the station where James Brown and the emerging sound lived in Minneapolis. And Prince listened to the revolution taking place on that station.[60] Meanwhile, there was insurrection in the streets. Prince witnessed the Black uprisings of 1966 and 1967 in response to police violence and the lack of economic opportunity.[61]

Prince was also listening to local funk musicians like Maurice McKinnies and the multitasking DJ Jack Harris, who also had a band and recorded on his label, Black and Proud. At a performance during the first leg of his final tour, "Prince: Piano & Microphone," in 2015, Prince told the crowd how much Harris's music meant to him as a kid: "Jack Harris had his own band. That's how funky he was. His band was tight as James Brown's band, or close. I always had to hear his music. He would choose what we listened to. And he had great taste."[62]

Hearing James Brown on KUXL made the "Godfather of Soul" the young musician's favorite singer. When Brown came to town in 1969, Prince and his friends saw him at the Minneapolis Armory. Legend has it that Prince was so excited by the performance that he got onstage and danced with the band before being removed by staff.[63]

Prince also heard another funk act that would significantly influence his musical career. He may have first got wind of them in the revolutionary year of 1968. Domestically and around the globe, the darker nations of the world were shaking off their colonial chains, demanding independence. Protests against the Vietnam War intensified as the US involvement escalated. Cities burned, ignited by the frustration of the "long hot summers" that Malcolm X predicted. The Black Panthers were organizing in Oakland, California, against police brutality and for jobs, education, and housing. The assassinations of Martin Luther King Jr. and Bobby Kennedy roiled the nation. In Chicago, police brutally beat protesters outside the Democratic National Convention.

That year, San Francisco–based Sly and the Family Stone hit number eight on the Billboard chart with their gospel funk single "Dance to the Music," followed by their most iconic song, "Everyday People."[64] No band had a more significant impact on Prince than Sly and the Family Stone. Their pop funk did much to spread the sound James Brown had invented. But whereas Brown's brand of funk was aimed at Black people, Sly Stone's big tent, the funk-is-for-everyone approach, demonstrated in his music and the makeup of his interracial band, inspired Prince profoundly. He especially loved bassist Larry Graham's innovative "slap" technique, where he used the thumb and forefinger to slap the strings, creating a percussive sound, as on their chart-topping hit "Thank You (Falettinme Be Mice Elf Agin)."[65]

Changes were happening at the Nelson home against the backdrop of Minneapolis's growing Black music scene. After his parents divorced in 1968 and John left the house, the prohibition on touching John's piano ended. Prince spent hours on the instrument, learning to play songs like the theme to the *Batman* television show, practicing things he'd seen John do. More and more, his musical abilities were taking shape. At the start of the new decade, however, things at home took a turn for the worse. In 1970, Mattie married Hayward Baker, who was also a musician. She received full custody of the children and the house on Eighth Avenue instead of child support when she and John divorced. Her second marriage brought love and financial security.[66] It also caused a profound break between her and Prince. "The day my mother re-married," said Prince, "was the day [I] decided [I] wanted 2 live with my real father."[67] He left the Eighth Avenue North home and moved into his father's apartment on Glenwood Avenue.[68]

Living with John didn't go well, either. The experiment was over in less than a year, followed by homelessness for the young musician. In the face of familial instability, school provided solidity and musical education that John couldn't offer. Moreover, school gave Prince something he'd never had: a place to play music. Although he had played in the living room or his bedroom, at school, Prince found spaces designed for music-making. Between seventh grade and high school graduation, Prince used these rooms to jam with other musicians, learn from music teachers, and find sanctuary in a world that was becoming increasingly unstable.

Chapter 7

SCHOOL DAYS

Eventually I would like to go to college and start lessons again when I'm much older.

—Prince Rogers Nelson

During his senior year at Central High School, Prince gave his first interview to student reporter Lisa Crawford. The article described his musical evolution—"Prince started playing piano at age seven—when his family broke up—and guitar when he got out of eighth grade." Leaning into the image of himself as gifted, he remarked, "I think I've had about two lessons, but they didn't help," while also saying that lessons would be "great."[1]

Schools hold little significance in the sprawling and ever-expanding writings on Prince and his musical evolution. However, junior high and high school were critical to his creative growth. Schools gave youths access to the queen of arts, allowing them to sing, play, and learn how music was created. However, the city's commitment to music education dwindled after the retirement of Thaddeus Giddings, the public school music director who democratized music education. Prince and his friends came up in a period when music education was no longer mandatory. Yet it was still available in many schools. Fortunately for Prince, the schools he attended—Bryant Junior High and Central High—had good music programs and committed teachers. They also had spaces where eager students like Prince could perform, jam, and find sanctuary.

The Twilight of Mass Music Education

Rhythm and blues, soul music, and funk came of age in the dwindling twilight of Giddings's experiment. By 1940, Giddings's proclamation that "participation is the path to appreciation" had made the city's school music program the nation's best.[2] With one in every six children in the city able to play an instrument, it was beyond question that his system worked.

Despite Giddings's impact, as he neared retirement, changes to the system he'd built appeared on the horizon. In 1942, his last year of work, the stickler for music pedagogy publicly chastised the school board director for what he saw as a deemphasis on music education. "A constant groping for something 'easy' has been carried to the point where many teachers spend a large portion of each class period teasing pupils to like to do something," he argued.[3] The change Giddings saw in 1942 came to fruition by the 1960s. School boards and superintendents of music moved away from his system. By the time Prince was born, art education had replaced mandatory music education. Music now competed with painting, poetry, sculpture, and dance.

Designed for Music

With hindsight, it appears inevitable that the music system Giddings created wouldn't last. Music education was the first of many trends in the Minneapolis public school system, now focused on STEM (science, technology, engineering, and math). Yet even though Giddings's system lost steam, music education still found its way into students' lives. How? Because several of the city's public schools, some still in operation today, were designed to facilitate music education. "All first-grade classrooms should have a piano," Giddings declared.[4] He also said every classroom should have instruments, even the gymnasium! For Giddings, if children were to be educated in and come to appreciate music, they also needed spaces designed and built for musical education and performance. Gidding achieved this through architecture. Design physically expresses values, history, culture, and politics. The construction of music venues in nineteenth-century Minneapolis, or concert halls in New Orleans or Paris, supported musical production by giving it a place. Minneapolis did this not only through halls, clubs, and bars but through its schools, too.

Minneapolis created a school board when the city was founded in 1849. The board designed and built the city's elementary, junior high, and high schools.[5] In 1915, the Architectural Department (Bureau of Buildings) helped the school board design new schools, launching the city's first education construction boom.[6] These new schools kept pace with the growing student population, which nearly doubled, from 45,000 in 1910 to 88,000 in 1930.[7]

The new schools also provided better physical environments for students: more natural light, ventilation, hygiene, sanitation, heating, fire safety, structural integrity, window design, and seamless interior design to make future structural changes easier.[8] E. S. Stebbins, who favored the "I" and "H" shape pattern and prominent central entries with Collegiate Gothic and English flair, designed many of the schools.[9] These schools also had another new design feature: specialized rooms like kindergartens, gymnasiums, swimming pools, and spaces for vocational training and domestic education.[10]

Specialized rooms for art were among the most common in junior high and high schools built in the 1920s. Many of them were music rooms. Nearly all twenty-three junior high and high schools built during Giddings's tenure had rooms for instrumental and vocal music. This musical architecture was more than a reminder of Giddings's impact on the city's public school system. It was a kind of insurance policy that guarded against the elimination of music from schools. Building physical infrastructure for music into schools ensured that students would have places to play even if music education lost support.

Between 1967 and the fall of 1969, Prince bounced from the neighborhood school, John Hay, to primarily white Kenwood after the "long hot summers" of 1965 and 1967 that set North Minneapolis ablaze. These were the years between the fourth and sixth grades, when Prince was one of the Black children bused from segregated neighborhoods to schools on the other side of the apartheid line. The racialized geography the city fostered in the early twentieth century, which created Black Minneapolis, was now pushing Black children like Prince away from their neighborhoods because they were too Black, to whiter ones because of their lack of diversity. Racism, it seems, is not without irony.

In 1969, on Prince's first day in the sixth grade at Abraham Lincoln Junior High School, he met Andre Anderson (who later became André Cymone).[11] Andre and Prince would become not only fast friends but also collaborators who pushed each other to be better musicians. Their work together over the next decade revolutionized popular music and elevated the Minneapolis Sound to the pop stratosphere. According to Andre, the two met as they received their schedules and were trying to make sense of their new world. Andre was searching the crowd for a familiar face when he saw a short, doe-eyed kid with a budding Afro. He went over and said, "Hey man, how are you doing? I'm Andre." "I'm Prince," the shy kid replied. "Prince. Okay.

What are you into?" Andre pressed. "I play music," he said, to which Andre responded, "That's interesting; I play music, too." After an exchange about what instruments each played—"I play piano and guitar," said Prince; "I play bass and drums, a little guitar," said Andre—Prince asked, "Why don't you come by my dad's house and jam?"[12]

A few days later, the two went to John Nelson's apartment and bonded as they fiddled with the instruments strewn around the small apartment where John's piano took up most of the space.[13] While jamming, Andre saw a familiar face in a photograph in the living room: his father. When John returned home from his job at the Honeywell Corporation, Prince's new friend asked John about the photo. John looked at it, then back at Andre. With a laugh, John said, "You're Fred's son!" John and Fred Anderson played together in the Prince Rogers Trio. Their sons' meeting and jamming together seemed destined.

After several afternoon jam sessions in John's apartment, the musical synergy between the boys was evident.[14] "We should start a band together," said Andre.[15] Prince agreed and introduced Andre to his cousin Charles "Chazz" Smith, whom he played with for years in the den of their Sheridan Avenue home. (Prince and Chazz would even perform for the neighborhood kids.)[16] The three were the core members of what would eventually become the band Grand Central.[17] But at this time, they called their band Phoenix. After winning Lincoln's talent show, the band caught the attention of Andre's next-door neighbor, Terry Jackson.[18] Jackson knew Prince from John Hay and remembered him from talent shows. "I remember seeing him tap dance. . . . And then, one talent show, he played [the theme from] 'Batman' on the piano."[19] After Prince, Chazz, and Andre won their school's talent show, Jackson joined Phoenix.

Abraham Lincoln Junior High was built in 1923 on a lot it shared with John Hay Elementary. The H-shaped building at Twelfth Avenue North was one of the Minneapolis public schools designed with specialized music rooms.[20] Before Lincoln, Prince practiced in his father's living room, played in his own bedroom, and had music instruction in regular classrooms. Lincoln was the first school Prince attended with dedicated music space. There were three: on the ground floor, two rectangular-shaped orchestral and band rooms that held forty to sixty students; and on the third floor, a general-purpose music room that also held forty to sixty students.[21]

The "architecture of a space," observes acoustic engineer Rob Metkemeijer, "can shape itself to sound. A good acoustic space is given shape and materials to serve music."[22] At Lincoln, the music rooms were designed to be shaped to sound. Their size and scale, the building materials, how the space was designed to accommodate instruments and singing, the chalkboards, and musical notation reveal the link between sound and design. This architecture of music had a profound impact on Prince. Indeed, throughout his junior high and high school days, he found solace in them. And even though he had several music teachers at other schools, he never had access to spaces for musical production as he did at Lincoln.[23] Those rooms gave him places to hone his craft and to jam with other musicians he met at school.

Bryant Junior High

In the fall of 1970, Prince switched schools and began attending Bryant Junior High. It is unclear why Prince spent only one year at Lincoln, but it is possible that his parents used the city's voluntary busing program, which grew out of desegregation efforts, to make the change. For unknown reasons, they may have recommended Bryant, located in South Minneapolis. Prince most likely wanted to attend Bryant because it had a reputation for having arguably the best music program among the junior highs.[24] Bryant was one of the few schools that still required all students to play an instrument, which elevated its musical pedigree and fostered a crop of multi-instrumentalists like Prince. Among them were future members of the Minneapolis funk band the Time and Jimmy "Jam" Harris, son of the prominent local pianist "Cornbread" Harris and later one-half of the songwriting and producing team Jimmy Jam and Terry Lewis.[25]

Although music likely drove Prince's attendance, he filled his plate with other activities. He played point guard on the basketball team and was a baller, too. Richard Robinson, his ninth-grade coach, said, "When we needed to kill something, we'd give the ball to Prince."[26] His handles, passing, and shooting made him the number six man in the rotation. He dreamed of playing at Central High, which had a tradition of winning. But the coach there wouldn't play someone Prince's size.[27]

At Bryant, Prince also developed his first relationship with a music teacher, James Hamilton, the music department chair. Hamilton taught Prince music theory for two years (1970–72) and encouraged his musical expression, which his father had never done.[28] In an interview given after Prince's passing, Hamilton said, "He was a seriously smart kid, and he just got music." The teacher was impressed by Prince and could see that he, even at thirteen years old, "really understood . . . what music was at the core, even from that early age." Hamilton saw that Prince was a "natural musician, he had the ear," meaning he could listen and play. Though the teenager was "introverted" and shy, when he played music, "he was a different person altogether."[29]

Hamilton confirmed what Prince would tell his high school paper: that he was primarily self-taught. When he arrived at Bryant, Prince was a good guitar and piano player. He'd spent years watching his father and soaking up lessons from previous music teachers. Hamilton's contribution was not to teach him how to play but to show him how music was structured and composed. So, rather than teach Prince the rudiments of playing, Hamilton focused on music theory, its concepts, and methods. Hamilton's theory lessons gave Prince tools to begin creating music. However, Hamilton's Business of Music course had the most significant impact.[30] Hamilton taught students the legal and financial aspects of the music industry. It was essential to understand music contracts; many artists who didn't were taken advantage of, which Hamilton believed had happened to Ray Charles. The course also explained how musicians could protect their interests.

Bryant was a critical period in Prince's musical development. He was now thinking more about his future. His musical skills were growing so rapidly that they became his primary language. And he'd joined a band. Prince was leaning into music in ways he hadn't at Lincoln. These factors made Bryant's music rooms essential spaces for the young musician. The school, named after American poet and journalist William Cullen Bryant, was built with music in mind. It had a long, rectangular band room on the ground floor and a music room on the third floor. The rooms could accommodate seventy-five and forty students, respectively.[31]

Prince spent countless hours in Bryant's music rooms, jamming and practicing. "He was at the band room at 8 a.m. sharp, waiting to be let in," said Hamilton. Before the first period, Prince would jam there with friends. And every day, Hamilton had to go in and "break up the session and make the kids go to biology class." Prince was the last student to go home in the afternoon. Those rooms were his sanctuary, where he was proficient and comfortable. The shy youth, who didn't speak much, spoke volumes through music. His sound engineer on several albums, Susan Rogers, said, "His way of being in the world was to express himself musically." Even as a seventh grader, music was the language Prince felt most comfortable speaking. "His eyes would light up when he started performing," said Hamilton.[32]

Kicked Out

Musically, things were going well for Prince in the eighth grade. He was even getting attention from girls. But things were not going well at home. Prince and John's living situation was rocky and soon came to a head. When he and Mattie were married, John was still working during the day and playing music in strip clubs at night. He couldn't give Prince the attention and guidance he needed.[33] After about six months of cohabitation, John kicked out his son for disobeying the no-girls-in-the-house rule, inaugurating a period of couch surfing and semihomelessness for the young musician.[34]

Prince stayed with his aunt Olivia (John's older sister) on South Fourth Avenue near the current George Floyd Square.[35] But that experiment soon ended; Prince didn't like his aunt's strict rules, and she didn't want his constant music playing. He bounced around after that, staying with different family members with the Stratocaster guitar his father bought him in tow. This time was difficult for Prince. At thirteen, he was homeless, "alone in a world so cold," as he would sing years later in his hit "When Doves Cry."

Prince found what he had been searching for with Andre's help. Andre told his mother, Bernadette Anderson, a respected community member, about his friend's troubles and asked if he could stay with them. Bernadette, who had recently divorced Fred, John Nelson's old bandmate and Andre's father, agreed. From eighth grade until high school graduation, Prince lived with Andre, his five siblings, and Mrs. Anderson in a bungalow with a rounded facade on a small grassy hill on Russell Avenue North. Prince and Andre lived and worked in the basement, which became a vital space for self-discovery and musical growth for Prince (fig. 7.1). He stayed because Bernadette Anderson acted as a surrogate mother, loving and caring for him like her own son.[36]

By the end of junior high school, the band Phoenix was showing promise. They were now a five-piece outfit, with Linda Anderson (Andre's sister) on keys, Andre on bass, Terry Jackson on congas, Chazz on drums, and Prince on lead guitar. They were getting a reputation as a good cover band, playing a mix of funk, rock, and R&B ranging from James Brown and Sly and the Family Stone to Chaka Khan and Rufus to Earth, Wind, and Fire, and Prince's favorite, Carlos Santana. They started gigging, playing school dances, the VFW, the YMCA, and even a few nightclubs, always with parents who were the band's managers and drivers. "My mom had a station wagon," said Terry Jackson, "so that became our road car for gigs."[37]

In 1972, Prince attended Central High School on the South Side instead of North High, most likely because Central had the best music program of all the city's public high schools. Even during Thaddeus Giddings's time, the school had a reputation as a band and choir powerhouse.

By this point, Prince had two years of music theory with Hamilton and had taken the teacher's Business of Music class. He now began plotting his future musical life. The young savant worked with Hamilton on complex arrangements and became very good on the piano and guitar, in no small part because of the time he spent in Bryant's music rooms.[38] Prince's band

Figure 7.1. Bernadette Anderson's home, where Prince and Andre lived. Photo by the author.

also changed its name from Phoenix to Grand Central, combining the names of the band Grand Funk Railroad and Prince's high school. Prince's musical growth perhaps soothed internal feelings about his parents' breakup and his period of homelessness. Music allowed him to speak, anchoring him in an uncertain world.[39]

Prince formed a close bond with his music teacher at Central, Katherine Doepke, who taught him voice, piano, and music theory during his sophomore and junior years. Doepke recalled that when she asked the students about their musical interests on the first day of voice class, the serious and quiet young musician said, "I want to become a rock-and-roll star."[40]

Prince, she recalled, was easy to teach. "I couldn't do a thing with him. He was good; he knew how to play amazingly well. . . . He was just so above the rest of them." But he did want more music theory. "He was the only music student I ever had who asked to study music theory," she recalled." Doepke let Prince take a synthesizer home one night, which was against school policy. Prince showed his appreciation by allowing her to play tambourine and maracas with his band. "I can say I played with Prince," beamed Doepke.[41]

Like Bryant, Central had some of the best musical architecture in the public school system, and Prince spent countless hours in its many music rooms. The school was one of the first designed after Giddings's tenure. Central had listening and practice rooms on the second floor and a large band and choral room on the third floor.[42]

Those music rooms had helped Central become a band powerhouse in the 1920s and '30s, providing students and teachers with a place for music appreciation and education.[43] Even after the school system deemphasized music education, the rooms remained a spatial expression of music's value. But although schools gave the young Prince rooms where he could grow musically (and find sanctuary), they weren't the spaces where he evolved the sound that would make him one of the world's most popular and successful musicians. In neighborhood basements, the backroom of a North Side community center, and recording studios between the North and South Sides, Prince and his friends incubated a new Minneapolis sound that would become world famous.

Chapter 8

THE ROOMS WHERE IT HAPPENED

Every building and every space has its own particular sound.

—Machiel Spaan

In the South Bronx, where hip-hop was born, its creators carved out space for its growth in public places: parks, subway stations, subway trains, street corners, and the sides of buildings. In Minneapolis, one of the places where youths like Prince grew musically was in schools. However, the basements, the backroom of a Near North Side neighborhood community center called the Way, and local music studios were equally important. It happened in these places because, like the South Bronx, Black people in Minneapolis had high rates of joblessness, lived near expressways that closed them off from other parts of the city, and dealt with the economic fallout of white flight to the suburbs. Bereft of resources, kids like Prince had few spaces to cultivate their musical interests and talents. What he and his contemporaries did have, like kids in the Bronx, were makeshift locations that incubated the sound that transformed popular music.

Basements, the Way, and recording studios were the creative birthplaces of the post–World War II Minneapolis Sound. In those places, Prince and several other Black youths midwifed a modern sound built on the funk and

R&B bursting from the radio, local bars and clubs, and the record shops in the segregated worlds of North and South Minneapolis. This chapter tells the story of the places where the postwar Minneapolis Sound was cultivated, with a focus on its leading composer and performer, Prince.

Basements

If school music rooms were sanctuaries where Prince could grow musically, basements were rehearsal spaces and early music studios. They gave him the isolation he needed to immerse himself in music while being large enough to accommodate band members to rehearse and jam. They would be important places for him well into the 1980s. Building codes in Minneapolis and the Midwest require foundations to be laid below the frost line.[1] If the foundation is built on the frost line, freezing and thawing will tear it apart. Geography determines the frost line's depth—shorter in warmer climates and deeper in cold areas. In Minnesota, basements were mainly used for storage, water heaters, and furnaces. In the 1950s, they were being turned into living and recreation spaces, including bars. But these perpetually damp and dank spaces that too often flood from heavy rains need lots of work and money to make them habitable.

Lack of wealth among Black residents made the cost of remodeling a basement a challenge. But even though they were not habitable, Prince and other young Minneapolitans used them to make music. The group first rehearsed in Chazz Smith's backyard. After a swarm of kids showed up to listen, police were called because of the crowd, and the band had to find another place to play.[2] Andre's house had a basement, so the young musicians cleaned it with Bernadette Anderson's permission and moved in their equipment. Prince took up residence in there. Living where he made music was a practice that would reach its most elaborate expression with the construction of Paisley Park, his estate and production complex in Chanhassen, a Minneapolis suburb. The Anderson basement gave Prince and his friends an intimate and private space. They found their chemistry and groove in the gumbo of rock, R&B, and funk that made up their sound. Prince had already developed his guitar skills during his long practice sessions at Bryant Junior High. He could play his idol Carlos Santana's "Soul Sacrifice" perfectly, to the amazement of Chazz, who had no idea he could play that well.[3]

Grand Central was one of the bands that defined the sound at the time. In 1972, they won a battle of the bands contest.[4] A buzz swirled around them, leading to gigs at high school dances, VFW halls, local clubs like Nacirema, the Way community center, and even the dedication ceremony to demolish the Minneapolis YWCA (see fig. 8.1).

Figure 8.1. Grand Central playing at the YWCA dedication around 1972. Prince is on the right with the guitar. Photo courtesy of the Hennepin County Library, Minnesota.

The band, however, needed another rehearsal space because Bernadette Anderson didn't like the noise emanating from her basement. Terry Jackson's mother agreed to let them use hers. A Grand Central member, William "Hollywood" Doughty, recalled how the ambitious teenage musicians spent their time: "Half the day in school, half the day in the basement."[5]

Grand Central was hot as fish grease, and several eager teens were angling to get in. One of them was Morris Day, a freckle-faced transplant from Springfield, Illinois, who'd encountered the band in the Central High lunchroom.[6] Morris's mother, LaVonne Daugherty, decided to move him and his sister from Illinois to California when Morris was about seven. South Minneapolis was supposed to be a stopover on their way west. LaVonne's cousin, Regina, took them in. After the Days got on their feet financially, they moved to the North Side, where they lived on the same street as Prince, Tyka, and Mattie.[7]

Morris and Andre Anderson attended Minneapolis North High School. They shared a mutual interest in "advanced music" and good weed.[8] While hanging out at Morris's house, the future Revolution bassist noticed Morris's drum kit. "Play something," Andre said, and the eager drummer obliged.[9]

Morris loved music. From a young age, it was the one thing he knew he cared about and could do well. The future leader of the Time had experienced the remnants of Bryant's still-solid music program, which he attended two years before Prince. In addition to his percussion and piano lessons, he spent thousands of hours listening to and trying to imitate his favorite drummers, like Billy Cobham, who played with Miles Davis and the jazz fusion band the Mahavishnu Orchestra.[10]

Morris was ready. He played some beats he'd learned from David Garibaldi, drummer for the West Coast band Tower of Power. A stunned Andre said, "Why didn't you tell me . . . that you could play your ass off?" According to Morris, Andre told him that the band had problems with Prince's cousin Chazz and that Morris should come by and audition. Morris happily accepted, and soon he was playing Sly and the Family Stone's "Dance to the Music," Carlos Santana's "Evil Ways," and Funkadelic's "Free Your Mind and Your Ass Will Follow" with the rest of Grand Central in Terry Jackson's basement. The band was as impressed with him as Andre was. Prince didn't say much, keeping his distance and focusing on the music. By the end of the audition, Grand Central agreed that Morris was what they needed. Chazz was out. Morris was in.[11]

It wasn't just Prince and Grand Central who used basements for music-making. In the early 1970s, basements were vital spaces for musical incubation in North Minneapolis. Bands used them for rehearsals and recording. Influenced by local and national R&B and funk sounds, they wanted to create their own music and used basements to develop it. Flyte Tyme, a band whose members included future music legends, had a friendly rivalry with Grand Central.[12]

Flyte Tyme's name came from the title of a song by jazz trumpeter Donald Byrd. The band's core members were Jimmy "Jam" Harris, a classmate of Prince's at Bryant, bassist Terry Lewis, and drummer Garry "Jellybean" Johnson.[13] All three would contribute to Prince's later projects, Jimmy and Terry in the Time, Jellybean in the New Power Generation. Jimmy and Terry would later form their own production company that worked with some of the most influential artists of the late twentieth century—Michael Jackson, Janet Jackson, New Edition, Alexander O'Neal, Britney Spears, Boyz II Men, Mariah Carey, Usher, Chaka Khan, the SOS Band, Sounds of Blackness, Mary J. Blige, the Spice Girls, and many more.

Jimmy and Terry met at the University of Minnesota's summer Upward Bound program. Terry was older and, to Jimmy, much cooler. The two became friends and soon discovered their mutual love of music. Though still in junior high, Jimmy played gigs around town, drumming for his father, Cornbread Harris. Terry linked up with a group of older musicians, one of whom was Jellybean. When Terry heard Jimmy jamming on the piano in the school cafeteria, he was impressed by the younger musician and asked him to join the band he was putting together for an Upward Bound event. After the performance, the two continued their friendship and developed a bit of a rivalry. Jimmy eventually joined a band called Mind & Matter, which allowed him to play the sultry, soulful ballads that were the stock-in-trade of his Philadelphia idols, songwriters and producers Kenneth Gamble and Leon Huff, famous for their work with the O'Jays and Harold Melvin & the Blue Notes.[14] Mind & Matter also spent countless hours rehearsing and recording in the basement of a group member on the North Side.[15]

Jimmy and Terry would join forces again in the band Flyte Tyme. Deeply inspired by Parliament Funkadelic's adventurous sounds and outrageous stage performances, Flyte Tyme had a three-piece brass section like them and other funk bands. The horns set them apart from all the other groups. They allowed the group to soar and create bright, crisp harmonic sounds. The band's vocalist, Cynthia Johnson, had a distinctive, soulful voice that made her an artist to watch toward the end of the decade. The group also featured saxophonist David "Batman" Eiland. Grand Central and tight, funky, and skilled Flyte Tyme vied for the top spot among the city's Black music groups.[16]

The Way

The Way, a popular community center for the Black community, provided a place for youth to jam, rehearse, perform, and be mentored by well-known musicians.[17] The Way was born in 1966. It was one of several community centers established in mostly Black urban neighborhoods as part of President Lyndon Johnson's "War on Poverty." Grants from the Economic Opportunity Act, handled by the Office of Economic Opportunities, channeled federal funds toward local antipoverty programs. Although Minneapolis and St. Paul had an unemployment rate of only 3.8 percent in 1966, Black unemployment in the Twin Cities was three times higher. Blacks were still locked out of unions and often found themselves in service work that didn't pay well or in jobs that didn't offer advancement, making owning a home nearly impossible. Joblessness was acute on Minneapolis's Near North Side.

Black North Siders also faced another pressing issue: enclosure from highways. Like Blacks on the South Side and in St. Paul's Rondo section, North Siders found their community cut off by highway construction. Sixth Avenue North, the cultural center of Black life on the Near North Side, was destroyed to make way for the Olson Memorial Parkway.[18] Before the parkway plowed through it, Sixth Avenue North was a hotbed of Black cultural life. "In the minds of the well-traveled," said the *Minneapolis Spokesman*, the picturesque block that housed the city's Black jazz scene was comparable to "Beale Street in Memphis, State Street in Chicago, Market Street in St. Louis, and Lenox Avenue in New York."[19]

In August 1966, violence erupted after a confrontation between an appliance store's Jewish owner and several Black youths. Over thirty police showed up in full riot gear. Residents felt the police response was excessive; some had heated exchanges with the officers. Black youths hurled bricks, smashed windows in the store, and looted items. Minneapolis's Jewish mayor, Arthur Naftalin, held meetings in the wake of the unrest, which local people said resulted from the lack of jobs, resources, and recreation facilities. Despite police claims that the unrest had been caused by "hoodlums," Naftalin responded with programs rather than punishment.[20] With the support of local civic leaders, businesses, and deep-pocketed and well-connected citizens, Naftalin provided jobs to Near North Side youth. Funding became available to lease an old bait-and-tackle shop with a leaky roof called Fishing Unlimited on Plymouth Avenue. That shop became the Way, the nerve center for community activities.

The Way was a beehive of activity for young people. Dances, basketball games (Prince played pickup), theater, mentoring, and job placement were part of the various activities. The community center was an extension of the North Side for residents. As Director of Community Education Mahmoud El-Kati said, "Wherever [the Way] ends up, that's where we [North Side residents] end up." El-Kati's proclamation was realized within the first year of the Way's existence.[21]

The Way's arts program helped elevate the local music scene and provided youths like Prince a place to rehearse and perform. The arts were central to the Way's work in the community. The center provided space for aspiring musicians in the building's back room. If you were part of the network of Black North Side bands in the late 1960s and 1970s, you came through the Way. Grand Central, Mind & Matter, and Flyte Tyme all practiced and performed in the backroom space packed with instruments that became known as the "music room."[22] One band was even born there.

Joe Lewis and Sonny Thompson met at the Way. Lewis was a drummer, and Thomas played piano and then guitar. The two listened to everything from Jimi Hendrix to James Brown to Wes Montgomery. When the Way opened, they spent countless hours trying to reproduce their favorite sounds on the instruments in the music room. Joe Lewis recalled the room as a laboratory of creative energy. "You've got nice instruments—you go to the back room, work on music four hours out of the day; it was something really to look forward to every day."[23] The music in the backroom was like a magnet.

It attracted young musicians, such as guitarist Randy Barber, keyboardist Calvin Cyprian, saxophonist Bill Perry, and vocalist Roland Willis Jr., who formed a band called Back to Black. Harry "Spike" Moss, the Way's first art director, managed them. In the early 1970s, they were the community center's house band, rehearsing during the week and playing on the weekends.[24]

Pierre Lewis, an accomplished jazz organist who'd been playing since seventh grade, was a member of Back to Black. Bandmate Joe Lewis called him a "child prodigy."[25] While playing in St. Paul, Lewis met the renowned jazz pianist and organist Bobby Lyle, who was in the audience and was impressed by the youngster's talent. "Yeah, it looks like I've got competition," Lyle remarked. Born in Memphis, Lyle grew up in Minneapolis, where he began his musical career playing in local clubs when he was sixteen. Between his international tours, Lyle would spend time at the Way, giving workshops, jamming, and mentoring the youths who hung out in the music room.[26]

Back to Black's sound mixed Parliament and Sly Stone funk with Hendrix's rock. They even dabbled in the sweet pop sounds of the Jackson 5. Despite their success, having "Black" in the title made white people nervous, limiting their opportunities to perform. So they changed their name to the Family.[27] It didn't take long for them to gain a reputation as a tight band whose music fused different sounds and styles. They accomplished this by logging long hours in the Way's music room. Their creative energy was so robust that Jimmy "Jam" Harris, Terry Lewis, Andre Anderson (who changed his name to Andre Cymone), Morris Day, and Prince were pulled in. The teenagers jammed, rehearsed, and traded musical knowledge Monday through Friday. Saturday nights were for performing at weekly dances in the Way's sizeable social room.[28]

North Side bands also played public concerts at a familiar site for music, the Phyllis Wheatley House. The long-standing social service organization hosted a battle of the bands contest showcasing local talent. The Family, Flyte Tyme, and Grand Central entered the contest. Each band competed for the crowd's approval and bragging rights as the best. The competition was fierce. "There was no prize," said Pierre Lewis. But that didn't matter; the real prize was "to sound better than the rest of the groups."[29]

The Studio

Basements were the location for early recordings by Prince and his contemporaries. Flyte Tyme, Grand Central, and the Family used these (literally) underground sites to capture their ingenuity and determination on tape. They recorded in basements out of necessity. Recording music in the early

1970s was expensive, and good studios were outside Black neighborhoods. That said, basements, with their damp conditions and lack of soundproofing, were hardly the best locations for recording. Bands ultimately had to turn to recording studios.

In the 1970s, many Black bands recorded at the Cookhouse, the Moon Studios, and Sound 80. Prince started recording at the Cookhouse through his cousin Pepé Willie, a Brooklyn-born and raised singer and songwriter who started as a valet for 1960s R&B singers like Little Anthony and the Imperials. After a stint in Los Angeles, Pepé, whose relationship with his wife Shantel had become strained, moved to her hometown, Minneapolis, so the couple could reconcile.[30]

When Willie arrived in December 1974, he was greeted by bone-chilling temperatures and warm greetings from his father-in-law, Eddie. Eddie had thrown a party in his honor and invited Grand Central to play. Little did Willie know, but the eager teens hoped he would mentor their band if he heard them play. Willie thought they were good and agreed to meet them the following week.[31]

Willie had much to offer; he'd spent more than a decade in music and had a wealth of knowledge to pass on. When he visited Grand Central during their rehearsal, he saw they were tight and moved easily between Earth, Wind, and Fire, and Sly and the Family Stone funk. He also heard some of their original material. The songs needed editing, but they were funky. Willie was impressed by the band's willingness to take advice and their professionalism.[32] He also was impressed by the dynamo fronting the band. During the rehearsal, Prince stopped the group, walked over to keyboardist Linda Anderson, and showed her exactly how he wanted her to phrase a song, playing the progression note-for-note. "Wow," thought Willie. "I didn't know he could play keys like that."[33] Prince then strolled over to Andre and asked for his bass. Willie was awed. At only seventeen, Prince had mastered multiple instruments. Pepé was so impressed that he invited Prince to join him and a few other musicians at the Cookhouse Recording Studios on Nicollet Avenue (see fig. 8.2). The quiet teenage prodigy agreed.[34]

The Cookhouse sessions were run by bassist Wendell Thomas and his sixteen-year-old half brother drummer Dale Alexander, vocalists Kristie Lazenberry and Marcy Ingvoldstad, and seventeen-year-old keyboardist Pierre Lewis of the Family, whom Prince knew from the Way.[35] They called themselves 94 East after the interstate that connected St. Paul and Minneapolis and upended the Rondo neighborhood.[36]

The band recorded several songs at the Cookhouse. The studio recorded local white rock and pop groups like the Trashmen and the Castaways. The city's apartheid kept music and people separate, even in recording studios.

Figure 8.2. Cookhouse Recording Studios, where Prince recorded with Pepé Willie and 94 East, 1970s. Photo courtesy of the Hennepin County Library, Minnesota.

Disrespect of Black talent by studio employees made recording an ordeal. "It took me three weeks just to be taken seriously," Willie lamented. "I was just some black kid from Brooklyn."[37] Recording costs were another barrier; for Black artists, they were prohibitive. Willie had to save every penny and pick up a second job (his main work was for the post office) as a teacher's aide at Prince's old junior high school.[38]

With no rehearsals, the impromptu Cookhouse sessions were dazzling. Each musician brought their best to the recordings. They recorded the lush funk ballad "If We Don't," the sultry pop of "I'll Always Love You," and the dirty Minneapolis funk of "If You See Me." Prince "approached the session like a seasoned professional," Willie remarked. On his first time in a recording studio he "played better than a professional session player . . . none of the guitar players I'd worked with played as well as Prince." After hearing the recordings, not only was Willie impressed, but so was band member David Wendell. He was astonished by the quality of musicianship and called Willie, shouting into the phone, "Did you hear what Prince was playing?!"[39] Willie secured a record deal for 94 East with New York–based Polydor Records on the strength of those recordings Prince played on.[40]

After the Cookhouse sessions, in the spring of 1976, Prince, Andre, and Morris recorded a demo at ASI studio in North Minneapolis, where the bohemian singer-songwriter Tom Waits had recorded just a year earlier. ASI was the creation of Dan Holmes and Wes Hayne. They released records by local R&B groups Purple Haze and Pound of Flesh.[41] Under the name Champagne, Andre, Morris, and Prince recorded "39th St. Party," "Grand Central," "Lady Pleasure," "Machine," "Whenever," and "You're Such a Fox." St. Louis Park resident David Rivkin, the sound engineer for those sessions, would work with Prince for years, including on the wildly successful *Purple Rain*.[42]

Shortly after these sessions, Prince, Andre, and Morris met British transplant Chris Moon, whose studio was one of the few places Black artists could record because of its affordable fees. Jimmy "Jam" Harris and Terry Lewis recorded there during their teenage years, as did other Black bands from the North Side.[43] Moon immigrated to the United States from Southampton when he was seventeen. After living in Hawaii for a few years, the family moved to Minneapolis.

Moon set up his first recording studio in the basement of a house he rented in South Minneapolis. He didn't charge for studio time as long as artists brought reel-to-reel tapes and credited him for his work.[44] It wasn't long before the rock, folk, polka, and country musicians who first recorded in his dungeon-like studio were replaced by R&B and funk bands from the South and North Sides.[45] In 1970, Moon's stock began to rise, and his basement was no longer suitable for recording. At Twenty-Eighth Avenue South, he opened a new recording facility, Moonsound Studios. Moon also began to think about songwriting while establishing himself as a producer and sound engineer. "I've always been a writer," he said. While recording his artists, he felt that "most of the lyrics these guys are singing are pretty dreadful. I know I can do better than that."[46] He came up with the idea to find a band, write songs for them, let them produce the music, and he would handle promotion.[47]

That band walked into Moonsound in the spring of 1976. Prince, Andre Anderson, and Morris Day recorded songs for a demo tape they wanted to use to land a record deal. After four or five hours of recording, the band left the studio to take a break, but Prince stayed behind. Alone in the studio, Prince moved from the piano to the bass to the drums. After a few minutes of listening, Moon thought, "He's not bad," better on some instruments than others, but Moon liked his confidence. Then it struck him: "If I have only one artist, I don't have to worry about the drummer not showing up and screwing up the whole session."[48]

When the band was finished for the day, Moon eased over to the painfully shy musician and gave him his pitch. "I'm a writer and producer and recording engineer and don't want to be an artist, and I wonder if you'd like me to package you up and promote you and write your songs and teach you how the studio works and see if you can make something happen for you?"[49] Moon handed Prince the keys to the studio. Moon would cover the recording costs and write for Prince if he was given credit for his work.

Not long after agreeing to work with Moon, Prince left Grand Central because of a disagreement with Morris Day's mother, LaVonne. Her deliberate pace and Prince's impetuous style clashed, causing his exit from the band.[50] The band floundered without its star. "Grand Central without Prince was like Desi without Lucy," Morris lamented. The crew tried to reconstitute itself as Champagne. However, without Prince's star power and hard-driving determination to be the best band in the land, they broke up, leaving Morris adrift and with no plans or skills other than music. It was a difficult road ahead for the drummer.[51] However, Andre Anderson (now Cymone) landed on his feet, thanks to his pal Prince.

For nearly a year, Prince took a bus from school to Moonsound, sometimes camping out in the studio over the weekend when Moon was away. His routine was like a band camp, sound engineering training, and songwriting practice every day. Prince arrived in the afternoon and began putting melodies to the lyrics Moon left for him, playing piano, bass, drums, and guitar. Once he graduated from high school, he spent even more time at Moonsound. He was relentless in his pursuit of the right sound and unwavering in his determination to get it right. There was mutual respect between Moon and Prince, but their relationship never went deeper. Each knew the other had something to benefit him, and each took full advantage of what the other could offer. Their mutual need for each other kept them working together, despite Prince's disapproval when Moon smoked a joint or enjoyed a rum and Coke between takes. (Prince's well-known abstinence was uncompromising even when he was a teen, which would make his death from a drug overdose even more shocking and painful.)

The two worked on songs around the clock. Prince found that the late-night hours were when he was the most productive. Both men were musically hungry and pushed each other creatively. Moon thought Prince needed a marketing strategy and suggested "naughty sexual innuendo." After a rum-filled night with two women, Moon staggered into the studio early on a Sunday morning (his day off), and as he lay in the studio recapping the wild night and nursing a severe hangover, "Soft and Wet" came to mind.[52] Moon penned the lyrics, and when he showed them to Prince, the singer began immediately working on the music.[53] Now that the producer and artist had a marketing concept and a song, it was time to find a record deal.

Prince flew to New York and stayed with his half-sister Sharon (John's daughter from his first marriage), hoping to find a deal. It didn't go well. He was either ignored, given the runaround, or offered terrible deals. Singer Cynthia Johnson spoke about the uphill struggle Black musicians from Minneapolis faced. "I don't think there's a black band in the Twin Cities that has a manager because there's not a manager that believes in the black music scene," she remarked.[54] It is perhaps not surprising that Prince strategically relied on white men, of which Moon was one, to help him land a deal.

The other was Owen Husney, a businessman and former musician who ran an advertising agency in Minneapolis. Moon approached Husney, telling him he'd found the next Stevie Wonder. Husney rolled his eyes. When Moon played "Soft and Wet" for him, he asked who the group was. With all the dramatic flair he could muster at this pivotal moment, Moon told Husney that the group was one eighteen-year-old playing all the instruments and doing all the vocals. Husney's interest was piqued. Seeing that an opportunity had just fallen into his lap, Husney organized a capital campaign, and within days, he raised $50,000 from his wealthy friends. Prince now would have a weekly allowance, new instruments, and a new apartment on Aldrich Avenue South in Uptown, leaving basements for good.[55]

Living in his first home as an adult and with Husney as his manager, Prince could focus exclusively on music. Husney had two priorities for his young musician: developing a band to perform shows and recording new demos. The sessions would occur at Minneapolis's premier recording studio, Sound 80, where Minnesota-born and raised Bob Dylan recorded songs for his *Blood on the Tracks* album in 1974. Local bands like the Suicide Commandos, the Suburbs, and Lipps Inc. also recorded there.[56] Located on East Twenty-Fifth Street, Sound 80 was established in 1969 by Tom Jung and Herb Pilhofer, who were also responsible for the Key Bank Studios, which became the Cookhouse. Sound engineer David Rivkin, who recorded songs for 94 East and was a former bandmate of Husney, ran the boards at Sound 80 and recorded the songs. When Prince began recording there in 1977, Rivkin introduced him to his younger brother Robert, a drummer who (under the name Bobby Z) would play in the Revolution for nearly a decade.[57]

Prince began recording his demo in March 1977. Pepé Willie had booked studio time there to record songs for his new deal with Polydor Records. On his first day of recording, he saw a familiar face: Prince. When Willie asked why he was in the studio, Prince replied, "Can I play with you guys?" "Are you kidding," Willie answered. "Absolutely." Prince played lead guitar on several of Willie's songs and sang backup.[58]

Prince may have been a one-person band in the studio, but he couldn't be one onstage. Longtime friend and collaborator André Cymone was the first to join, followed by Bobby Z.[59] Their jams, free-flowing instrumental playing that alternated between dirty Minneapolis funk and jazz, demonstrated the musical range Prince was developing. These sounds were not the pop songs he recorded at Sound 80; they were closer to John Nelson's avant-garde jazz but funky and accessible. Prince played lead guitar and the Moog synthesizer, which he increasingly relied on in the coming years. These recordings also demonstrated his new skills as a sound engineer and producer.[60]

This period of sustained growth and productivity was herculean. Prince added skills to his sonic repertoire that reached beyond the promise he had shown in high school, the band Grand Central, and his early recordings. That growth was evident in the Sound 80 recordings. "Baby," "Just as Long as We're Together," "My Love Is Forever," which Moon worked on, and "Soft and Wet" all were significantly improved at Sound 80. Armed with new tracks, Husney and Prince flew to Los Angeles to seek a record deal.

Getting a meeting with record executives wasn't easy. So Husney played them against each other by telling them he had met with their rivals. The gamble worked. The executives scheduled meetings with Husney in the hope of signing Prince first. CBS Records, A&M, RSO, ABC, Dunhill, and Warner Bros. lined up.[61] The labels began to salivate at the possibility of getting "the next Stevie Wonder." CBS gave Prince studio time to see if he was the one-man-band Husney sold him as. Executives watched him move from instrument to instrument, playing and singing. He recorded "Just as Long as We're Together" before their eyes. They dropped their skepticism and made him an offer. A bidding war erupted among CBS, A&M, and Warner Bros.[62] Husney and Prince sat through meetings and lavish dinners with expensive wine that the strait-laced musician didn't touch. Each company promised to make him the next star, offering lucrative contracts and multialbum deals. A&M's offer of two albums was rejected, which left CBS and Warner Bros. CBS offered a three-album deal but wanted the first album produced by another musician, a dealbreaker for Prince.[63]

Warner Bros. remained in the running, but negotiations were tense. Top executives Mo Ostin and Lenny Waronker were confronted with the question all record executives face: Could this unknown new artist make hit records that would justify their investment? After deliberation, they gave Prince what he wanted—a three-album deal and a six-figure signing bonus. There was one caveat: He'd have creative freedom, but he would have a coproducer on his first album. On June 25, 1977, three weeks after his nineteenth birthday, Prince signed a Warner Bros. contract for $250,000. It was a remarkable achievement. The teenager from the Near North Side of Minneapolis had done what no Black recording artist in Minnesota history had done—sign a record deal with a major label.[64]

The tension over creative control began shortly after the ink dried on the deal. Warner Bros. wanted Maurice White, the lead singer and songwriter for Earth, Wind, and Fire, to coproduce Prince's album. But Prince didn't want to be limited to R&B or funk music. He was a Minneapolis musician from the city's Black community, and Black music there was more expansive than the music industry's racially restrictive genres. Prince was creating new music by fusing different genres. Labels like "R&B," "soul," and "funk" didn't capture the music he was making. His musical marriage of Sly Stone, Carlos Santana, Joni Mitchell, and Fleetwood Mac put his sound beyond category. It was his sound, a Minneapolis sound.

A heated exchange with Waronker captured the tensions over creative control. Prince famously told the Warner executive, "Don't make me black; my idols are all over the place."[65] This statement might sound like Prince was distancing himself from being Black and from Black music. But Prince refused to be pigeonholed by narrow definitions of Black music. Prince listened to and loved Black music. It was in the DNA of his sound. But Prince was a Minneapolis product, meaning he could play that dirty Minneapolis funk, croon R&B, and pound out the new punk and indie rock pioneered by young white suburbanites like Hüsker Dü, the Suburbs, and the Replacements. These new sounds, which Prince first heard in junior high and high school, were antiestablishment and combative. They also were wildly inventive and energetic. Young Blacks like Prince from North and South Minneapolis, though not invited to join in, watched from afar, soaking up the sounds they would incorporate into their music.

Chapter 9

PLANNING, PUNK, AND INDIE ROCK DOWNTOWN

No one in the Minneapolis city government saw this side of the Gateway. All they saw was a fetid slum that unless cleared, could forever poison attempts to reinvigorate an aging, dormant downtown, rapidly losing business and population to the suburbs.

—Larry Millett

Within a few years, the primordial pronto-punk scene rapidly expanded to include dozens of musicians, performing indie rock, punk, new wave, no wave, art rock, and more. Minneapolis was on a parallel path with the few scenes cropping up across the United States.

—Cyn Collins

As Prince began to work on the songs that would appear on his 1978 debut album, *For You*, another sound was brewing in Minneapolis. This one was not on the North and South Sides where he'd grown up and gone to school but mainly downtown; it emerged from the west bank of the Mississippi River's folk, blues, and classic rock scene that eclipsed jazz at the beginning of the 1960s. The young musicians who birthed this new sound were inspired by the music coming out of New York—artists like the New York Dolls and, from London, David Bowie. The musicians and fans who created Minneapolis's punk and indie rock scene rebelled against what they saw as the drab and boring sounds of the previous generation. They ignited a local scene that, although influenced from afar, was homegrown.[1]

The location of this musical revolution is just as important as the sounds that emerged from it. For decades, the city's epicenter of commerce and culture had been at war with itself. Minneapolis's growing middle class and expanding suburbs were fighting the saloons, flophouses, old grocery stores, boardinghouses, pool halls, and pawnshops housed in architectural relics of the past that made up the downtown Gateway district. This new scene washed ashore downtown. City planners eager to eliminate the city's skid row and white flight to the suburbs were crucial factors in shaping its musical geography. City leaders and urban planners saw the old neighborhood as an impediment to development and capital accumulation and wanted the area cleaned up. They regarded its existence as incongruent with the middle-class, business-friendly city they wanted Minneapolis to be. But the women and men who lined the streets of Nicollet Avenue didn't see it that way. They saw the Gateway as home, a place that reflected their values and desire to live the way they wanted.

By the time Prince was born in 1958, the city had won the battle against the Gateway; the neighborhood was razed at the end of the 1950s. But this didn't stop whites from leaving the city for the suburbs. These forces set the stage for the birth of punk and indie rock downtown. The children of the parents who exited the city as the Gateway was razed created this new scene. Musically, punk and indie rock grew out of the vacuum created by the staleness of 1960s rock. Economically, these sounds were enabled by white flight, which depressed land values and left empty storefronts throughout downtown. Young white entrepreneurs took advantage of the low prices and opened music venues to serve up the sounds emanating from the suburbs.

Planning the Destruction of the Gateway

When the Mississippi River sustained Minneapolis's life, making it a titan of flour production, the tens of thousands of men and women who worked in the industry clustered around the mill district and made it home. The neighborhood was called Bridge Square. It eventually took on the name "the Gateway" because the bridge was a gateway into the city. It was where Nicollet and Hennepin met near the city's oldest bridge, which was built in 1854. An entire economy arose to meet these laborers' needs: laundries, groceries, furniture stores, sex workers, bars and taverns, cobblers, teachers, hatmakers, printers, lawyers, and more.[2] Bridge Square was a thriving, densely packed community. For the city's first half century, its people provided the labor that powered its mill industry. By the 1880s, the class identity of this population began to shift. For reasons not entirely clear, perhaps density, noise, or pollution, those with economic mobility—the teachers, lawyers, cobblers—began leaving the neighborhood for less densely packed parts of the city. Left over was the "underclass." Male day laborers lived in boardinghouses that offered little privacy or comfort. Bars, restaurants, theaters, pool halls, and cheap hotels also sprung up along Washington Avenue to service the new proletariat that walked the streets looking for work.[3]

As the mill industry dried up in the early twentieth century, "fears and anxiety about these idle men haunted many a good Minneapolitan and seemed to signal the decline of the center city," writes historian Annette Atkins about the Gateway.[4] Progressive reformers decided to plan their way out of this crisis. In 1917, the city created a blueprint to "revive decaying downtowns."[5] The "Plan of Minneapolis" sought to reorganize the downtown in alignment with business interests and disappear the people and architecture of the old downtown. The Gateway's commercial district had old warehouses that stored the city's flour production in the nineteenth century. The district's crown jewel was a twelve-story Gothic building constructed in 1890 at Third Street and Second Avenue. When it was built, the *Minneapolis Journal* called it "the most magnificent office building in the whole round world." But by the end of the Second World War, observers like the attorney for the Minneapolis Housing and Redevelopment Authority called the building "a monstrosity in the eyes of most observers."[6]

By the mid twentieth century, Minneapolis newspapers regularly ran stories about the Gateway's crime, unemployment, and social ills. Working-class white men continued to fill the neighborhood, leading lives that contrasted with the image of a business-friendly city attractive to finance capital.[7] By the 1930s, blight was seen less as an eyesore and more as a social ill. Blight contradicted the efficient use of land; it illustrated the presence of social and public health problems. So, city planners convinced city leaders that such areas should be demolished. Plans to radically transform the area were put in motion.

Enter urban renewal. In the late 1940s, the federal government created a nationwide program to solve urban centers' "blight." Cities received vast funds to demolish old areas to make land available for new development. Modern, business-friendly buildings, the elimination of blight, and more drivable streets were the immediate effects of urban renewal. With decisions about how to spend the funds made at the local level, with little federal oversight, urban renewal was a financial windfall for cities.[8]

In 1957, Minneapolis Mayor P. K. Peterson received federal funding to demolish the Gateway. Within two years, the city began acquiring property, razing the old warehouses, and relocating the commercial district elsewhere. During the two decades of construction that followed, city officials moved people from rental properties. Nearly 200 buildings, spread over seventeen blocks, were demolished. Forty percent of the historic nineteenth-century landscape disappeared. In 1961, wrecking balls turned the nineteenth-century Gothic Metropolitan Building into rubble.[9] By the early 1960s, Minneapolis had bought and torn down many buildings in the Gateway and replaced them with parking lots.[10] By the early 1970s, the grimy area many called home was just a memory. It would be decades before the economic hopes of urban renewal in the Gateway bore fruit. That's because, by the 1950s, downtown Minneapolis was being hollowed out. The view of the Gateway as a place of social ills helped push white residents away from downtown. Their exodus meant they no longer looked to the city center for entertainment, culture, and shopping and instead spent their money in the suburbs. At the start of the exodus, a group of concerned businessmen started an association to advocate for the financial interests of downtown. They could see that white flight would significantly impact the city's economic viability.

The Downtown Council for Minneapolis

As the Gateway was being razed, Minneapolis's white residents had already decided they wanted out. Government policies subsidized their exodus. Between the 1950s and the early 1970s, Minneapolis's white population declined by 4 percent, while the Black population grew. The postwar housing boom that gave returning white GIs and white workers access to home loans in developing suburbs facilitated white flight. Golden Valley, Bloomington, Edina, Egan, and Chanhassen (where Prince would build his multiplex studio Paisley Park) absorbed many white people fleeing the city. After civil rights legislation struck down racially restrictive housing covenants and housing discrimination, the exodus only increased.

White flight not only moved white people and reinforced the color line but also removed economic resources from the city, especially its downtown. Jobs moved to suburban office complexes, corporate headquarters relocated, and the consequent financial drain shrank the city's tax base, and thereby support for schools, hospitals, parks, and recreation.

In 1955, as the city was planning the destruction of the Gateway, the Downtown Council for Minneapolis was formed to focus on long-range planning for downtown's future economic growth. The council advocated for the razing of the Gateway.[11] As white flight reached its apex, the council faced economic fallout from nearly two decades of urban renewal. A 1970 survey asked suburban residents if they preferred to come downtown to shop or shop closer to home. More than two-thirds said they preferred the suburbs to the city.[12] That preference also extended to dining and entertainment. The suburbs were seen as superior to downtown even though they lacked the diversity of downtown's shopping, dining, and entertainment options. The Downtown Council realized this was an existential threat to business interests and the city's economy. If white suburbanites with high disposable incomes didn't come into the city, this would wreak havoc on the tax base. In the aftermath of the survey, the council launched an advertising campaign to lure suburbanites to the city to spend money. Full-page ads appeared in the *Minneapolis Star* with images of the city's bustling and beautiful downtown. Some advertising tried to entice white suburbanites with retail sales or events like Downtown Day at the Nicollet Mall.

During this period, the Downtown Council confronted its most significant challenge in generating urban wealth. The Minnesota Vikings football team was looking for a new stadium, and the council lobbied them to move downtown.[13] For decades, the team had played at the University of Minnesota near the west bank of the Mississippi River in Minneapolis's Dinkytown neighborhood. The frost-bitten winters exposed the team and its fans to the brutal cold as they sat on backless wood benches. The proposed stadium would be located across from the Falls of St. Anthony in the heart of the old Gateway district. It would be domed and climate-controlled. The council argued that the 70,000-seat stadium would bring tens of millions of dollars to downtown and help resuscitate the area.[14] The council lobbied hard, pressuring the city council to give tax concessions for the stadium. The Vikings took the city's offer and began building the Hubert H. Humphrey Metrodome.

The Downtown Council's efforts to lure suburbanites to the city succeeded with the stadium opening in 1982. Their teenage children began to come to downtown Minneapolis, but not for shopping, dining, or football games. They went there to participate in the thriving music scene in bars and, notably, in an old bus station transformed into a music venue at First Avenue and Seventh Street. Buoyed by white-flight prices that enabled them to survive hard times, these venues gave birth to a new sound that produced national acts and fed the Minneapolis Sound that Prince created in the late 1970s and 1980s.

The Depot

A folk and blues scene emerged in Minnesota in the West Bank area, concentrated in bars and cafés like the New Riverside Café on Cedar Avenue and the Ten O'Clock Scholar in Dinkytown. Inspired by renowned artists like Pete Seeger, Woody Guthrie, and Joan Baez, Minnesota's folk scene helped propel Minnesota native Bob Dylan to national fame.[15] (Dylan, for a while, lived and performed in Dinkytown.) The blues scene featured established stars like B. B. King and young, up-and-coming artists like Bonnie Raitt.

Local rock bands emerged in the early 1960s as R&B took off in the South and Near North Sides. Nicollet and Lake Streets were rock centers, but the scene was displaced by urban renewal.[16] Their models were the Beatles, Led Zeppelin, the Rolling Stones, the Doors, Neil Young, and the Grateful Dead. Though short-lived, groups like the Del Counts, the Castaways, the Accents, Danny's Reasons, Crow, and the Trashmen (famous for their hit "Surfin' Bird") defined the 1960s rock scene.[17]

This brief period set the stage for the indie rock and punk scene that came after. As the 1970s began, the city's downtown was experiencing the effects of two decades of white flight and urban renewal. Schools, the Way community center, and North and South Minneapolis gigs sustained the Black music scene. The downtown indie rock and punk scene was financed by wealth generated in a housing market that excluded Black people—decades of home appreciation lined the pockets of music entrepreneurs who created venues for the city's newest homegrown sounds.

One such entrepreneur was Allan Fingerhut, the son of Jewish immigrants who moved to North Minneapolis in the early twentieth century and then to St. Louis Park after the Second World War. Their mail-order company (a nondigital precursor to Amazon) relied on credit, one-month grace periods, and installment payments. Though they initially sold plastic seat covers, their sales model opened them up to thousands of other products, as evidenced by the thick catalog that graced my great-grandmother's nightstand when I was a child. The company's national success made the Fingerhuts one of the wealthiest families in Minneapolis.[18]

Allan didn't show much interest in the family business. He was more interested in photography and fashion, which led him to the New York School of Design after graduating from high school. After a stint in the Army as a truck driver, Allan asked his father to help him open a nightclub. "My parents didn't care what I did as long as I was happy," said the young entrepreneur. "I wanted to [open a club] for a long time, and when I returned from the military, I pursued it."[19] The support of deep-pocketed parents led to the opening of the most essential music venue in Minneapolis's history.

As the Downtown Council ran ads in the *Tribune* to entice suburban shoppers to spend money downtown, Allan Fingerhut began looking for a venue to invest his parents' money. In 1970, he and his business partner Danny Stevens leased an abandoned Greyhound bus station and transformed it into the Depot, the city's first club dedicated to rock 'n' roll.

Shuttered for two years before Fingerhut and Stevens leased it, the bus station was in terrible shape, needing remodeling, plastering, and painting. The two young entrepreneurs worked tirelessly to get the place in shape for opening night as the Depot, with British rock singer Joe Cocker as the new venue's first act. The local press coverage of the Depot's opening was uniformly negative. "What started out as a good idea has definitely gone sour," said the *Minneapolis Star*. The paper observed that "the thought of having rock concerts at the old Greyhound bus depot was one that could have blossomed," but the lack of planning, unfinished remodeling, and short supply of alcohol on opening night sank all hopes.[20] Journalists lambasted the planning and execution of opening night and said it was a harbinger of things to come. They were right. The first year was rocky, and the club made no money. But the Depot was popular with young people hungry for rock and excited by the gritty atmosphere and being able to stand close to the stage as bands played. "There wasn't any other music venue like it in town," said one fan.[21]

Despite negative press coverage, the Depot survived for just over a year, mainly because of the acts it presented, among them Cocker, Rod Stewart and the Faces, Frank Zappa, shock rocker Alice Cooper, and punk rockers Iggy and the Stooges. The venue's acts weren't all white male rockers. Among the Black artists to appear were jazz pianist Ramsey Lewis, the soul band Rotary Connection (featuring a young singer, Minnie Riperton, whose breakthrough hit was "Loving You"), jazz and soul singer Al Jarreau, Ike and Tina Turner, and blues musicians John Lee Hooker and B. B. King.[22]

Local artists also played there, but the Depot maintained the apartheid system that went back decades. This system was a boon to them, as was the case for past white acts. Singer-songwriter Curtiss A, blues artist Willie Murphy, rock bands Rubberband and White Lightning, and many more local groups played the Depot. The club gave local artists a chance to perform, and some of the acts were recorded for a 1970 compilation album. The recording engineers came from Sound 80, where Prince recorded his demos for Warner Bros. *Gathering at the Depot* featured summer-of-love, hippie-inspired bands whose groovy, sunny sounds had titles like "It's for You / Wake Up Sunshine," "Sunshine Day," and "Take Me to the Sunrise."[23]

But despite finding an audience, presenting top acts, and supporting (white) local bands, Fingerhut found himself deep in debt, and he shuttered the Depot fifteen months after Joe Cocker inaugurated the bus station–turned–rock venue. (The site reemerged in 1972 as the discotheque Uncle Sam's, which for the next seven years projected itself as a safe place for suburban white people who wanted a disco party-fueled night in the city.) But the end of the Depot didn't mean the end of rock in downtown Minneapolis. Its demise was only a temporary pause in the downtown music scene.

Filling the Void

When the Depot closed, rock and punk musicians scattered around the suburban rim, searching for places to play. St. Louis Park, Bloomington, and other suburbs began to host them.[24] Though no longer a rock venue, Uncle Sam's continued offering some live music—the rock bands Cain and Cheap Trick appeared there in the early 1970s.[25] But these shows were rare, and with a few exceptions, disco DJs ruled during these years.

In the mid-1970s, a short-lived bar emerged to fill the void. Blitz Bar was the only downtown venue providing space for emerging rock bands—a dive bar in the basement of a strip club. Blitz offered sonic shelter to the musical vagabonds roaming the suburbs, especially punk rockers. The Suicide Commandos, the city's first real punk band, played there often. Their volatile, clashing sounds, influenced partly by the New York Dolls (who played at the Minnesota State Fair in 1974), revolutionized the city's rock scene and made them icons, the "Godfathers of Minneapolis Punk." A trio made up of guitarist Chris Osgood, bassist Steve Almaas, and drummer Dave Ahl, the Suicide Commandos were known for their outrageous, audacious shows.[26] In her oral history of the birth of the Minneapolis punk and rock scene during the mid-1970s to the mid-1980s, *Complicated Fun*, journalist Cyn Collins shares the stories of the people who watched the scene unfold. Speaking about the Suicide Commandos, one fan said they "were really the grandaddies of the whole Minneapolis music scene."[27]

Hailing from Lake Minnetonka, a wealthy, white suburb northeast of downtown, the trio started out playing in the suburbs, small towns, a club in downtown St. Paul called Kelly's Club, and Blitz in downtown Minneapolis. It was at Blitz that their popularity soared. The band's success signaled the beginning of a new era of Minneapolis indie rock and punk. Even though the scene was growing, it wouldn't be until 1977 that rock and punk found a foothold downtown. That year, a young, deep-pocketed entrepreneur named Jay Berine purchased a downtown bar and handed the stage to local indie rock and punk bands.[28]

Performances by the Suicide Commandos, Flamingos, Curtiss A, and Thumbs Up rapidly spread the word that Jay's Longhorn Bar was the new indie rock and punk epicenter.[29] Soon the venue was bursting at the seams with fans eager to sample the local musical fare. It wasn't long before national acts were playing there like Blondie, Iggy Pop, Gang of Four, Elvis Costello, Talking Heads, Mink DeVille, and the band from Queens, New York, that popularized punk, the Ramones.[30] Located on Fifth Street, Jay's Longhorn was the spot for new sounds. "People wanted to hear something new and different," Collins recalled. "Jay's was that place."[31] The former steak house and jazz club had a basement where bands performed (on the first floor, a DJ spun records). It created intimacy between the bands and the audience, often filling up quickly. But like the Depot, making money on music was difficult. The bar opened for lunch to keep the doors open, attracting the suburban business crowd who worked downtown.

While food kept the doors open, music made Jay's Longhorn the city's top venue for white rock acts between 1977 and the early 1980s. The Suicide Commandos were the house band, while newer ones, like the aptly named Suburbs, were coming up. Their fusion of indie rock, punk, soul, and jazz tapped into the sounds germinating in Black Minneapolis for years while intensifying the new musical energy gripping young people on the city's edge. Like the Suicide Commandos, who significantly influenced them, the Suburbs had an exciting stage presence. Their wild shows at Jay's Longhorn added to the venue's growing status and gave the band a reputation on par with their idols.

The Birth of First Avenue & 7th Street Entry

Jay's and Blitz filled the void created by the demise of the Depot, the one-time rock spot rebranded itself. The Depot became a discotheque called Uncle Sam's at the end of the 1970s, then gradually rebranded itself into a venue featuring indie rock, punk, and eventually funk. This change began on November 29, 1979, with the Ramones. Fans, including local bands like the newly formed Hüsker Dü, showed up to see the leather clad quartet, who put on a show legendary for its volume.[32] Though the band had performed in the city before, this show set off something transformative. The underground scene that grew out of the ashes of the Gateway, suburbanization, jazz, and 1960s rock and folk reached its creative apex the night the New York–based quartet took the stage at Uncle Sam's. The city's local scene was no longer waiting for the next big moment that might ignite a smoldering fire. The Ramones show lit the fire and pushed the venue to remake itself yet again.

After the Ramones' performance, Uncle Sam's manager, Stephen McClellan, told Allan Fingerhut he should wash his hands of the business because the corporation that backed the venue was pulling out. Fingerhut would have to sink more money into the club to keep it going. But McClellan understood the significance of the Ramones show and bet long in the hopes that he could convince Fingerhut to sell Uncle Sam's to him. To his surprise, Fingerhut did. McClellan and his accountant formed a company to run Uncle Sam's. They called it 2M, a play on 3M (originally Minnesota Mining and Manufacturing Company), the industrial conglomerate headquartered in the St. Paul suburb of Maplewood. The two men began making the club into an edgy indie rock venue.[33]

But every night, there was a battle over the venue's direction. Punk, new wave, indie rock, and a new sound from the Bronx, rap, competed with disco despite claims of its death on the multicolored, neon dance floor. Uncle Sam's DJ Kevin Cole said, "There was a period where I would play a half hour of disco, then get into the rock set and completely lose the dance floor."[34] Not even the groundbreaking show by the Ramones and changes to the DJ set were enough to transform the venue's musical culture.

The venue needed to demonstrate it was moving in a new direction, turning over a new leaf. McClellan thought the dank former coatroom space could be better utilized. With barely enough money to cover the construction, McClellan and his crew began building a smaller, intimate space perfect for accommodating local bands like the Suicide Commandos and up-and-comers Hüsker Dü and the Suburbs. The new area would add another stage to a growing list of downtown venues hosting local artists. And it would be different from the main stage. It would be edgy and experimental, presenting music that didn't draw as many patrons as the main stage. In 1980, the former "dark, ugly, filthy room" became 7th Street Entry (after its location at that street's side of the venue).[35] The space accommodated about 250 people, fostering intimacy between performers and audiences and reducing costs.

The new club was a massive success. Minneapolis indie rock and punk acts like Hüsker Dü, the Replacements, the Suburbs, and the Hypstrz played there. But opening 7th Street Entry also helped rebrand the entire Uncle Sam's venue into the edgy place McClellan imagined.

The first big move came in April 1980, when "Sam's & 7th Street Entry" first appeared in the press.[36] McClellan and Myers dropped "Uncle" from the moniker, and McClellan started booking Black artists that same year. This forever cracked the musical color line and opened the venue to music that sustains it to this day. Local R&B groups Flyte Tyme and the Family appeared at 7th Street Entry in 1980 and 1981, respectively. Prince's funk band side project, the Time, fronted by former Grand Central drummer Morris Day, played the Entry on October 7, 1981.[37] On March 9, 1981, Prince played his first show on the main stage. The change had less to do with antiracism politics than with innovative art. "Everybody was talking about" 7th Street Entry, recalled André Cymone. "It had a buzz. It was an edgy venue."[38] For Prince, Cymone, and other Black artists, Sam's & 7th Street Entry was a place where they could make experimental music that fused R&B with punk, indie rock, and new wave.

Figure 9.1. First Avenue & 7th Street Entry, looking south, ca. 1988. Photo courtesy of the Hennepin County Library, Minnesota.

When Prince first played Sam's main stage in 1981, he had three albums under his belt. He showed the primarily white crowd who hankered for indie rock and punk how local Black artists were mixing those styles with R&B and funk, creating an entirely new sound. Prince's performance was a revelation for the few who saw the show. The young star dazzled the audience with his stage presence, dancing, flawless falsetto, and instrumental skills. *Minneapolis Star* music critic Jon Bream said Prince "has been crowned as rock's latest contender for the throne."[39]

As the calendar turned to 1982, Sam's was renamed after the location of the former bus depot: First Avenue (see fig. 9.1). That year, the Minnesota Vikings played their inaugural game in the Hubert H. Humphrey Metrodome. Decades of advocacy by the Downtown Council and planners' efforts to make the city hospitable to business interests by razing the old Gateway neighborhood brought the National Football League downtown and pulled suburban capital back to the city's core. This convergence of capital and culture downtown set the stage for Prince's musical genius to take root and for the Minneapolis Sound to reach new heights.

Between 1981 and 1983, Prince held court on First Avenue's mainstage, gaining new fans with the funky music that had been brewing in school rooms, basements, and the Way community center on the Near North Side for decades. First Avenue & 7th Street Entry were the intersections where the city's diverse music scene and its sonic geographies of Black and white converged to produce a new sound.[40] This sound, born in the city's fraught terrain, defined Prince and Minneapolis.

PART 4

The Rise

1977–1987

★

Chapter 10

MAKING A DIFFERENT SOUND, PART I

I wanted to make a different sounding record.

—Prince

Dick Clark was dumbfounded. It's not hard to imagine the *American Bandstand* host standing in the studio audience with the dozens of teenage fans watching Prince and his band with his incredulous look that suggested he had no idea what they were playing. And from Minneapolis, of all places? But Clark's statement that Prince's music isn't the kind that comes from Minneapolis wasn't dismissive. No one outside of Minneapolis had heard anything like it before. It was a shock to the soundscape of popular music. And it inaugurated a transformation, a new sonic turn.

Clark had no idea about Minneapolis's rich music tradition dating back over a century. The city's music scene was largely unknown, except for Bob Dylan and the 1940s vocal group the Andrews Sisters. Clark and his viewers hadn't heard about the city's Black music scene and its innovations from 1950 to the 1970s, nor were they aware of the city's indie rock, punk, and new wave scenes. The *American Bandstand* host and his audience would never have guessed that a gifted young Black musician would come out of Minneapolis.

Prince and his contemporaries cultivated their talents in school music rooms, North Side basements, and the Way's backroom, then recorded in

South Side studios. When indie rock and punk found a home downtown, Prince broke the apartheid line and began to perform at 7th Street Entry and then the main stage at First Avenue. From the city's racial and musical geography, he created a distinctive sound in his first three groundbreaking albums: *For You*, his 1978 debut; *Prince* (1979); and his critically acclaimed *Dirty Mind* (1980).

"Produced, Arranged, Composed, and Performed, by Prince"

When Prince won over Warner Bros. executives by proving he could produce his music, he began a career-long process of controlling it. Throughout his career, Prince directed every inch of his musical life. He was an early adopter of digital distribution and fought Warner Bros. for nearly a decade to control his master recordings. His efforts changed how musicians engaged with record companies by helping them get more money and control over their master recordings. But his famous declaration printed on the back of all his albums, "Produced, Arranged, Composed, and Performed, by Prince," is partly legend. Although Prince did most of the work on *For You* and successive albums, other musicians who contributed to his sound—a guitar riff, a synth chord, or a lyric—weren't always acknowledged. But Prince focused on his role as the auteur. In one of his first interviews, Prince told staff writer Tim Carr of the *Minneapolis Star* that he composed, arranged, played twenty-seven instruments, sang all the vocal parts, and recorded the overdubs and multitrack parts.[1]

The talent and control of his art facilitated his sound creation. The combination of sounds and his use of the studio as an instrument gives *For You* the "illusion of a full orchestra," said Carr.[2] The multiple synthesizers, guitar riffs, bass lines, and the R&B, funk, and rock rhythms show that this youngster from Minneapolis was a different kind of cat. As someone who had an intimate relationship with the sounds of the city, it made sense that he would want to control the production of his world, too. So, even though he received help, he gave himself production, engineering, and cover design credits. Prince primarily wrote the songs on *For You*, but some were cowritten with Chris Moon. Singer and keyboardist Patrice Rushen and her boyfriend Charles Veal contributed to the song "Baby."[3] Warner Bros. executive Tommy Vicari helped to engineer the record, but Prince reportedly erased his name and replaced it with his own. When Prince asked Vicari if he would get credit for it, the executive said, "Look, why don't you press the record and take the pictures, too?"[4]

Prince doing everything on his albums was one of many myths he used to separate himself from other artists and show how rare the "Minneapolis genius" was, a savant who lived his music rather than performed it. Although the album was recorded at the Record Plant in Sausalito, California, that "dirty Minneapolis funk" filled the nine-song LP. "Soft and Wet," the album's first single, was pure Minneapolis: The funk was lean and mean, the synthesizers added intensity, while the bass drove the sound with an unrelenting heavy groove.[5] Chris Moon and Prince wrote the music, and Prince wrote the lyrics.[6]

The first track, "For You," is one minute of Prince harmonizing with himself, his voice multitracked. The a cappella performance introduces him to the world, carving a new sonic lane for a unique artist.[7] Prince's vocal arrangements also dabble in jazz and gospel, and he shows off a falsetto that linked him to great R&B singers like Marvin Gaye and Smokey Robinson.

After its first track, the album moves from synth-driven pop funk ("In Love") to bossa nova ("Soft and Wet") to Minneapolis funk ("Just as Long as We're Together") to straightforward rhythm and blues ("Baby" and "My Love Is Forever") that contain the sonic elements that Prince would perfect over time: his falsetto vocals, understated bass lines, percussive synthesizer parts touched with piano chords, electric and acoustic guitar riffs filling the spaces between the instruments. The synthesizers, played by an uncredited Patrice Rushen, are essential to the song; they stand in for a string section and give the track an orchestral feeling.[8] "My Love Is Forever" uses the same formula as "Baby," with synthesizers replacing the horns Prince originally planned to use on the track. He remarked, "It's really hard to sound different if you use the same instruments." So, instead, he "created a different kind of horn section by multitracking a synthesizer and some guitar lines."[9] With falsetto vocals, this up-tempo disco-dipped song, cowritten by Chris Moon, outlines the path down which Prince would take his Minneapolis Sound.

"So Blue" signals the influence of his favorite artist, Joni Mitchell, and her iconic 1971 album, *Blue*. Using simple chord progressions, subtle bass lines, brushed drums, and falsetto vocals, this song demonstrates the artist's range and the Minneapolis Sound's ability to bend into different sonic shapes and colors. "I'm Yours" displays Prince's formidable rock guitar skills and the influence of another of his music heroes, Carlos Santana.

But despite its artful and original mix of different styles and sounds, *For You* struggled to navigate the apartheid system that had controlled the music industry, radio, and racially coded sales charts since the early twentieth century.[10] White acts dominated the Billboard Hot 100 and 200 charts; Black music was largely segregated on the R&B chart. *For You* barely entered the Billboard 200 charts, peaking at 163. "Soft and Wet" made it to 92 on the Hot 100. But on the R&B chart, the single hit number 12. The album sold well in the Black South, too.[11] And when he visited Black communities to sign autographs, he was mobbed. White record buyers, for the most part, didn't gravitate to the album. This racial disparity motivated Prince to defy music categories even more.

Prince's music, like his idols, like Minneapolis's music scene, was diverse. Although the city's music scene was organized by its racial geography, Minneapolis never had one sound that ruled. Black kids like Prince were exposed to all kinds of music. *For You* was his attempt to create a different sound that reflected his musical roots and the city's musical geography. It leaned heavily on Black music but incorporated classic rock. But it didn't find the kind of audience he had wanted. The segregation of the recording industry in racially inflected genres clashed with his blended sound. His next album would sell more copies. But first, the one-person band needed a group to take his music on the road.

Making a Revolution

Even though Prince could play all the instruments, he needed a backing band to perform. Just before the release of *For You*, Prince's manager, Owen Husney, began organizing rehearsals for potential band members at Del's Tire Mart in the old Scandinavian neighborhood, the Seven Corners.[12] Prince wanted good players who were funky, creative, and musically "unobtrusive," as well as a rainbow coalition to visually reflect the diverse range of his sound.[13]

The band that would eventually become the Revolution had five members. The first to join was childhood friend Andre Anderson (now Cymone) on bass, followed by St. Paul–born Dez Dickerson, a guitarist who played on *For You*.[14] When Prince began assembling the rhythm section, his ideas on crossing over and representation shaped his decisions. Prince was influenced by Sly and the Family Stone's mixed race and gender lineup and felt that would help him reach beyond the boundaries that the record industry, including Warner Bros., had set for him. Instead of hiring Morris Day, his longtime friend and drummer for his high school band, Prince chose Bobby Rivkin, who went by the stage name Bobby Z. As Pepé Willie remarked, "Prince wanted a white drummer" for his rainbow coalition.[15]

The Revolution wasn't only about visual representation. Prince also wanted a diverse group of musicians who could realize the new sounds he wanted. This line of thinking also played a role in his selection of keyboardists. When Prince's cousin Chazz brought in St. Louis Park–born and raised Gayle Chapman, Prince was amazed by her subtle style and ability to create rhythms in the spaces between notes.[16] She was immediately added to the fold. Even though she'd been practicing for months, she was surprised when she got the job. When she asked Prince why he hired her, he said,

"You're white, you're blond, you have blue eyes, and you can play funky keyboards."[17] With the hiring of another St. Louis Park musician, Matt Fink, whose jazz fusion keyboard playing worked well with the guitarists' soloing, the Revolution was born.[18]

Twelve-hour rehearsals four to five days a week expedited the sonic melding among the band members.[19] The extended hours also enabled something he'd rarely allowed himself: collaboration. Though Prince was a fiercely independent artist, the band significantly influenced Prince's sound. The band's original members helped expose him to new music, including the sounds of the growing downtown musicscape. Dez, who was close to Prince at the time, was a big fan of punk, which was surging downtown. He also loved rock acts like Fleetwood Mac, the Beatles, the Who, the Rolling Stones, and Led Zeppelin, whose music he shared with Prince.[20] Then-newer bands like the Cars and Van Halen, heavy metal and new wave, and Matt Fink's jazz fusion filled Prince's ears and fed his creativity.[21]

Prince wasn't a hit at home despite being released by a major label. By 1978, Hüsker Dü and the Replacements were better known in Minneapolis.[22] Prince and his manager, Owen Husney, were at odds over *For You*'s low sales and muted chart impact. Prince believed Husney wasn't doing enough to promote the album, and tensions grew between them. Prince ended their relationship. His cousin, Pepé Willie, took over management for a while.[23] The band used Willie's basement for rehearsals, harkening back to their high school days in such spaces. After many long hours rehearsing in Willie's basement, Prince approached his new manager and said, "Pepé, we're ready. I want to do a show."[24]

Willie booked a two-night showcase at the Capri Theater on the Near North Side during the bone-chilling month of January 1979. The first night was a dress rehearsal; the second show was for fans and Warner Bros. executives. The Friday dress rehearsal went well, but the Saturday show was plagued with problems from the start. The night of the performance, the weather had dipped to 20 degrees below zero by the show's beginning, and the half-century-old building didn't hold heat very well. Dez's wireless amp malfunctioned, there were sound issues, and the band was out of sync. Ultimately, Warner Bros. told Prince to work more on his stagecraft; perhaps the band could tour to promote the next album. Prince was devastated. However, the experience also motivated him never to have a show like that again.[25]

Getting Out of the Hole

Lackluster sales from his first album motivated the young recording artist to make hits, which ultimately meant crossing over to the white market.

However, he didn't want to achieve crossover success by watering down his music; it had to come from the uniqueness of his sound. Also, the lengthy recording time of *For You* pushed him to streamline the process and record his second album in a fraction of the time and with less money.[26]

Prince began working on his eponymous second album, *Prince*, in April 1979.[27] It was completed in just twelve weeks. Like his first album, he recorded it in California at the little-known Alpha Studio in Burbank.[28] The studio was in the home of engineer Gary Brandt, a friend of Warner Bros. executive Bob Cavallo, who managed Prince from 1979 to 1989.[29] Bobby Z and André joined Prince in the studio and offered vocals and advice, but Prince largely controlled the process. By this time, Warner Bros. had faith that the young artist could produce himself, if only because Prince was impervious to all suggestions from the company.[30] Feeling that *For You* was overproduced, *Prince* was recorded on a sixteen-track board rather than the twenty-four-track one used on his first album. This production change limited his ability to add more textures, resulting in a sleeker and crisper sound.[31]

Prince's first single, "I Wanna Be Your Lover," hit the airwaves in August 1979, just weeks after Michael Jackson released "Don't Stop 'til You Get Enough," the first single from his debut solo album, *Off the Wall*. Jackson, the lead singer of the original boyband, teamed up with longtime producer and composer Quincy Jones to create a disco/funk mashup with supple grooves that were perfect for Jackson's fantastic dancing. The album was hot, and the reviews said as much. The *Los Angeles Times* called *Off the Wall* the "best R&B album of the year."[32]

Prince was a fan of the Jackson 5. But he wanted to be just as good, if not better. It might be here where the lifelong rivalry of the two wunderkinds began. Whenever it started, album reviews most certainly fueled it. Prince's album didn't get the same accolades as Jackson's. That said, *Prince* was well-received. The *Los Angeles Times* called Prince's music a "regal mixture of pop" that was beyond category.[33] The *Amsterdam News* raved about it, citing the young Minneapolitan's hybrid sound and his ability to play without reading music as evidence of his "genius."[34]

This tension between Jackson's ability to make some of the best R&B of the time and Prince's expansive compositions marks the difference in their music. On Prince's first album, the young composer could stretch musically, playing twenty-seven instruments and composing much of it independently. But the lack of record sales had, as he told a *Los Angeles Times* reporter, "put himself in a hole," and he needed hits on the follow-up.[35]

Prince was his attempt at making hits, and it was also the album where he began to cultivate the sounds that defined his career sonically. Its nine tracks, more than *For You*, display the range of his talent and unique sonic mix. The album's bright, unencumbered sound set the stage for Prince's future projects.

The first single, "I Wanna Be Your Lover," was Prince's first big hit, reaching number twenty-two on the pop charts and five on the R&B chart. What made the song such a hit was its marriage of funk, disco, and pop. Guitar, synthesizer, and percussive piano drive the track and maintain tension. The precise drum pattern came from a drum machine he began using on the album and would maintain throughout his career. The bass is interesting; it's noticeable and funky but doesn't anchor the song like traditional funk (think anything by James Brown or Sly Stone). The understated bass makes the song more like a Beatles tune or white pop music, where the bass hangs out, and the guitar plays the lead role.[36]

"Why You Wanna Treat Me So Bad?" is a rock tune that evokes Fleetwood Mac. It has both major and minor chords, up-tempo drumming, bass, and falsetto vocal parts. The final rafter-reaching guitar solo echoes the rock gods of the early 1970s. On "Sexy Dancer," you can hear the North and South Side funk and R&B that Prince grew up on. Over a bass line that would make Funkadelic leader George Clinton proud, the song is an ode to the city that raised him. "When We're Dancing Close and Slow" demonstrates his R&B chops. Subtle C-sharp, B, and D chords played on the piano, paced by the drum machine, give the song an airy quality. He continues this feeling on "With You," with its country-inspired guitar riffs reminiscent of his favorite artist, Joni Mitchell.

"Bambi" is the "Let-me-show-you-what-I-can-do" song, a "rock guitar statement" that would make Carlos Santana proud (or look over his shoulder).[37] The album's last three tracks, "Still Waiting," "I Feel for You," and "It's Gonna Be Lonely," are steeped in R&B with sonic traces of Joni Mitchell, Chaka Khan, and Fleetwood Mac.

Prince tunes our ears to the Near North Side and the quixotic mixtures of funk and R&B that he experimented with at school, in basements, and in the back room of the Way community center. *Prince* is a statement about his hometown's musical landscape as much as an album focused on commercial success. It's a music map of sonic pleasure.

Prince earned him Billboard status, respect as a songwriter, and radio play. It brought him the fans who, as he put it, "check you out when you have another hit."[38] Warner Bros. gave him the green light to tour in support of the album, and he and the band hit the road, playing gigs up and down the East Coast and the Southeast. These shows leaned into rock and new wave and began to garner him an audience, including Black fans. His appearances on *American Bandstand* and another national network program, *Midnight Special*, exposed him to the white rock fans he wanted to cultivate.

Prince was digging the artist out of the hole. However, the young rock star wanted more than that; he craved an audience that was flexible and amenable to the changing musical reality of his life, which mirrored Minneapolis's musical geography. He achieved this on his next project and, in the process, gave his best expression to date of the dialectic of sound germinating in his hometown.

"Somewhere in Uptown"

Prince recorded his first two albums in California studios. His third album, *Dirty Mind*, was recorded in Minnesota, in his home studio eighteen miles west of Minneapolis in Wayzata, a small city on idyllic Lake Minnetonka. Prince converted the house's bedrooms and kitchen into a home studio, recording much of *Dirty Mind* there and overdubs at Hollywood Sound in Los Angeles.[39]

Many fans, critics, and scholars consider *Dirty Mind* the first of his great albums. That it was recorded at his home studio is not a coincidence; *Dirty Mind* is grounded in the sounds of Minneapolis. It's the album where he achieves the sonic braiding of different musical genres he'd heard most of his life and worked on in *For You* and *Prince*. Laura Fissinger of the *Twin Cities Reader* recognized how important Minneapolis is to the album's sound. "Prince's music is a hodgepodge," she wrote. However, this mixture happened not because of "extensive touring and exposure to new places, but from being allowed by the record company to simply hibernate in his Minneapolis studio."[40] Indeed, Prince didn't need to find musical inspiration in California or New York. He developed his unique sound not by leaving home but by staying there. A few years after wanting to leave Minneapolis because he thought it would be too hard to make it there in the record industry, Prince realized that Minneapolis had musical virtues worth sticking around for. "When I think about it," he told *Rolling Stone* journalist Bill Adler, "I'm here for a purpose."[41]

Dirty Mind's title track grew from jam sessions with his new band in late 1979. Prince noted some chords Matt Fink was playing and asked him to remember them. They rehearsed the song, and after Fink went home, Prince worked and returned the next day with the song mostly completed.[42] "Dirty Mind" opens with four measures of quarter-note drum machine beats; then come the percussive R&B rhythms from the synthesizers. The sound of "Dirty Mind" set the tone for the rest of the album. It also lays the foundation for the sound Prince would bring to its peak with *Sign o' the Times* in 1987.

Prince's first two albums had experimented with combining funk, R&B, and rock. But *Dirty Mind* was a giant leap forward; it mixed these styles to create something entirely new. Prince began recording *Dirty Mind* after coming off the road as the opening act for Rick James, the artist who first linked funk and R&B. Opening for James was a big step up for Prince. The two artists, who prided themselves on their arrogance and competitive nature, got under each other's skin. Prince used the tension to fuel his songs, many of which found their way onto *Dirty Mind*.[43]

He recorded *Dirty Mind* in the spring of 1980 at breakneck speed compared to *For You*.[44] But if the tension between him and Rick James fueled his songwriting, the tour also created tensions between Prince and keyboardist Gayle Chapman. She left the band in May over the increasingly sexual onstage performances and risqué outfits Prince demanded she wear.[45] Chapman was replaced by Lisa Coleman, the daughter of Gary Coleman, a member of the renowned Wrecking Crew of Los Angeles session musicians, who had worked with legendary artists like Marvin Gaye.[46] Coleman grew up in Los Angeles and had close connections to the music industry because of her father. Coleman made a demo tape that Prince loved. He met her at the airport when she arrived in Minneapolis days after listening to it. Lisa had more influence on Prince's sound during his "golden age" than any other band member. During the making of *Dirty Mind*, Lisa lived in his house in Wayzata. The two developed a deep and intimate musical relationship that lasted until the end of the Revolution in 1986.[47]

Dirty Mind is Prince's "alchemistical blend" of funk, rock, and R&B, which critics termed the "Minneapolis Sound."[48] For some, that was just a catchphrase; for others, it was a way to talk about Prince and the multiple streams of music he created during the 1980s.[49] Some critics said it was just a marketing label for the Black and white music coming out of Minneapolis, while others said it didn't exist. Regardless, a distinct Minneapolis Sound can be identified: electronic dance music with new wave influences blended with funk, punk, and R&B. It has its characteristic sounds—crisp rhythm guitar parts that give way to hard rock solos, synthesizers instead of horns, drum machines, falsetto vocals, and understated funk bass lines.[50] Many of these elements can be heard on Prince's previous albums. Each album brought him closer to the mix of sounds he was trying to create, but they were inconsistent and lacked cohesion. *Dirty Mind* is where it all came together.

Music critic Randy Anderson of Minneapolis's *City Pages* called the album "punk funk."[51] Prince listened to local musicians, and it stands to reason that he was paying attention to punk's emergence. He knew about Hüsker Dü, the Replacements, and the Suburbs, who performed at Jay's Longhorn, Sam's, the Blitz, and 7th Street Entry. He saw punk's popularity, felt its energy, and respected its sound. Prince also listened to Warner Bros. albums the company sent him and absorbed the influences of his rainbow coalition bandmates and friends.[52] But Minneapolis provided him with a primer on how to blend all the sounds that caught his ear.

"Minneapolis," said Terry Lewis, "is totally out of touch with the rest of the country." He observed that "the lack of Black radio has been a help in some ways in shaping our sound or the Minneapolis Sound."[53] Indeed, being geographically and sonically outside the main currents of Black music allowed Black musicians to draw on their resources to innovate. Jon Kirby, a member of Nero, a band headed by André Cymone, put it this way: "Rather than regurgitating the music being played on the radio, [Black bands] were recycling the ideas of their peers and other players, so you get a feedback loop where everybody's feeding off each other."[54]

Because Prince's music grew from Minneapolis's soundscape, it was flexible, malleable, and wide ranging. *For You* trafficked in R&B and funk but was influenced by classic rock of the early 1970s. Prince dove more into rock while making inroads into new wave as it found residence downtown. As a Minneapolis musician, the DNA of musical mixing was part of his sound from the beginning; evolution and musical growth were always there. *Dirty Mind* represents the first significant leap in his music-making.

The title track is only one of an album's ingenious stylistic fusions. "When You Were Mine" evokes 1960s bubblegum pop with brightly played E, B, and A electric guitar chords, while the bass line dabbles in James Brown funk. The track is built on a riff created on the Oberheim Ob-SX synthesizer, an instrument that would become a mainstay of his musical arsenal, appearing on hits like "Little Red Corvette."[55] Falsetto vocals give the song an R&B edge, mediated by the poppy guitar riffs. The funk-R&B hybrid "Do It All Night" features funky keyboards over F-sharp, A-sharp, C-sharp, E, and D-sharp chords in minor and major, climaxing with a screaming synthesizer solo.

"Uptown" combines disco, funk, and punk with bass guitar played in the slap style of Prince's favorite bassist, Larry Graham from Sly and the Family Stone. "Head" is just funky as hell. Percussive synthesizer parts over slap bass, programmed drums, lusty falsetto vocals, and otherworldly synth solos make this four-minute-and-forty-second track irresistibly sexy. The album's penultimate track, "Sister," is the most punk. The mix of sung and shouted vocals reflects the style's considerable influence, as does the frantic tempo, paced by the programmed drums and guitar riffs. The album ends with "Partyup," a funk number driven by simple bass lines, electric guitar riffs, and emphatic A, C, and D keyboard chords.

Dirty Mind didn't sell well, moving just over 400,000 copies. Radio wouldn't play it because of racy lyrics about oral sex (from a woman on her way to the altar who ends up with semen on her wedding gown), sex education of a young man by an older sister, and a two-timing girlfriend who left stained sheets as evidence of her betrayal. Prince let his dirty mind run free on an album that one critic called a manifesto for a "pervert's crusade."[56] *Rolling Stone* and the *New York Times* praised *Dirty Mind*'s innovative sound and lusty lyrical content. By the time Prince and his band began their tour in December 1980, he was the artist to watch, and the crowds of young Black fans who packed his shows proved as much.[57]

The long hours of woodshedding in preparation for the tour paid off, as evidenced by the reviews. Gene Gillis of the *Amsterdam News* called the January 1981 show at the Ritz "epic."[58] Cultural luminaires such as Nile Rodgers, the rock band Kiss, Andy Warhol, and Mick Jagger were in attendance, as were young Black fans who screamed when Prince soloed on guitar.[59] Reviewing another show at Manhattan's Palladium, Gillis evoked one of Prince's heroes: "He's the biggest and best thing to happen to music since Jimi Hendrix."[60]

The band had grown in sonic cohesion and stage presence. Prince's demanding rehearsals, which could last twelve hours or more, paid off. By the time *Dirty Mind* hit stores, the band was tight, and their stagecraft was exceptional. This helped spread the word about the album despite its stalling at forty-six on the pop charts.

Myths to Match the Music

In addition to bringing the Minneapolis Sound to the fore, *Dirty Mind* is also the album on which Prince begins to craft his mythology, that confusing mix of stories, beguiling half-truths, and flat-out falsehoods that followed him throughout his career. The self-mythologizing made him pop music's greatest enigma and created a cottage industry of writers, critics, and researchers hell-bent on finding the "real Prince." Prince told so many stories about who he was that they all, at some point, contradicted each other. Frustrating as this was, the wunderkind from Minneapolis was fully aware of what he was doing, or at least he said he was. But when it came to Prince, truth and fiction were intertwined, and trying to separate them was and remains impossible.[61]

Many Prince scholars have spent entire books trying to understand the truth behind the myths. I applaud their work. But there's another way to see Prince's tales: Rather than just misinformation, his myths primarily related to his music. Prince said that one of the reasons he told these outlandish and confusing stories was to make people pay more attention to his music than his life.

A *New York Times* article by music critic Robert Palmer described Prince as a "mixed black-Italian" from a "racially integrated neighborhood in

Minneapolis." Palmer said this racial mixing made his music a "biracial" sound. In February 1981, Prince told *Rolling Stone* reporter Bill Adler that he "grew up on the borderline" between Black and white Minneapolis. According to Prince, "I had a bunch of black friends, and I had a bunch of white friends. I never grew up in any particular culture."[62] Prince wasn't mixed-race. His mother wasn't Italian (he reproduced this myth in the semiautobiographical film *Purple Rain*). Nor did he live in a mixed neighborhood, except for the white family that lived next to him when he was little. Prince was born and raised in Black Minneapolis.

Prince's mythmaking was part of a geographic narrative about his sound's ethos. Echoing Terry Lewis's point, the "normalcy and remoteness of Minneapolis," which removed him from centers of popular culture, especially Black popular culture, fed his artistic expression and fueled his desire to create a different kind of sound. *Dirty Mind* is the sonic culmination of that effort. Integration for Prince has nothing to do with racially mixed parentage or neighborhoods. There was never any living on the "borderline" for him. But integration is fundamental to *Dirty Mind*. Prince integrated Minneapolis's turn toward punk into the album, creating a "black-white synthesis" of sound, making it the album's sonic cornerstone.[63] "That's what 'Uptown' is all about," Prince told music journalist Bill Adler. In that place—real or fictional, physical or sonic—"residents" could "do whatever we want."[64] "Uptown" was where "white, Black, Puerto Rican / everybody just a-freakin." But more important than the lyrics, the story of "Uptown" is heard in the musical arrangement of punk, funk, and disco wrapped in the Minneapolis Sound's substitution of synthesizers for horns, the understated bass lines, crispy guitars, electronic drums, and falsetto vocal arraignments. Recorded in isolation "somewhere in Uptown," *Dirty Mind* is as much a musical map of Minneapolis in the late 1970s and early 1980s—fusing the geographies of downtown, South Minneapolis, and the Near North Side—as it is a hedonist manifesto.

Lyrically, sex is the album's core. The young musician created a mythology for this, too. He claimed he would sneak into his mother's bedroom and read the "spicy novels" she hid under *Better Homes and Gardens*. He said these novels inspired him to "write his own."[65] Lust runs through *Dirty Mind*, but as *Rolling Stone* critic Ken Tucker in his glowing review argued, it "may be dirty . . . it certainly isn't pornographic."[66] More than the sex, the album's biracial sounds are its most striking and significant element. These myths Prince promoted about himself and his background were a way to contextualize his sound and sexual lyrics. Of course, a mixed-race kid living in a mixed-race neighborhood on the margins of Black life who read his mother's sexy novels would make an album like *Dirty Mind*. The stories were made to fit the sound.

When Prince began working on his fourth album in the spring of 1982, he was clear about his new sound. Over the next two years, it would continue to evolve. Two more albums, two acts he created to perform his music, and the production work of childhood friends Jimmy "Jam" Harris and Terry Lewis would change the direction of popular music in the 1980s.

Chapter 11

MAKING A DIFFERENT SOUND, PART II

With no high voicing used and an atypically restrained beat propelling the surprisingly sparse arrangement, on first listen, "Annie Christian" sounds more like it could be something from the Suburbs excellent *Credit in Heaven* double LP than a Prince cut.

—Chuck Helm

Music critic Chuck Helm was right: "Annie Christian," on Prince's 1981 album, *Controversy*, sounds more like something by new wave punk disciples the Suburbs rather than Prince. But in recognizing the similarities between the artists, Helm was illustrating something important about Prince's sound: Even in the face of the geographic and musical apartheid that shaped the city for decades, he found ways to bring the sounds of the city together to create new music. *Controversy*, *1999*, and music from his side projects, the Time and Vanity 6, are testaments to the new sound Prince created in the early 1980s. More than individual genius, Prince's Minneapolis perch—that out-of-touch-with-the-rest-of-the-country place that lacked the kind of Black radio other epicenters had—afforded him the space to merge genres in ways others hadn't. Minneapolis liberated him from the hegemony of sounds coming from Motown, Stax, and rap. His rock-oriented, punk-influenced, new wave–inflected sound married the funk and R&B created by Minneapolis's small Black community. Black music in Minneapolis in the late 1970s and throughout the 1980s experienced hybridization—a merging of different genres separated by race and place. Between 1981 and 1983, Prince composed multiple albums that embraced this hybridization. The success of that sound shifted the pop music landscape and made the city a hotspot for musical creativity.

Pioneer

If *Dirty Mind* introduced the world to the Minneapolis Sound, Prince's first show at Sam's introduced his version of it to Minneapolis. Though the album received critical support nationally, it was not hot at home. Maybe the popularity of groups like Hüsker Dü, the Replacements, and the Suburbs lessened its impact. But all that changed on March 9, 1981, when Prince and his new band held their first show on the main floor at Sam's.[1]

The show happened just weeks after they tore up the stage on *Saturday Night Live* with "Partyup." The city was eager for their return home, too. "Something about Minneapolis," said drummer Bobby Z, "if you go away and come back, you're appreciated more." People in Minneapolis are "impressed if you make it and come back."[2] That's exactly what Prince did. And even though Prince had been performing on the Black side of the city's color line since the early 1970s and had given several performances since signing with Warner Bros., his 1980 show at the Orpheum Theatre, which was just a few blocks away from Sam's, started the buzz with local music scribes. Despite not selling out the venue and seats that prohibited dancing, Minneapolis music critic Martin Keller said Prince was a "phenom in the making. A hometown kid brewing a delicious batch of rock and soul music." Sam's DJ, Kevin Cole, got wind of the Orpheum show from his boss at the Hot Licks record store on Hennepin, who described Prince as a mix of "Marc Bolan meets Bowie meets Sly Stone meets Hendrix." On the heels of this praise, Cole began spinning Prince records at Sam's and approached the venue's co-owner, Steve McClellan, about booking him.[3]

A Prince show at the city's best-known venue was considered risky in 1981 because no local Black acts had graced the checkered floor of the main room, a holdover from the decades of musical apartheid that hadn't abated. Dress codes, bookings, and playlists kept local Black acts off the big stage and many Black people away from the venue.[4] Even though Black acts had more opportunity at 7th Street Entry, where Flyte Time and Prince had performed, the main stage was another story. Despite the venue's history, Black artists wanted to perform there. Of the venue, André Cymone said,

"Everybody was talking about it . . . it had a buzz. It was an edgy venue. We wanted to be edgy and considered ourselves at the time to be getting edgier and pushing the envelope a little bit."[5]

Tickets sold out quickly. Curtiss A opened for the band. Before tearing the roof off the club, Prince walked out onto the stage in his trench coat and stockings and quoted fellow Minnesotan Judy Garland: "There's no place like home." "Do It All Night" kicked in, and Prince and the band commenced to give what some say was his best performance at the venue.[6] Part homecoming, part coming-out party, the March 1981 show was the beginning of Prince's reign over the venue, and just as Michael Jackson did for MTV, it forever broke the apartheid system that kept Blacks off the main floor.

The Time

Dirty Mind was the best example of the Minneapolis Sound in 1981. But the lack of radio play and the lackluster sales, despite the glowing reviews by critics and sold-out shows, stalled its popularity. Prince responded by writing songs for a new band he called the Time. The band became the pipeline for the dirty Minneapolis funk that was part of Prince's sound. They opened for him at his second show at Sam's in October 1981.[7]

The Time grew out of a promise made to the former drummer for Grand Central and childhood friend Morris Day, who had written "Partyup" on *Dirty Mind*. When he played the song for Prince, the artist offered him money or a record deal. Day took the deal. At the time, Day served as Prince's videographer and played in local bands for thirty-five dollars a night.[8] After the *Dirty Mind* tour ended, Prince began working on his follow-up, fulfilling his promise to Day and getting him a deal. "It all happened in a flash," said Day.[9] However, Prince's vision was not for Day to be a solo artist but part of a band.[10]

Prince tapped his former musical rivals and friends from Flyte Tyme as the band to back Morris. It consisted of Jimmy "Jam" Harris on keys; Terry Lewis on bass; Jellybean Johnson, a funk drummer in the James Brown tradition; white soul singer and synth player Monte Moir; and Illinois import Jessie Johnson on guitar. The Mississippi-born soul singer Alexander O'Neal was considered to front the outfit, but ultimately, Prince chose Morris Day. Morris was reluctant. He didn't see himself as a lead singer, especially not on par with O'Neal, but Prince encouraged him to front the new band, and the drummer obliged.[11]

Within days of inking the deal with Warner Bros., Morris and Prince locked themselves in Prince's new Kiowa Trail home studio in Chanhassen, about twenty-one miles southwest of Minneapolis, and recorded the Time's first album.[12] The members of the band never played on it. Prince composed most of the songs and played guitar and bass. Morris played the drums. Matt Fink added synths. And a young woman who'd begun hanging around the band, Wendy Melvoin, did some vocals and a little writing.[13]

The Time's sound was Minneapolis funk. The "less is more," "high and tight" funk rhythms and grooves were born of sizzling synthesizers, undistorted drums, clean guitars, and funky but understated bass. Their hit, "Get It Up," trafficked in the Minneapolis Sound Prince was creating. It had extended synthesizer parts that exceeded anything Prince did on his albums. Morris's alto voice (with Prince on backing vocals) and funk grooves over punk and rock rhythms separate the album from other Prince projects. It's only on "After Hi School," which sounds like an attempt to recapture the magic of Prince's "When You Were Mine," with its heavy reliance on Beatles-era rock, that Prince's rock fusion becomes audible. "Oh, Baby," where Prince's backing vocals and vocal influence are most pronounced, and "The Stick," with a Prince rock guitar solo, are some of the heaviest R&B and funk tracks on the seven-song album. And Like Prince's previous albums, the chords are simple. The album proved what Prince and others had known for years: that R&B, funk, and soul could be done in a way that leaned into the unique left-field music coming out of the Land of 10,000 Lakes. Radio play, album sales, and packed performances proved as much. Released in July 1981, *The Time* did well on the R&B charts. The album went gold and yielded three hit singles. The band was so tight, and the music was so well received that the Time opened for Prince on his *Controversy* tour.[14]

Renegade

On the heels of the Time's success, Prince returned to the studio to record his fourth album. And like number three, he recorded it at his home studio (with overdubbing at Sunset Sound in Hollywood). It was in his new place on Kiowa Trail in Chanhassen this time. Prince began to enjoy the anonymity of the suburbs and the city's proximity, and he would continue this way of living and recording until he died in 2016.[15]

Controversy built on the sound Prince developed on *Dirty Mind* and *The Time*. The album dips its toe into the electronic sounds of bands like the Düsseldorf pioneers Kraftwerk and the Akron-based electro-punk band Devo. Prince also roamed Minneapolis clubs and listened to local bands.[16]

These influences can be heard on *Controversy*. The album was built around four sonic pillars: punk, new wave, funk, and R&B. *Controversy* was polished. Although it was not the critical success of *Dirty Mind*, the album's first single, "Controversy," did give him his highest-charting single—twenty-one—on the pop charts.[17] And hometown music critics who fell asleep during *Dirty Mind* gave full-throated support to the fourth album. Randy Anderson of the *City Pages* said it demonstrated that "1981 was the year of Prince."[18] Michael Anthony, music critic for the *Minneapolis Tribune*, called it "one of the most interesting albums of the year."[19]

National music critics gave *Controversy* positive marks, too. Stephen Holden of *Rolling Stone* gave it four stars and compared Prince to Sly Stone, Rick James, and George Clinton.[20] Much talk about *Controversy* swirled around the more politicized lyrics attacking racism, Ronald Reagan's "Morning in America," nuclear proliferation, and the Cold War. Evocative lyrics, which shout,

> I just can't believe all the things people say
> Controversy
> Am I black or white? Am I straight or gay?
> Controversy
> Do I believe in God? Do I believe in me?

However, this is not what makes this song unique. *Controversy* is a sonically complex album that combines the sounds of Minneapolis in the early 1980s with the electronic music coming out of Germany and Akron. Indeed, the Minneapolis Sound proved to be a flexible and dynamic musical form.

The album's title track begins with four-beat electronic drum machine pulses over synthesizer riffs that replace horns in traditional funk. Prince's use of the drums to drive the track makes the synthesizer "slave" to the rhythm, generating irresistible tension and creating harmony.[21] The rhythmic elements leave space for vocals that move between singing and speech. The subtle guitar riffs that lay on top of the drums and between synth chords sound like an eight-year-old randomly fiddling the ninth and tenth frets on the G, B, and E strings. But this smooths the tension in the song's harmony. The bass line is steady but light under the weight of the drum machine. These aural contradictions make "Controversy" a sonically sophisticated, funky track and the best song on the album.[22]

"Sexuality" clarifies that Prince is leaning hard into his newfound sound and making small changes in each track to give them their personality. Driven by a drum machine with beats that sound like fists hitting the hood of a car, this up-tempo track, unlike "Controversy," merges the keyboards and the percussion. The muted bass line and short-winded guitar riffs hover in the background and only emerge when the rhythm section drops out toward the song's conclusion. "Sexuality" also employs vocals that shift between falsetto singing and talking. They are purposely choppy to create a staccato effect and mirror the rhythm section.

The Minneapolis Sound's harmonics also find their way into the album's best ballad, "Do Me, Baby," which, according to many, was written by André Cymone.[23] The song has computerized drums and understated bass lines. But rather than being synthesizer-heavy, the arrangement introduces a sultry piano part into the sparse rhythm section that mimics Prince having sex. The song also has a vocal rendition of the act, which gives it a visual quality. But even with all this, "Do Me Baby" is a 1970s soul ballad. Prince's crooning falsetto, full of shouts and orgasmic screams that fall in line with the rhythm section, puts his voice at the forefront of the track and makes him sound like an instrument in the song's sexual orchestra.

None of the instruments Prince uses on this album have the impact of the Linn LM-1 drum machine. Created by California-based engineer Roger Linn and released in 1980, the drum machine revolutionized music. It appears on numerous pop hits, like "Beat It" by Michael Jackson, "Take on Me" by A-ha, and "Don't You Want Me" by the Human League. But Prince made the most inventive use of the instrument and showed it on *Controversy*. The Linn LM-1 first appears on the album's fourth track, "Private Joy."[24] The intricate percussion of the Linn makes the synthesizers sound even more electronic. Still, the more pronounced bass line, mixed with the falsetto and alto vocal arrangement and the heavy rock guitar riffs toward the climax, gives the track a feel like some of the songs on the Time's debut album. It's funky electronic, and it rocks all at once.

"Ronnie, Talk to Russia" uses the flexibility of the Minneapolis Sound to lean more in the direction of rock, with traces of gospel. The one-minute-and-fifty-eight-second up-tempo track has soaring guitar riffs and churchy choir-like vocals with acoustic drums and understated bass lines. This ability to pull music in different directions based on instrumentation and wherever Prince's creative mind takes him is the real power of the Minneapolis Sound, which no other sound in the late twentieth century could match for roominess and flexibility.

"Let's Work," which sounds like it came right from the Time's album, is another example. The song is heavier on the synthesizer and has more pronounced bass-line vamps that funk up the track. The falsetto vocal arrangements over the lean and mean funk, sizzling synthesizer, with hard and heavy grooves that don't let up, make the song another strong entry in the canon of dirty Minneapolis funk. "Annie Christian" does what the track before it did: connect the song to Minneapolis. With its sparse arrangement, inflected with rock and new wave rhythms, guitar riffs in the background, and chanting/talking vocals, "Annie Christian" is pure Minneapolis in both form and content. As music critic Chuck Helm stated, the song is far from much of the music Prince had made to that point. That said, it resonates with Minneapolis. Its sound—sparse, electronic, even mechanical at times—could easily be found in the music of bands like the Suburbs, the Suicide Commandos, the Replacements, or Hüsker Dü. That's not surprising since, as André Cymone said, he and Prince spent much time checking out those bands, and those sounds became part of *Controversy*.[25] "Jack U Off," the last song on *Controversy*, could just as easily have been a track on a Suburbs album. It leans into the funk while also being punkish.

Rise and Fall

On October 5, Prince and his band returned to Sam's for back-to-back shows to kick off the *Controversy* tour. The Time opened. The show was a tune-up to prepare for the national tour. Prince was also breaking in a new bassist. Nineteen-year-old Mark Brown, whom Prince renamed Brown Mark, took over for childhood friend André Cymone, who left the band after their brief European stint. Creative tensions between André and Prince began to engulf their relationship. Cymone felt Prince took credit for music he helped write, namely "Uptown," "Controversy," and "Do Me, Baby." After these snubs, André left the group to start a solo career. The March show was the first and last time André and Prince performed at Sam's. The musical collaboration that had begun on the first day of school at Bryant Junior High ended.[26]

The Sam's show was electrifying. It sold out in forty-five minutes just by word of mouth. And even though it was a tune-up, it quickly became a whole show. Fans lined up around the block in anticipation. The ten-song set included "Sexuality," "Jack U Off," "Annie Christian," "Let's Work," "Controversy," and tracks from *Dirty Mind*. Hüsker Dü, the Replacements, and Prince's father, John, were in the audience.[27]

After the high of the Sam's shows, Prince and the band played opened two shows for the Rolling Stones. They were disastrous. After catching his New York performance, Mick Jagger asked Prince to open for the Stones. The rock legend was mesmerized by his sound and stage presence. Prince jumped at the chance to open for the rock legends. But once he and the band got onstage, the white crowd full of bikers, seeing the mixed-race and -gender band in punkish, sexy spandex, stockings, with a lead singer in a bikini and a trench coat, booed, screamed insults, racist and homophobic taunts, and hurled projectiles.[28] The band ran off the stage, and Prince flew to Minneapolis. When they arrived for the next show, the crowd was ready for them and treated them worse. They made it through a truncated set and rushed from the stage as thrown objects followed them.[29]

The disastrous performances, said *Minneapolis Tribune* music critic Chuck Helm, revealed something important about Prince and the musical landscape from which his music emerged. California's conservative "Reagan watchers," he observed, lacked the sonic diversity of Minneapolis, where punk, funk, rock, and R&B were central to the city's musical code and where Prince's album "rages." Helms's assessment was an essential lesson for the Minneapolis composer. Though people at home got him, others in different places might not. And if he wanted to achieve his dream of superstardom, the people who booed him off the stage would be the ones he'd have to win over.[30]

The *Controversy* tour was, by all accounts, successful. But all was not good. Tensions between the Time and Prince grew during the term. The Time were spoilers and upstaged Prince in the same way he did Rick James. The Time had three hit singles, and their set was tight and funky. The group's impact threatened Prince, and according to Morris Day, sabotage set in.[31] A fight between the Revolution and the Time broke out, which damaged a hotel room. Prince wanted Day to pay for the damage, but Day claimed Prince had instigated the fight. This tension amplified the band's concern about pay. Despite achieving some measure of success, Day was broke. He felt Prince was holding out on him financially, adding to the tension between the longtime friends. These events all but broke the relationship between the Time and Prince.[32] But despite their frustrations, Day and the members of the Time had to temper their frustration with Prince and remain subservient to his demands to remain employed.[33]

The Idol Maker

Between 1981 and 1982, Prince was a river of music. His output was dizzying. He was so prolific that he created another band to absorb some of the deluge. In 1982, work was underway on the Time's second album. Like the first, Prince wrote, arranged, and performed all the songs on the album, most of which were created at his new home on Lake Minnetonka. The house was known by the color it was painted—purple. A large, imposing black gate surrounded it.[34]

While living there, Prince became a fan of a little-known film called *The Idolmaker*. The film was based on the life of rock promoter/manager Bob Marcucci, who discovered the singers Frankie Avalon and Fabian. In the movie, Vinnie, the visionary idol maker, takes two local Brooklyn boys and turns them into stars through authoritarian control over their careers. Dez Dickerson said Prince wanted "to do an updated version of that" movie by becoming a Svengali.[35] This was Jamie Starr, the persona Prince created for the behind-the-scenes producer, writer, arranger, and composer who created the music for the Time and his new all-woman group, Vanity 6.[36] Denise Matthews, one of Rick James's backup singers, led the group until she defected to Prince's camp after he left James's tour. Prince was recording a song per day, according to his Sunset Sound engineer Peggy McCreary, and the Jamie Starr persona allowed him to use the various genres of music coursing through his mind and channel them into different groups.[37]

The Time was a classic Minneapolis funk band that played their dirty Minneapolis funk, high and tight, catering to Black listeners. The Revolution was more experimental; their music ran the gamut of punk, funk, classic rock, new wave, R&B, and all the hybrid forms circulating in the city. The Revolution allowed Prince to access more white listeners, while Vanity 6, a sexy synth-pop group with funk influences, was a female version of the Time that catered to Black listeners.

The Minneapolis Sound was hitting on all cylinders, evinced by all the Prince songs climbing the charts. The Time's sophomore album, *What Time Is It?*, was released on August 25, 1982. It was recorded between January and June of that year at Prince's home studio, with overdubs at Sunset Sound. Most of the album was created by Prince. Dez Dickerson is credited with cowriting "Wild and Loose." "777-9311," a funky synth track (the title was Dez Dickerson's home phone number), "The Walk," and "Gigolos Get Lonely Too" were the album's best tracks and helped land *What Time Is It?* at the number two spot on the R&B charts and twenty-six on the pop chart. Vanity 6 was equally successful on the strength of their singles "Nasty Girl," a synth-pop funk track with breathy vocals, and "Sex Shooter," a rock funk mashup. Both songs reached number six on the R&B chart and forty-six on the pop charts.[38]

These three groups made up what their members called "the purple family," a three-act revue that would voice all parts of the Minneapolis Sound. The Time represented Black Minneapolis with its funk and R&B rhythms. Vanity 6 also was Black Minneapolis but with downtown rock and new wave inflections. The Revolution incorporated all aspects of the city's sound: rock, new wave, funk, punk, and R&B. If albums are maps, as music critic Martin Keller suggested, then *What Time Is It?*, *Vanity 6*, and Prince's new project, *1999*, map Minneapolis in the late 1970s and early 1980s.

The Electronic Turn

Prince's fifth studio album, *1999*, culminated with relentless experimentation, musical evolution, and sonic geographies he'd been tinkering with since his first album. It was a massive success. Its four singles—"1999," "Little Red Corvette," "Delirious," and "Let's Pretend We're Married"—charted at twelve, six, eight, and fifty-two on the Billboard charts. The album reached nine on the pop charts and four on the Black chart.[39] It was the first of Prince's albums to cross over to white audiences, realizing the goal Prince had set for himself the day he signed with Warner Bros. His desire not to be locked into any genre but to explore Minneapolis's diverse sonic landscape laid the groundwork for the album's commercial impact.

Released in October 1982, 1999 was Prince's first double album. Like most record companies, Warner Bros. didn't like double albums but eventually agreed to release 1999 in that format.[40] Prince recorded it in his Kiowa Trail home studio, with overdubs again at Sunset Sound with Peggy McCreary.[41]

The album is a symphonic expression of the Minneapolis Sound, fully invested in the electronic music of bands like Kraftwerk and Devo. The music sounds grand, like multiple musicians performed, but Prince played all the instruments. He achieved this through his electronic turn.

The Oberheim synthesizer and the Linn LM-1 drum machine are the instruments he used to give his music its digital ethos. No track on the album demonstrates the impact of these instruments better than the celebratory opening salvo, "1999." The track's heavy organ-inflected sound, created by the Oberheim synthesizer, gives way to a gospel feel over the funky percussion from the Linn-LM1 drum machine. Well-placed guitar riffs fill the spaces between the other instruments, including understated but funky bass. Multipart vocal arrangements with Lisa Coleman, Jill Jones, Dez, and Prince marry the Minneapolis Sound to electricity. The vocals and bass fall out at six minutes, leaving the Linn drum machine percussion and Prince's guitar. A digitally distorted voice asking, "Mommy / why does everybody have a bomb?" closes this song that challenged all comers in 1982: As far as songs about dancing during the end of times go, "1999" stands second to none.

The album's second track, the slow-building but up-tempo ballad "Little Red Corvette," scored Prince his first big hit. Dez Dickerson's epic guitar solo helped the song find a sweet spot between R&B and rock, and radio play on rock stations helped it rocket up the charts. Rhythmic handclaps generated by the Linn drum machine enhance the song's electronic vibe; Prince would use this device on many songs throughout his career.

"Little Red Corvette" also had a visual impact. The song's video was added to MTV's playlist in 1983, making Prince (who appears in it clad in a metallic purple trench coat) one of the first Black artists to break MTV's musical apartheid.

Prince's electronic turn on 1999 coincided with the rise of new wave, a postpunk-inflected sound purveyed by Talking Heads, Blondie, Duran Duran, and other late 1970s and 1980s bands. Simple arrangements and heavy reliance on synthesizers characterized new wave. When German bands like Kraftwerk played it, they amped up the electronic component.[42] Minneapolis bands played this style in downtown clubs in the early 1980s, as Prince was working on *1999*. Its influence on *1999* is evident in tracks like "Delirious," a pop-rock-inflected song that sounds like it was recovered from white rock radio and run through a computer, with its rockabilly influences and synthesizer notes that can only be described as a *Star Wars* droid trying to harmonize. The percussive synthesized organ riffs are funky and playful with a blues quality. Linn LM-1 drums and booming bass drive the song, and computerized handclaps give it a gospel feel.

"Let's Pretend We're Married" uses this sound, too. This song is so deep in the electro-pop, new wave style it makes the body want to dance the Carlton.[43] The Linn drum machine pushes the sound forward with some of Prince's best programming, bringing funk by playing the role of a James Brown–style horn section. At the other end of the spectrum is "D.M.S.R. (Dance, Music, Sex, Romance)," a Minneapolis electro-funk track that could have been on one of the Time's albums. Like "Let's Pretend We're Married," synthesizers hold the keys to the funk kingdom by playing the part of the horn section. The synths and computerized call-and-response vocals make "D.M.S.R." one of the Minneapolis maestro's funkiest productions.

The album continues with "Automatic," a nine-and-a-half-minute R&B-inflected new wave number with electronically enhanced vocals. "Something in the Water (Does Not Compute)" sounds like something Devo might have created.

"Free," a somber tune Prince sings in a raspy falsetto, is a rock ballad with sweeping guitar parts, operatic piano chords, and slow-tempo drum programming. Prince's crescendo of screams as the song reaches its dramatic ending makes it sound more like the hard rocker Meatloaf than Prince. "Lady Cab Driver" is classic dirty Minneapolis funk, while "All the Critics Love U in New York" is a deep plunge into new wave. The double album ends with "International Lover," a waltz-like ballad driven by elegant piano chords. Hovering between R&B, funk, and new wave, it is the least synthesized song on the synthesizer-heavy album.

Dissonance is also another vital element of *1999*'s sound. Clashing rhythms and harmonies work brilliantly on "Something in the Water (Does Not Compute)" and "Lady Cab Driver." The album also leans into polyrhythms—two or more different rhythms played simultaneously on "1999," "Little Red Corvette," "D.M.S.R.," and other tracks.

Prince's vocals on *1999* departed from his previous albums. His first four albums showcased his falsetto, but on *1999* he favored his alto, sometimes electrified, and incorporated spoken parts. These new elements demonstrate an expanding conception of what his Minneapolis Sound could do.

Finally, 1999 is the album on which Prince formally introduces the Revolution. On the album cover, in the eye-shaped part of the "i" in "Prince," the words "and the revolution" are printed upside-down, lowercase, and backward.

The cultural impact of 1999 was immediate and has proved long-lasting. It continues to be rated among the best pop albums of all time, and many of its songs are still played on radio and are available from streaming services. The 2019 super deluxe reissue includes dozens of songs Prince recorded and released as B-sides of singles ("How Come U Don't Call Me Anymore") or socked away in his vault ("Purple Music").

The album's lyrics also demonstrated the young composer's expanding worldview. The sacred and the profane converged in his songwriting, as they did in the music of Marvin Gaye, Ray Charles, Aretha Franklin, and countless blues women and men before him. But he also wrote about war and the threat of nuclear destruction. He situated these themes in layered and textured sonic landscapes that transcended what fellow Minnesotan Bob Dylan or most other pop musicians achieved. As Minneapolis music critic Jon Bream put it, "The cleverness of his synthesizer work, the irresistibility of his rhythms and his flair for a variety of instrumental hooks rank Prince as one of the brighter young composers in popular music."[44]

1983

In 1983, the cult following Prince had built over his first five albums became a national sensation, and soon the Minneapolis Sound was everywhere. The year got off to a rocky start, however. Although critics praised 1999, it wasn't the breakout album Warner Bros. hoped for. Sales lagged, and the single "1999" slipped down the charts.[45] Prince was about to hit the road for his most extensive tour, from November 1982 to April 1983. It featured Prince's full revue—the Time, Vanity 6, and the Revolution. January tour dates in Texas and Louisiana sold moderately well to his fanbase. Prince flew between shows to Los Angeles and Sunset Sound to mix a twelve-inch single version of "Little Red Corvette." Peggy McCreary wasn't available, so Bill Jackson stepped in as the sound engineer. Prince kept Jackson up all night to finish the mix. He also recorded "Gigolos Get Lonely Too" with the Time.[46]

The tension between Prince and the Time that had erupted on the *Controversy* tour continued. Now, with two albums, lots of stage experience, and a solid following, the Time had become a Frankenstein monster. Prince had created the Time, but the band came into their own. Drummer Jellybean Johnson recalled that Prince "made music and told us what to play, we came in and played, a lot of times better than what he had. And in concert, it went over better than what it did on the record, and after a while, he resented that shit."[47] That resentment fueled the Time, who took every opportunity to show up their boss. "They were really good," said Prince keyboardist Matt Fink. "They were so tight and would put on such a great show that Prince in some respects thought they were showing us up. When Prince didn't receive the same kind of response from the audience that the Time did, he was hurt."[48] Jimmy Jam put it bluntly: "The Time kicked his ass in almost every city we played in." And Prince knew it. "They were, to be perfectly honest, the only band that I was afraid of," he admitted. "And they were turning into like . . . Godzilla."[49]

Things were also tense with Dez Dickerson, Prince's lead guitarist, the Keith Richards to Prince's Mick Jagger.[50] He was an exceptional guitarist. His solo on "Little Red Corvette" proved as much. The source of the tension was partly spiritual. Dez had a religious experience that profoundly affected his moral compass. He felt conflicted about performing Prince's sexually explicit songs, leading to arguments about the band's direction and about what Prince asked his musicians to do onstage. Dez also wanted to lead his own band and began to tire of being second to Prince. And as Prince's star rose, things began to resemble "a movement, and I didn't want to be involved in the movement."[51] Dez started to distance himself from Prince and the band. He didn't want to do sound checks, and throughout the tour, he became moody and difficult to be around.[52] Prince kept him on the tour, but the writing was on the wall—his time with the band was ending. Fortunately, Prince didn't have to look far for his replacement.

One night, while the tour was in New York for the Christmas holiday, Prince heard guitar-playing coming from Lisa Coleman's hotel room. He knocked on the door and asked, "Who's playing guitar in there?"[53] It was Lisa's girlfriend, Wendy Melvoin.[54] Lisa and Wendy were childhood friends. (Wendy's father, like Lisa's, was one of the Wrecking Crew session musicians.) Wendy had been working with Prince since 1981. She played on *Controversy*, sang on *1999*, cowrote songs for the Time's first album, and played keyboards on one track. Prince knew Wendy was a solid keyboardist and songwriter, but he had no idea she could play guitar until he heard her in the hotel room that night. Prince was hooked. He asked her to sit in with the band as they did a run-through of "Controversy," and before the song ended, it was evident that she "was the future," according to Bobby Z. Prince hired her for the rest of the tour, and though she didn't perform in the shows, she jammed with the band daily. When Dez left the group at the end of the tour, Wendy stepped in.[55]

Wendy changed the nature of the band. The fact that she was not a Minneapolis musician created a bit of rancor. Some resented what they saw as her easy pathway into the band. Others found her presence exciting. What's certain is that after she joined, nothing was the same. With Wendy, they were more than just Prince's backing band for tours. After Wendy joined, they became a cohesive band. Wendy's addition also changed Prince's sound, laying the groundwork for *Purple Rain*, Prince's best-selling album. Dez brought a 1970s hard rock sound to the band with his soaring solos and stunning technique. Rock was where he lived; he wasn't a fan of the new wave, pop funk music Prince was composing.

Wendy was more flexible and open to many styles, which fit well with Prince's hybrid Minneapolis Sound. She could phrase songs in many voicings without adhering to any one style. Moreover, as Prince began to change up the set list of shows based on audience response, he needed a flexible lead guitarist who could adapt quickly, and in this regard, Wendy was a better fit than Dez.[56] She also helped him move away from the rock and synthesizer mix that shaped his first five albums toward more complex musical arrangements that reached their peak with his 1987 masterpiece, *Sign o' the Times*.[57] Lisa Coleman said Wendy had this "funky little black girl" quality to her playing, while her chords sounded like Joni Mitchell's. Soon, sound checks turned into "chord class," where the weirdest or coolest chord won.[58] Prince and the Minneapolis Sound blossomed under this experimentation.

The new band members, Wendy and Brown Mark, created a different feeling in the group. Prince trusted and felt comfortable with them, so much so that he began collaborating with them in ways he'd never done before. In contrast, Dez (and André Cymone) dreamed of solo careers, which frustrated Prince. Wendy and Brown Mark didn't have the same aspirations. They were committed to the group, allowing the band to gel in ways the previous versions hadn't. According to Bobby Z, "It wasn't until Wendy joined that it really became the band he wanted it to be."[59]

If I were to pick a date when the Minneapolis Sound and Prince entered popular culture, I would choose February 9, 1983. On that day, Warner Bros. released the twelve-inch single for "Little Red Corvette." Dez describes the release as a "turning point."[60] Indeed, the song—Prince's first to hit the *Billboard* top five—boosted lagging album sales and helped fill concert arenas almost overnight, selling out shows in Tallahassee, Jacksonville, and Pittsburgh.[61] One month later, the video hit MTV. The combination of the single and the video thrust Prince into the public eye more than any of his previous records. And "Little Red Corvette" brought him the more extensive white fan base he sought. According to Jellybean Johnson, "He could do 'Little Red Corvette' and all that pop shit. He could do it and have the white folks and stuff. And that's what he wanted. And that's the reason when he made *Purple Rain*, it exploded. Because he had everybody."[62]

Even with the tour going well, tensions between the Time and Prince continued. Prince was paying them poverty wages, prompting Jimmy Jam Harris and Terry Lewis to find alternative sources of income. They flew to Atlanta between shows to work with the L.A.-based funk group, the SOS Band. While they were there, a snowstorm hit and stranded them at the airport, forcing them to miss a tour date. Prince, Lisa, and Wendy filled in for them. Prince then fired them.[63] In an attempt to prevent this tour from devolving into conflict like on the *Controversy* tour, Prince's L.A.-based management team Cavallo, Ruffalo & Fargnoli hired Alan Leeds, a music industry veteran who'd been around Black music for decades and had been James Brown's road manager. Leeds was able to hold things together for the remainder of the tour, but the damage was done.

Jimmy and Terry's firing was probably one of the best things that could have happened for them and the Minneapolis Sound. Freed from Prince, Jimmy and Terry created their own production company in Minneapolis, which they called Flyte Tyme Productions, after their old band. Influenced by the city's Black sound in North and South Minneapolis, Jimmy and Terry created R&B and funk music that drew from the Minneapolis Sound: synthesizers instead of horns, drum machines, and muted bass lines. Some of the biggest names in Black music, including Aretha Franklin, New Edition, and Michael Jackson, wanted it. Their most successful productions were for Michael's younger sister, Janet. *Control*, *Rhythm Nation 1814*, *Janet*, and *The Velvet Rope* were influential pop albums that sold millions of copies and put the Minneapolis Sound on Black and pop radio stations and MTV. Those albums thrust Janet into the pop stratosphere and the Rock and Roll Hall of Fame.

Over the first five months of 1983, the Minneapolis Sound had become part of the pop music lexicon. Music critics began to write about the city's sound and Prince's masterful musical creations. And the changes in the band helped usher in new sounds that would change his music and popular music. All the while, Prince continued to produce music. Alan Leeds watched Prince write and record at a feverish pace. He wrote, recorded, or worked on twenty-five songs during the 1982–83 tour. Though Leeds had been around many other great musicians, he thought Prince was the most impressive he'd ever seen. "The music was just pouring out of him," said Leeds.[64]

Music wasn't the only thing pouring out of Prince. The film fan who hosted screenings at his home for his band began to think of ways to bring his music and love of film together. During the tour, band members saw him scribbling ideas inside a purple notebook. As the tour concluded in May 1983, he told the band what he'd been writing. To their surprise, it wasn't a new song or ideas for a new album but a screenplay. Prince told them, "We're gonna make a movie."[65]

Chapter 12

1984

It was my baby. . . . I knew what it was going to be. . . .
it was just like labor, like giving birth—in '84.

—Prince

No album since Funkadelic's *Let's Take It to the Stage* has
so amorously bedded down black and white pop. . . .
It's the record Prince had been wanting to make all along,
since the music sounds like the kind of mulatto variation
he probably was piecing together and performing
in Minnesota before he got his deal.

—Greg Tate

In 1984, everything changed for Prince and the Minneapolis Sound. After five albums and years of knocking on the door of pop superstardom, he broke through that year. Prince knew the album and movie he was working on would be enormous. And he recognized that seeing music, not just hearing it, was the avenue to do this. *Purple Rain*, the album and movie, made the Minneapolis Sound the most impactful musical force of the decade. The visual representation of the Minneapolis Sound created a narrative backdrop to a city and its music scene, which, for more than a century, had existed on the margins. But it was that marginal status, that "totally out of touch place" that no one ever considered to be a hotbed of musical innovation, that launched what the late music critic Greg Tate called the "mulatto variations" that had been brewing in the segregated city for over a decade. The album gave the public a masterful example of this new sound that Prince had composed in North and South Minneapolis spaces since high school. Indeed, in '84, all the pieces came together.

"Video Killed the Radio Star"

Prince's love of movies may have informed his desire to make one, but the birth of MTV inspired the idea of marrying an album and a film. Without MTV, it's hard to imagine the concert film format of *Purple Rain* happening. Launched August 1, 1981, the cable channel revolutionized music and pop culture. The first video played was the aptly titled pop song "Video Killed the Radio Star" by London's new wave duo, the Buggles. It seems unfathomable now, but some musicians balked at the idea of music videos. Some saw them as cheap commercialism that undermined music. Bruce Springsteen, for example, initially refused to do them, only to change his mind by 1984 when he released the video for "Born in the USA."[1] But up-and-coming artists like Cyndi Lauper, Duran Duran, and a young woman from Michigan named Madonna embraced it. Michael Jackson saw the opportunity MTV posed from the start. When he released *Thriller* in 1983, his videos "Beat It," "Billie Jean," and, most important, "Thriller," transformed how music videos were used, demonstrating to other artists (like Springsteen) how important they were. Yet Jackson had to break through the channel's apartheid to get his videos played.

If Jackson could use a music video to make a short film, Prince would use film to make a music video movie. Prince saw MTV as a chance to scale up his sound and fan base. According to Lisa Coleman, "Instead of thinking 'Ugh, MTV ruined music' he was like, 'MTV!' Prince embraced it; he was always very visually oriented."[2] When Alan Leeds joined the camp, he quickly realized how Prince thought of music and visuals simultaneously. "I'll never forget," said Leeds, "when I went in, and he was playing a new song." With the music blaring, he began "describing a video treatment for the song." Astonished, Leeds said, "You just wrote it this morning! You've already got the video?" Prince replied, "Alan, you don't understand. Today people don't hear music; they see it. It all comes together for me."[3]

Purple Rain brought everything together in the seamless harmony of Minneapolis Sound compositions and concert filmmaking. It expanded what Jackson did for "Thriller" (the song), and in doing it, Prince showed that video did not kill the radio star. Instead, it made him into one.

The Dream

By his twenty-fifth birthday, on June 7, 1983, Prince and the Minneapolis Sound were breathing the rarefied air of pop stardom. His ambitions, talents, and the eclectic diversity of his music finally aligned with the cultural moment. The hard work and dogged experimentation paid off. He and his sound were gaining notoriety. *Saturday Night Live* star comedian Eddie Murphy said, "I think Prince is five years ahead of everybody." He made the cover of *Rolling Stone*, too. The article is a kind of cultural and musical history. Not only did they call him a "musical wizard," but for the first time, the venerable rock publication talked about the "Minneapolis Sound," which it described as a "technofunk rock blend."[4]

In this cocoon of success, Prince began to seek a cinematic outlet for his sound. This wasn't his first attempt. Prince had been thinking about making a movie since at least 1981. "I knew he had this idea pretty early on," said Bobby Z. Lisa Coleman knew about it, too. Prince tried his hand at filmmaking in 1982 during the *Controversy* tour.[5] The part concert film, part drama was directed by Chuck Statler, who'd done promotional videos on MTV. The project, titled *The Second Coming*, was abandoned due to Prince's demands for more takes.[6] It wasn't until after the 1999 tour that he tried again.

Prince began to meet with Warner Bros. executives and directors about a film script he'd been writing, tentatively called "Dreams." A rock star hadn't made a decent film since the Beatles' *A Hard Day's Night* and *Help!* And though Prince, with his Minneapolis Sound, had broken new ground and gained a larger fanbase, it was exceedingly optimistic to think such an endeavor would work. When he shared his idea for the movie with Matt Fink, the keyboardist thought, "Do we have the following to create a movie that's going to generate enough people to come out and see it, create the revenue needed to support something like that?"[7] Alan Leeds thought the idea was "nuts." Label executives were equally bewildered. But Prince wasn't going to be denied. His vision, work ethic, discipline, and sheer unadulterated belief in his art not only pushed him to make his dreams come true but everyone in the camp. "Prince had to make it happen . . . he was compelled, and he knew how to make everyone else feel that compulsion, too," said Wendy Melvoin.[8] And those on the fence he forced to get on board. According to Prince's manager, Bob Cavallo, Prince told him he would not retain his services "unless we got him a movie." And it had to be with a major studio.[9] In response, the management team raised half a million dollars to start the process.

Even though Prince was a star, meeting with potential filmmakers went nowhere. That's because the "Dreams" script was horrible. Its mix of music, murder, suicide, jealousy, toxic relationships, domestic violence, fame, fortune, and redemption was too erratic for potential filmmakers.[10] When the script landed in the hands of a University of Southern California film school graduate who'd only made one student film about jazz musicians, even he rejected it. "It's terrible," Albert Magnoli told Prince's manager, Cavallo, "and I won't do it."[11] But the two agreed to meet again to understand why Magnoli rejected it and what could be done to turn things around. At the meeting, Cavallo offered the poor film graduate $75,000 to make the film. Magnoli passed again. Frustrated and angry, Cavallo asked him for help on the script. Magnoli agreed, and a week later, the young filmmaker showed up with a different perspective. His excitement bubbled over, and within minutes, he pitched the film to the manager, and the two agreed to move forward.

Magnoli began formally working on the script in July 1983, one month after Prince's twenty-fifth birthday, which he celebrated at First Avenue. That month, the USC grad flew to Minneapolis to meet with Prince. He had to convince him that his script "sucked" and that his version was better. Despite controlling all his previous projects, Prince agreed.[12] Magnoli began furiously rewriting the script. To do this, he had to spend time with Prince and the principal characters in the film. Magnoli didn't know much about Prince at all. Through late-night meetings where he constructed an "emotional biography" of the guarded musician, Magnoli gleaned just enough to begin writing Prince's character, The Kid.

"Dreams" was a composite of Prince's real-life biography and the mythology he had constructed about himself. The Kid, a talented, driven, but troubled musician, has a tenuous relationship with his musician father because of their musical rivalry and his father's abuse of his white wife. The Kid's desire to lead the best band in the Minneapolis music scene without compromising his art is the second plot line that drives the film's drama. The Kid's band, the Revolution, made up of the members of the Revolution, has a rivalry with the Time, made up of members of the Time. The bands duke it out at First Avenue & 7th Street Entry, which is a character in the film in many ways. Creative tensions in the Revolution, which The Kid rules autocratically, bubble to the surface as Wendy and Lisa (played by Wendy and Lisa) create their music, which The Kid rejects because of his need for creative control and fears of abandonment.[13] Finally, The Kid and Morris, the lead singer of the Time, vie for the favors of a beautiful young singer named Apollonia. When she joins Morris's band, The Kid's fears of abandonment are unloosed, and he attempts to control her with the physical violence he witnessed his father use against his mother. In the film's climactic scene, the father, depressed from his contentious relationship with his wife and frustrated about his musical career, attempts suicide. In the aftermath, The Kid discovers his father's written compositions and realizes they are more alike than he thought, so to become the musician he wants to be, he must not follow his father's path.

The film concludes with the Revolution and the Time battling for musical supremacy at First Avenue. In a show of faith in his band and his willingness to be open to the input of others, The Kid performs the music Wendy and Lisa compose in the most crucial musical moment in the film. Fearful of vulnerability, The Kid bolts from the stage at the song's conclusion and doesn't hear the roaring applause until he's in the alley behind the club. The song is a stunning success. The audience erupts from the beautiful and painful power ballad. The Kid learns to trust his bandmates and does it while not compromising his art. Through a montage, the film concludes with The Kid and Apollonia reconciling and his mother by the side of her husband, who survived the suicide attempt.[14]

Before the script was complete, Prince's managers secured $2 million from Warner Bros. Chairman Mo Ostin to begin production. The funds were to be used against future royalties, which, according to Ostin, "seemed incredibly safe."[15] Magnoli was still writing the script when the shooting began in October 1983. Things were a bit chaotic. Between the time Magnoli came on to the project and the beginning of production, Prince and all the cast members took acting and dance lessons. During the summer, the band also diligently worked on the music and choreography for a benefit concert Prince agreed to do for the Minnesota Dance Theater, where he'd studied dance and movement in high school. The concert at First Avenue introduced many of the songs that would end up on the soundtrack for the film, which was still titled "Dreams." Rehearsals for this show took place in an old industrial warehouse in a Minneapolis suburb.

The Warehouse

No place was more important in creating the music for the film and the connection built between Prince and the Revolution than a large warehouse with an open floor plan located along Highway 7 in St. Louis Park. It was important because, in that space, many of the songs that appeared on the album were rehearsed and recorded. Built in 1945, the GSW Manufacturing Company first occupied the building, headquartered at 1310 East Franklin Avenue. Between 1954 and 1956, the Midwest Metal Manufacturing Company, which did metal stamping, occupied it. Over the years, the space changed hands multiple times. In the early 1980s, the Kennel-Aire Company, which made "dog equipment products with that pedigree quality," held the lease. In 1983, they leased the space to Prince.[16]

Its remoteness (which Prince was fond of when it came to work), the timing, and changes in the band were the factors that midwifed new directions in the Minneapolis Sound. And those involved in the production of the album could hear it. Changes in the recording process, how he edited songs, and the time he took to create them demonstrated this. However, the greatest impact on his musical evolution came after Wendy Melvoin joined the band.[17] Lisa Coleman also played an essential role in the growth of the Minneapolis Sound by contributing funky keyboards and string arrangements.

Besides being a place where Prince and the Revolution could work out the kinks in their routine in rehearsals, the warehouse also was where the Revolution could "write as a band," Coleman recalled.[18] Prince would bring outlines or parts of a song and allow the other musicians to add chord progressions, change keys, or even reconfigure how Prince himself arranged certain parts. The most important and undoubtedly most iconic of the songs recorded there was the power ballad "Purple Rain." Because of the way it functions in the film, there's a misconception that Wendy and Lisa wrote it. Melvoin said they didn't write it, "But . . . did we help? Yes, we did." They, along with the rest of the band, were critical to the birth of that song.[19] The idea for it first came to him on the 1999 tour. Prince said the inspiration came from Journey's song "Faithfully," a staple in the Top 20 in 1983.[20] Prince even reached out to the songwriter, Jonathan Cain, to make sure the music wasn't too close to his, to which the "super-flattered" Cain responded by wishing him good luck.[21]

Whatever its inspiration, it came to life at the warehouse. According to Bobby Z, Prince introduced "Purple Rain" toward the end of a rehearsal. "I want to try something out before we go home," he told the group. "It's mellow." He had been working on the song since the 1999 tour, Fink later explained, "but the arrangement wasn't quite finalized yet and I don't think the lyrics were finished. So, he brought it to us and said, 'play what you feel'"—a startling invitation from the artist who, just six years earlier, had played twenty-seven parts himself.[22] Melvoin recalled playing the song during that session and making a significant suggestion. "Prince's chords were much more simple then. We kept all those suspended chords in there and then I put a 9 in." The addition of the 9th note gave the track its reflective, melancholy vibe, like a country song—which stunned the First Avenue audience when it was played at the August 3 benefit concert.[23] They were used to eclecticism from Prince but not to something like the haunting and twangy "Purple Rain."[24]

"We were seriously camped out in that warehouse working out those songs," enthused Lisa Coleman. "And we would really write them as a band, and we were so tight that by that time, and Wendy fit in so well and added such beautiful color in her guitar playing" that it added just the right sound to bring "Purple Rain" to life.[25] This is where Wendy's impact on the evolution of the Minneapolis Sound comes into focus. Her musical training and ability to bring different colors and phrasing expanded Prince's version of the song. Her use of big, luscious chords and suspended notes produced a richer sound, and her use of a chorus pedal made it feel orchestral.

Two songs were recorded at the warehouse. Prince wanted to experience the feel of having the entire band play the songs and record them that way. Doing this enabled Prince to work out parts of the music on the fly and have multitrack recordings. These recordings not only became the masters but also documented the songs' evolution. In August, Prince asked engineers David Leonard, Rick "Hawkeye" Henriksen, and newly hired Susan Rogers to convert the rehearsal space into a recording studio. After wiring the space for recording and laying out a large carpet in the middle of the room to trap echoes, the basic tracking and overdubs for "Let's Go Crazy" were worked on at the warehouse in August. "It wasn't ideal," said Leonard, "but the results were legendary."[26] The next day, "Computer Blue" was recorded there. The song was inspired by a bass groove Matt Fink played in rehearsal. Prince worked on it and had Wendy and Lisa add vocals ("Is the water warm, Wendy? Yes, Lisa"), and a bridge from a song Prince's father, John, wrote was added.[27]

Testing Ground

If the warehouse was where the new Minneapolis Sound was cultivated, First Avenue was the "testing ground."[28] Between 1981 and 1983, Prince's shows there gave the city "claim to a star."[29] (Evidenced by the large golden star that bears his name on the venue's famous facade; see fig. 12.1.)[30] On the cusp of this new film, Prince returned to First Avenue to test his latest sonic concoction and secure the funding he needed to make the movie happen. The twelve-song set debuted new songs that Prince had written for the film. "Baby I'm a Star," "Let's Go Crazy," "Computer Blue," and especially "Purple Rain" sealed the deal for the Warner Bros. executives in attendance.

The city with no musical center on the nation's musical margins, with little Black radio, was an appropriate place for his musical gumbo. As the geographic epicenter of the city, First Avenue facilitated the creative intersection that mixed Near North and South Minneapolis funk and R&B with downtown indie rock, punk, and new wave. The story of the 1983 show links

Figure 12.1. Prince's golden star on First Avenue's star wall. Photo by the author.

Prince and the place where he grew up. Perhaps the greatest pop musician of all time was collaborating on multiple levels—not only with his bandmates but with the histories that created the city itself.

Prince liked First Avenue because it "felt big and theatrical"—like the warehouse.[31] He appreciated that it was friendlier to Black artists than other downtown clubs and functioned as a middle ground between the North Minneapolis Black community in which he had grown up and the South Minneapolis Black community where George Floyd would be murdered in 2020. He liked the flawless acoustics, its hometown vibe, and the fact he could not only perform there whenever he wanted but also walk in unannounced and watch a show without being bothered, even after he became a superstar.[32]

At the benefit concert, the crowd sang along to hits and inhaled the new work on offer. However, the set's penultimate song earned Prince the backing for his film and made the performance legendary. Ablaze with stage light, Wendy Melvoin strummed a B-flat suspended 2 chord with a D in the bass, a sound that contradicted the show's punk/funk/rock/R&B/new wave groove. It was wistful and, in a distinctive way, sounded like the prelude to an anthem, a mode that Prince had been tinkering with.[33] The "unusual" chord subdued the audience, and the band filled the empty space.[34] After nearly two minutes, Prince's melancholy voice entered: "I never meant to cause you any sorrow / I never meant to cause you any pain."

As the band walked offstage, Albert Magnoli, who was still writing the script, exclaimed, "That song . . . that could be the song!" "It's really not done yet," Prince responded.[35] The director told him that this song would make the film. "Dreams" needed a song to anchor it, and Magnoli felt he'd just heard it. The director asked Prince the song's title, and Prince replied, "Purple Rain." "Can we name the movie 'Purple Rain?'" Prince asked the filmmaker, who answered, "Yeah, that's the name of the movie."[36]

Reign

Purple Rain began filming on Halloween 1983. It was already winter in Minneapolis, and the bitter cold made shooting difficult. Actors huddled around heaters in between scenes. In addition to the weather, right before shooting began the lead actress, Denise Matthews (Vanity), who was to play The Kid's love interest, left the project because of tensions in her on-again-off-again real-life relationship with Prince. Her role had to be recast. Hundreds of women showed up at an audition, clad in leather for the part. But none of them fit. Time was of the essence, and panic began to set in. "We had no one," said Magnoli, "then one day Apollonia walks in" fresh from the gym "in baggy sweats, no makeup."[37] The Southern California–born Patricia Kotero, who took the name Apollonia, was a former Oakland Raiders cheerleader and daytime TV actress.[38] She had no singing experience, however, so getting her ready to be lead vocalist of the now-renamed Apollonia 6 would be a steep hill to climb. Nevertheless, Magnoli and Prince thought she was a good fit and offered her the role. "I can work with her," Prince said, and he did coach her extensively.[39]

The fact that this film was being made in Minneapolis was a remarkable feat, a testament to Prince's star power. *Minneapolis Tribune* music journalist Jon Bream's reports on the film's development and shooting put the city in the limelight. More than 600 extras were used. For a period, Minneapolis was the center of the pop world.

How the soundtrack was recorded was critical to the album's sound. "Let's Go Crazy" and "Computer Blue" were recorded in the warehouse after the August benefit concert. The rest of the soundtrack was recorded while the filming was underway. Sound engineers David Leonard and Susan Rogers oversaw the recording. One of the things that makes Rogers unique, in addition to her sublime ear, was that she was trained not as a studio engineer—someone professionally trained to record—but rather as a technician, someone who sets up the recording equipment. She helped Prince turn the warehouse into a recording studio when she arrived. Soon after, he asked her to record. Her first session was "Let's Go Crazy." Rogers also recorded "Darling Nikki" at Prince's Kiowa Trail home studio along with Robert "Cubby" Colby and Don Batts. When Colby and Batts moved on, Rogers became his full-time engineer and part of the engineering team that worked on the album's title track.[40]

As the album took shape and the editing of the film reached its conclusion, Magnoli told Prince he needed a song for a montage that voiced the emotional pain about The Kid's "father, his mother, loss, redemption, salvation—all the themes we were dealing with in the film. The next morning, he called me and said, 'Okay, I got two songs.'"[41] After a night at the Grammys, where he was nominated but lost to Michael Jackson, Prince perched himself inside Studio 3 at Sunset Sound and began working on "When Doves Cry."[42] Prince spent two hours in the studio laying down the basic tracks for the song. Much of that time was spent creating the song's hypnotic drum pattern on the Linn-LM1 drum machine. "Prince was one of the very best drum programmers," argued Bobby Z, "because he could get very warm sounds out of machines."[43] By the next day, Prince had a complete working version of the track after a sixteen-hour studio session, lyrics included. But he wasn't satisfied with it. "It just wasn't sounding right," the composer recalled.[44] Prince began stripping the track of its many sounds. This included the bass. "When he was playing with it before he did the vocals, he took the bass out," according to Peggy McCreary. He knew no one in pop music would "have the balls to do this. You just wait, they'll be freaking out."[45] And history proved him right. No pop song has ever reached the top of the charts without a bass line.[46] Even band members couldn't believe it. After hearing it, Matt Fink said, "There's no bass on that thing. It's just all kick drum." To Fink, it sounded "too empty." But in retrospect, he realized it was "pure genius, because it was so different."[47]

Purple Rain was a forty-three-minute-long, nine-track album that didn't waste a note. Every song expressed Prince's new musical direction. And Wendy and Lisa's impact was noticeable. The use of strings, complex chord voicings, and the different colors they brought to the music pushed the Minneapolis Sound in a new direction and played a significant role in the album's success. They turned the Minneapolis Sound away from the digital ethos that dominated previous albums. Incorporating acoustic instruments, more intricate harmonies, and dynamic songwriting, Wendy and

Lisa gave it a rich, elastic flavor. Because of this, says Alan Leeds, "Wendy and Lisa were more involved in Prince's recording than the other band members." Lisa had a musical range on the keys that Prince couldn't match. "And in Wendy's case, it wasn't that she could outplay him, but she had a distinct kind of sound" that helped to expand his music.[48] The result of this collaboration was, as Greg Tate wrote in the *Village Voice*, an album that "bedded down black and white pop" in ways that Prince had been working toward since playing in the basements, backrooms, and band rooms during his teenage years.[49]

Purple Rain was sequenced sometime in late April or early May 1984. "Sequencing for the record was a big deal," according to Susan Rogers. Creating segues and stitching the songs together creates a unique sonic experience that his previous albums lacked. "On those earlier records, you hear that unrestrained, unfiltered rawness on some of the tracks, whereas *Purple Rain* was carefully arranged. It's a masterpiece," said Rogers.[50]

The first single, "When Doves Cry," hit the airways in May 1984. It exploded. Within six weeks, it sat at the top of the charts—Prince's first song to reach that plateau—and held that position for five more weeks. As the single burned and the film reached the final stages of postproduction, *Purple Rain* hit stores in June, one month before the film was released. The album held the top spot on the pop charts for twenty-four weeks, deposing Bruce Springsteen's *Born in the USA*. And it hit number one on the Black music charts, pushing aside Tina Turner's *Private Dancer*.[51] The album produced three chart-topping singles—"When Doves Cry," "Let's Go Crazy," and "Purple Rain." The response to the album was electric and immediate. It sold 1.5 million copies in its first week. Over the next year, 13 million copies fled from record stores, and the album would eventually sell 25 million copies worldwide, making it one of the biggest-selling albums in music history.[52]

The album opens with "Let's Go Crazy," a shot across the bow of '80s rock that showed a new guitar hero was on the scene. The song begins with a gospel-inspired organ playing behind Prince's opening sermon ("Dearly beloved, we are gathered here today to get through this thing called 'life'"). The song perfectly declared the unique sound and band that the album represented. Prince sparingly used the elements that made up the Minneapolis Sound between 1980 and 1983. But what remained was the blending of musical genres, which was its foundation.

"Let's Go Crazy" is a deep dive into rock. With suspended chords (Wendy's influence), the guitar-playing departs from the more straightforward rock guitar he played on previous albums. Lisa's keyboard arpeggios over Matt Fink's rhythmic synthesizer with Brown Mark's funk-inflected bass create a rock funk rhythm section that Wendy's rhythm guitar and Prince's lead fit into brilliantly. But the song's most significant statement is the half-minute guitar pyrotechnic shredding that evokes Santana and Hendrix. To say it reaches for the rafters is an understatement; it's a career-defining solo that ranks among the best in rock history.

The second track is the "breezy" and bouncy pop ballad "Take Me With U."[53] This duet with Apollonia was Prince's first and the first time his costar had ever recorded as a vocalist.[54] Getting her to the point where she was comfortable enough to sing took a lot of coaxing and preparation, and she spent much time in the studio to get it right.[55] It opens with a complex drum solo played on the Simmons SDS-5 electric drum kit. It could produce acoustic effects, and Prince loved its sound. The Oberheim keyboard created the repetitive rhythm that gives the song its bouncy feel. The rhythm section is rounded out with a steady but unobtrusive bass line, a holdover from the previous Minneapolis Sound. Prince's alto vocals and Apollonia's, with backing by Jill Jones and Lisa Coleman, fit succulently with Coleman's open, airy string arrangement.[56] The result is a pop song full of character with complex arrangements that offer beauty and accessibility. "Take Me With U," said Bobby Z, "is just a beautiful song."[57]

"The Beautiful Ones" is Prince fully in sync with his creativity. What makes the song special is its unique orchestration. According to Matt Fink, the combination of "synthesizers, guitars, pianos, lots of digital delay, and reverb," as well as a powerful vocal arrangement, make this one of the album's best tracks. "Computer Blue" was inspired by British electro-pop musician Gary Numan. Prince created the song's cold and isolated feel through the vacant industrial space of the warehouse. The track opens with Bobby Z soloing on the Simmons SDS-5. A screeching electric guitar boldly enters behind Lisa and Wendy's spoken word parts. The guitar pyrotechnics shift the song toward a funk new wave sound. The mix of funk, rock, and new wave that Prince used on previous songs reemerges in "Computer Blue" but in fresh ways that lean more toward rock while also being funky.

No track on the album generated as much controversy as "Darling Nikki." Its sexually daring lyrics upset Tipper Gore, the wife of then-Senator Al Gore, who had bought Prince's album for her daughter. She made a federal case out of it. At her urging, the Senate held hearings that resulted in parental advisory warning labels put on so-called objectionable records. Risqué lyrics aside, the production and sparse sound distinguish the track. It features acoustic drums with Linn-LM1 embellishments, keyboard riffs, and guitar accents, all recorded by Prince at his home studio. The song moves down the musical scale, leading to a sonic explosion at the track's conclusion.

"When Doves Cry" is the album's most exciting song and the simplest, with fewer instruments and fewer technical elements than the other tracks.[58] Stripping out the bass line included made it stand out.[59] Prince's vocals, switching from singing to speaking, come through with sonic and emotional clarity.

"I Would Die 4 U" and "Baby I'm a Star" are separate tracks, but they're joined on the album and provide a penultimate up-tempo blast before the deep emotion of "Purple Rain." Prince's best-known song crystallizes the flexibility and capaciousness of the Minneapolis Sound. When first played onstage at First Avenue, it came in at just under fourteen minutes; for the album, it was edited to eight minutes and forty-one seconds. Although the song may have been inspired by Bob Seger, echoes of Joni Mitchell ring even clearer in this purple anthem. "I can hear my influence on 'Purple Rain,' said Mitchell, "but I don't know if it's coming from him [Prince] or Wendy or Lisa because they also assimilated some of the modality of open tunings."[60] (Open tunings make changing major and minor chords easier and simplify fingerpicking.) Prince often acknowledged her impact on his work, telling MTV, for example, that "Joni Mitchell . . . taught me about color and sound."[61] But it was most likely Wendy's idea to change the tuning for "Purple Rain," which gives it a folky, country sound. Prince's stunning guitar solos, which evoke deep emotion, remind the listener of the guitar hero on "Let's Go Crazy." The vocal arrangement mixes his voice, spoken parts, and rafter-reaching primal screams, producing a powerful emotional effect. The song ends with a guitar solo and a beautiful string section peppered with piano arpeggios. The live crowd it was recorded in front of can be heard whistling and screaming as the strings fade to close.

Music critics were enthusiastic about the album. The *New York Times* called it a "winner" and said that Prince's working with the Revolution as his equals made the "music sound more alive and sensual."[62] Kurt Loder of *Rolling Stone* described Prince as cut from the same cloth as Jimi Hendrix and Sly Stone and gave the album four stars.[63] Jon Bream of the *Minneapolis Star Tribune* raved that "the album is simply further proof that Prince is one of the most original visionaries on the contemporary music scene."[64] The album was on numerous lists of best albums of the year, with three chart-topping singles. It bested Michael Jackson's *Victory* album, Springsteen's *Born in the USA*, Stevie Wonder's *Woman in Red*, Lionel Richie's *Can't Slow Down*, and Cyndi Lauper's *She's So Unusual*. There was simply nothing like *Purple Rain*. Its combination of rock, gospel, and R&B was unparalleled. It was the most sonically original album of the year and, for some critics, the decade. Prince's mixed-race music that blended Black and white rhythms was more than just the album he wanted to make; it was also a recipe for his Minneapolis Sound.

As if creating *Purple Rain* wasn't enough, Prince also wrote and arranged for his new protégées Sheila E. and Apollonia 6, as well as producing the final album with the Time. Recorded in the spring of 1984 at his home studio in Chanhassen and Sunset Sound, they all were released before the film hit theaters. The albums channeled the Minneapolis Sound as expressed between 1981 and 1983, which leaned toward new wave, funk, R&B, and electronic dance music with heavy synthesizers, understated bass, drum machines, and taut guitars. Sheila E.'s "The Glamorous Life" (from the album of the same name), Apollonia 6's "Sex Shooter" (from *Apollonia 6*), and the Time's "Jungle Love" (from *Ice Cream Castle*) employ this sound, with a heavy dose of that dirty Minneapolis funk on the Time's album.

But once again, Prince's heavy hand and need to control the music-making process brought things to a head. After the 1999 tour, relations with the Time permanently soured. Morris Day was heartbroken over the firing of Jimmy "Jam" Harris and Terry Lewis. To make matters worse, Prince replaced them with musicians the band had no hand in picking. The success of "Jungle Love," "The Bird," and "Ice Cream Castles," which sent *Ice Cream Castle* double platinum, and Day's prominent role in *Purple Rain*, which critics responded to positively, weren't enough to cool the tensions. After the premiere of the film, Morris broke with the band and with Prince. He sought a solo deal and used the movie's success to begin auditioning for acting roles.[65]

"A Cinematic Valentine"

The premiere of *Purple Rain*, a month after the soundtrack's release, was held on July 26, 1984, at the legendary Mann's Chinese Theatre in Hollywood. The star-studded event attracted the likes of Eddie Murphy, Steven Spielberg, Stevie Nicks, Kevin Bacon, Lionel Richie, Little Richard, and members of Kiss and Talking Heads. Prince arrived in a purple Rolls-Royce, clad in his purple trench coat and holding a rose he'd picked before arriving at the theater. An MTV-sponsored afterparty followed the showing. For the members of the Revolution, it was an exciting moment. They performed at the afterparty, along with Sheila E. Journalists interviewed them. They'd entered a new world. After years of "write, record, tour," seeing the massive crowd, the stars, and the reaction from the audience as they watched the movie, Lisa Coleman wondered aloud, "Wow, where is this gonna go?"[66] Where it went was to the top of the box office.[67]

After screen-testing the film, Warner Bros. opted for a wider release than originally planned. The bet paid off. On the movie's opening weekend, it grossed $7.8 million at the box office, recouping its cost. *Purple Rain* replaced *Ghostbusters* as the week's top movie. The film also sent the album sales through the roof.[68] A significant portion of *Purple Rain* happens onstage. "It was the first long-form music video," said Alan Leeds.[69] The marriage of music and film had not captured the public in this way since the Beatles' *A Hard Day's Night*. Young people flocked to theaters and saw it repeatedly, which kept the film a hit at the box office until the fall and kept the album atop the charts until January 1985, nearly six months after its release.

Many critics praised the film. Sheila Benson of the *Los Angeles Times* said it succeeded "beyond even its own audacious dreams."[70] For Geoffrey Hines of the *Washington Post*, the movie "reveal[ed] the emergence of a new multiracial youth counterculture." Charles Rogers of New York's *Amsterdam News* wrote that the "live concert footage places this film in a class all its own."[71] It was, he said, a "Prince of a film."

But the reviews were not all glowing. *New Yorker* critic Pauline Kael called *Purple Rain* "pretty terrible." *New York Times* writer Vincent Canby was equally acerbic: "The offstage stuff is utter nonsense," he wrote, and "the only things that count" were the musical performances. The treatment of women also concerned Canby. He argued that the female characters were written as "suckers for men who knock them around with brutal regularity."[72] Charles Rogers said women in the movie are "relegated to punching bags, sex machines and even trash."[73]

Despite being made in Minneapolis, the movie never mentions the city. (When I first saw it, I had no idea where it occurred.) Lake Minnetonka and First Avenue & 7th Street Entry are the only geographic references. This is because the screenplay was written by Magnoli, who was from California and didn't feel it was essential to make the city more visible. The lack of geographic specificity didn't detract from the city's primary role in the film. More than just the backdrop, "the attitude and tenor of the local music scene have shaped the look and essence of this picture," wrote Jon Bream of the *Minneapolis Star Tribune*. And even though, according to Bream, "the acting is erratic, the violence and sexism is excessive, tasteless and gratuitous, and it takes too long for viewers to become emotionally involved," *Purple Rain* is, nevertheless, "a cinematic valentine to Minneapolis from our most prominent rock music figure."[74]

The album and movie *Purple Rain* landed in the Reagan presidency's grim political and social landscape. Reagan's election was due at least in part to the "Southern strategy" that Republicans employed to attract white voters in the South by appealing to anti-Black racism. Words like "welfare," "busing," and "states' rights" cropped up repeatedly in campaign rhetoric to galvanize Southern whites under the Republican banner. The strategic defense system known as "Star Wars" sent the Cold War into a new technological phase, expanding the possibility of nuclear destruction that Prince had sung about only a year earlier in "Ronnie, Talk to Russia." The excess of Wall Street and the myth of "trickle-down economics" unleashed growing poverty, especially among Black Americans. In the Iran-Contra Affair, the Reagan administration secretly enabled arms sales to Iran, using proceeds from the arms sales to fund the Contras, a right-wing and drug-dealing rebel group in Nicaragua. (Most of the Contras' funding up to then had been from cocaine sales.)

The album and movie also landed in a particular time in pop culture. Madonna's "Like a Virgin" performance on the MTV Music Awards and albums by Bruce Springsteen, Culture Club, Michael Jackson (the juggernaut *Thriller*), Deniece Williams, Billy Idol, Huey Lewis and the News, Ray Parker Jr., Talking Heads, and Duran Duran all happened that year. Oprah Winfrey began broadcasting her morning show out of Chicago. *Beverly Hills Cop* was a top box office draw. Marvin Gaye was killed by his father after delivering the coolest version of the "Star-Spangled Banner" ever at the NBA All-Star Game. And MTV moved from a marginal cable channel to the center of the pop culture world.

This political and cultural context created a fertile ground for *Purple Rain*'s cultural explosion. Bucking the commercial pop sounds firmly cemented in established racially organized genres, the album's mixed-race sounds, and the film's visual representation of the music scene from which it sprang made the album and the movie outliers. Except for Prince's previous albums and the music of the Time, *Purple Rain* had no sonic peers. It didn't sound like anything on the radio. Moreover, the mixed-race representation of First Avenue & 7th Street Entry, with The Kid having a Black father and white mother, and the "mulatto variation" of Apollonia, along with the mixed-race dating happening at the club, was far afield from the segregated stories of Black and white life in popular film.[75]

Purple Rain turned the 1980s upside down by injecting a new kind of sound that emerged from a place far from the centers of US music-making, Los Angeles and New York. Since *For You*, his 1978 debut album, Prince had been putting his city on the pop music map, inviting listeners to hear the heterodox Minneapolis sounds grounded in a landscape and produced over a century. With each album, Prince honed and perfected his musical mapping of the city's sound, moving closer to the music "he . . . was piecing together and performing in Minnesota before he got his deal."[76] *Purple Rain* was his cinematic gift to Minneapolis, but it was also a platform for its sound. Against the backdrop of increasing racial segregation, the conservatism and white supremacy of the Reagan administration, and the segmenting of music along racial lines, *Purple Rain*, the album and the film, captured the zeitgeist of a unique political and cultural moment. It achieved this status by leaning into hybrid sounds coursing through Minneapolis and its most important composer.

Chapter 13

ANOTHER VERY EXPERIMENTAL KIND OF RECORD

I try not to repeat myself. It's the hardest thing in the world to do. There are only so many notes one human being can master.

—Prince

Lisa Coleman called *Parade*, Prince and the Revolution's third and final project, "another very experimental kind of record for us."[1] Indeed, the post–*Purple Rain* period was one of growth and creativity. Warner Bros., Prince's fans, and many critics wanted another *Purple Rain*. But Prince saw that as a trap. The album had won three Grammy awards and an Oscar for Best Original Score. It sold more copies than all his previous work combined. Prince had become a household name on the level of Michael Jackson and amassed great wealth in the process. He'd taken the Minneapolis Sound to the peak of musical fame. But this presented creative problems. "What happens if you reach the mountain peak?" asked bassist Brown Mark. "Where do you go from there?" If you're Prince, you make one album that mashes up psychedelic rock, funk, and gospel and another that synthesizes jazz, classical, and funk.

Prince had grown weary of *Purple Rain*. He loved making new music. The ninety-plus shows he and the band played from late 1984 to 1985 to promote the album got in the way of that. The tour was a massive success. *Rolling Stone* called it the best of the year. Charles Rogers of the *Amsterdam News* called it "extraordinary."[2] The tour broke attendance records in nearly every city it landed. In some cases, the demand was so high, extra shows were added. On March 30, at the Carrier Dome in Syracuse, New York, in front of 90,000 fans, Prince and the Revolution gave a live broadcast show that reached 12 million people in Western Europe through the Eurovision broadcasting company. But even though the songs were new to the public, he'd played them for years. According to Coleman, "he got bored."[3] Prince realized the album's success was double-edged: "In some ways, *Purple Rain* scared me . . . It was too successful and no matter what I do, I'll never top it . . . It'll be hanging around my neck as long as I'm making music."[4]

The purple albatross motivated him to move past it as soon as possible. That opportunity came on April 7, 1985, during the tour's final show at the Orange Bowl in Miami. Heavy rains created a soggy ground, and the stage slowly began to sink as the band nervously finished their set. They made it through, and when it was over, Prince broke with *Purple Rain* and "never looked back."[5] Having completed new albums by Sheila E. and the Revolution made moving on easier. In 2004, he told *Entertainment Weekly* why moving on and not making the same sounds defined his career: "I'm about the present and moving forward. New joke, new anecdote, new lesson to be discovered. You know that old lady on Sunset Boulevard, trapped in her mansion and past glories? Getting ready for her close-up? I don't run with that."[6]

With his need to constantly push the boundaries and never repeat himself, he created music that baffled some, exhilarated many, and carved new sonic grooves that would influence pop music moving forward. Writing at an even more feverish pace, Prince leaned heavily on the collaborative sprint that marked his most recent project. Between 1985 and 1986, with the help of Lisa Coleman and Wendy Melvoin, Prince pushed his sound in new directions, drawing on jazz legends like Bill Evans, Clare Fischer, Miles Davis, and Duke Ellington and classical musicians like Paul Hindemith and Ralph Vaughan Williams. He composed music that took him and Minneapolis Sound miles away from *Purple Rain*. Prince turned the Minneapolis Sound into orchestral pop music on two sonically experimental albums—*Around the World in a Day* and *Parade*. No longer just electronic dance music that replaced horns with synthesizers, used crisp guitar licks and drum machines, and kept the funk dirty and tight, the Minneapolis Sound had become a kind of sonic zeitgeist that reflected the era's culture and the possibilities of what pop music could be.

Between April 1985 and March 1986, Prince's music continued to evolve in revolutionary ways. Although I have previously referred to Prince as a composer, it was during this period that he fully became one. He changed his recording process to capture the ocean of music flowing through him. Rather than writing down his compositions as European composers like Mozart did, he used his recording engineers, Susan Rogers and Peggy McCreary, to capture the sound. Prince also employed his growing band and collaborators like composer Clare Fischer to create arrangements for his orchestral pop music. Prince pushed his compositions in a new direction, incorporating Middle Eastern flavors, psychedelic rock, classical, jazz, and, for the first time, horns.

"Another Groove"

After the success of *Purple Rain*, Prince began "a new process of creative growth."[7] To call Prince's output during this period exceptional would be an understatement. The stuff of legends would be a more apt description. As he once remarked, "I am energized by music. Music is my reason for existence."[8] Prince was pumping out music at a pace never seen in popular music. It was a period of little sleep, long sound checks, even longer rehearsals with hours-long jams that stretched until five or six in the morning, recording sessions that kept Susan Rogers up around the clock, and constant writing. Prince's girlfriend, Susannah Melvoin, said he didn't "get tired," and "sleep was unnecessary because the adrenaline of his creative self kept him going."[9] Prince was pushing his creative impulses to the maximum. "Anyone who was around back then," Prince remarked, "knew what was happening. I was working. When they were sleeping, I was jamming. When they woke up, I had another groove."[10] This period produced a burst of material that helped him move past *Purple Rain* so quickly that it left little time for reflection. It also expanded his catalog, much of which still has not seen the light of day.

During this period, his sound moved into its most experimental phase. As far back as *Dirty Mind*, jam sessions had been an essential source of musical generation for Prince. But in the aftermath of *Purple Rain*, he leaned on them even more. His composing process involved riffing on chord progressions—"Groove in A. Everybody groove in B-flat," he would say. Susan Rogers recorded every second of the jams, which he would mine for song material.[11] Brown Mark recalled, "We would jam all night and then he would be like, 'Susan Rogers, roll tape.'"[12]

Another vital element in Prince's new groove was his band. A salon of musicians that extended beyond the band's core members was informing his sound.[13] Wendy Melvoin, Lisa Coleman, and Susannah Melvoin raised his interest in rock music, which began as a teen, by adding Led Zeppelin, the Beatles, and the Rolling Stones to his list of influences.[14] Alan Leeds and his saxophonist brother, Eric, exposed him to Duke Ellington, Miles Davis, and Charles Mingus, while Sheila E. introduced him to the jazz fusion band Weather Report.[15] These influences increased his musical vocabulary and helped him become a more capacious composer.[16]

But the most crucial element in this period was how he leaned into collaboration. Though still in charge of his compositions, Prince sought more input from the band than ever, especially from Wendy and Lisa. The three had become writing partners throughout *Around the World in a Day*. "He'd have us go in and do arrangements—string arrangements, vocal arrangements—and the guitar and keyboard parts. That's really where it started—our writing together," observed Wendy Melvoin.[17] She and Lisa helped to push his sound in more experimental directions, and Prince was open enough to welcome their assistance. Soon, he began handing over master recordings of ideas and asking them to finish them. But this collaborative attitude didn't extend to the rest of the band. The men—Brown Mark, Matt Fink, and Bobby Z—were not asked to collaborate. Why? Alan Leeds said, "Prince has been traditionally more comfortable with women." He wrote songs for them. He collaborated with them. And much of his inspiration stemmed from working with women.[18] This might have to do with vocal register, bad experiences with men, or the fluid gendering of his persona. Whatever the reason, he made Wendy and Lisa partners in the creative writing process while the men became session players.

These processes dramatically shaped the sound of *Purple Rain*'s follow-up, *Around the World in a Day*. Prince and the band recorded most of the album as *Purple Rain* was still fresh in theaters and record stores. More than just a departure from its predecessor, *Around the World in a Day* represented a genuine turn from the sounds that dominated his previous albums. The first track, "Pop Life," was recorded in April 1985 at Sunset Sound and engineered by Terry Christian.[19] Prince didn't record the next song until July 23, when he laid down the basic tracking for "America" with Susan Rogers at the Flying Cloud studio in Eden Prairie, Minnesota. Three weeks later, he did the basic tracking for the title track.[20]

"Interesting but Not Commercial"

The album was his most collaborative project yet. It was also the most sonically adventurous expression of the Minneapolis Sound. But when Warner Bros. suits heard the album on February 25, 1985, expecting *Purple Rain 2*, they listened with trepidation to the psychedelic funk rock album while Prince, holding a flower and sitting on the floor of the conference room with his father and Wendy and Lisa in tow, pensively watched the room. Warner Bros. didn't like the record at all. After the disastrous listening session, which Prince exited before the album finished playing, the executives wondered aloud, "What are we going to do with this? It's interesting but not commercial."[21]

Their reaction didn't bother Prince at all. "I kind of had an f-you attitude about the whole thing," he remarked. The album was, indeed, sonically interesting. It demonstrated that the Minneapolis Sound could do many different things and incorporate diverse textures while adhering to pop formats.

The genesis of the album's title track was a birthday gift Prince gave to David Coleman, Lisa's brother, who worked with Prince on *Purple Rain*. Prince paid for two days of recording time at Sunset Sound, where, among other songs, David recorded his song "Around the World in a Day." When Lisa and Wendy heard the track, they loved it and suggested he play it for Prince, who "was floored by it." David agreed to hand the song over to Prince, who then changed the lyrics, keeping only the "Around the World in a Day" parts. According to Susannah Melvoin, the sounds David used in his recording inspired the entire album. An excited Prince quickly booked studio time to record the song with the Revolution, Wendy, and Lisa's brother.[22] It has the most diverse section of instruments on a Prince track—finger cymbals, darbuka, and an oud, all played by David Coleman. The track opens with Coleman arpeggiating notes on his cello to evoke the Middle East. A Princely cry precipitates the warm percussive sounds of the darbuka, a goblet-shaped Middle Eastern and North African drum. Finger cymbals, an oud, an acoustic guitar, and the Linn-LM1 drum machine fill out the rhythm section. At the two-forty-two mark, the sizzle of synthesizer chords lifts the song's tempo, adding a touch of the dirty Minneapolis funk. Multiple backing vocals move between falsetto and soprano. The earthy, globally inspired psychedelic funk sets the tone for what will come.

"Paisley Park" is the most psychedelic track in the corpus of the Minneapolis Sound. The song came together through rehearsals as the band was preparing for the *Purple Rain* tour. Like many of the songs on *Around the World in a Day*, the entire band plays on it. The track also relies on acoustic instruments. Acoustic drums and elongated feedback-heavy electric guitar open the song. Echoed Linn-LM1 drums are accented with finger cymbals played by Prince while feedback guitar riffs in the background. Prince's soprano vocals, with backup by Wendy and Lisa, and Novi Novog's violin add to the song's hippie-inspired feel.

"Condition of the Heart" is a slight departure from the album's psychedelic funk rock. It's also the only song performed entirely by Prince. "Condition of the Heart" is a melancholy ballad that opens with a mix of airy piano chords and spacy synthesizer notes that sound like the score for a Flash Gordon movie. The piano chords, rooted in B major, merge into a melodic progression and are accented by falsetto vocal arrangements. Subtle finger cymbals, acoustic guitar, and kettle drums fill in the open spaces between piano chords and voice. Near the song's conclusion, all the instruments and voices come together in an epic crescendo that lifts it to the rafters while deepening its melancholy vibe.

"Raspberry Beret," a song whose genesis goes back to when Dez was in the band, was first recorded in 1982 during the 1999 period. Perfectly placed, "Raspberry Beret" lifts the emotion and tempo of the album. Because of when it was initially recorded, it's the only song on the album with the pre-1984 Minneapolis Sound, with prominent synthesizers, subtle bass, electronic drums, and taut guitar parts. Wendy and Lisa changed the song's arrangement, and Prince and the band added new elements they began experimenting with on *Purple Rain*. The three-minute-and-thirty-one-second song begins with Prince counting off the beat with echoey Linn-LM1 drums, organizing his timing. When he hits the fourth minute, the full corpus of instruments used in the song enters. This burst of orchestral sound holds until Prince's soprano vocals enter. Airy synthesizers, acoustic guitar, sweeping violin, funk-fueled bass, and cello combine to give the song a symphonic sound that's equal part Mozart and pop.

One of *Around the World in a Day*'s markers was the increased use of acoustic instrumentation. "Tamborine" has a funk-heavy rhythm section with prominent bass and understated synthesizer. "America" has rock guitar riffs that hearken back to 1999 and a funky bassline played by Brown Mark that would make Funkadelic leader George Clinton proud. Sheila E.'s drum pattern lays down the funk hard. Borrowing from the pre-'84 Minneapolis Sound, guitar riffs, low-key bass lines, and mystical-sounding synthesizer chords swirl around the percussion, producing a full but not overloaded sound. "Pop Life" might be the strongest track on the album. The first song recorded for the album, it features Sheila E. on drums. But it is the lush and echoey vocal arrangements that distinguish "Pop Life." Wendy's and Lisa's voices are upfront and mixed with Prince's vocals, making the song warm and inviting.

No song in the corpus of the Minneapolis Sound is as orchestral as "The Ladder." With seventeen musicians and sixteen instruments, this is a gospel orchestra, which is evident from the opening string arrangement by Lisa Coleman. The soothing, classical sounds of the string section are disturbed by atonal guitar chords followed by slams on the snare drum, electric guitar, and piano, all of which come together to create a kind of gospel funk. Like "Let's Go Crazy," Prince gives a sermon over the melody built from a chord progression by his father, John. Bright saxophone riffs played by Eddie Mininfield from Sheila E.'s band float over the melody, filling open spaces and helping to elevate the music toward a crescendo. The vocals are epic. Prince's shouts and screams, some of the most expressive he's ever recorded, mix with spoken and alto vocals and engage in round singing with a choir of Wendy, Lisa, Bobby Z, Susannah Melvoin, and Taja Sevelle. "The Ladder" is a mix of classical, gospel, and funk that leaves the listener breathless by the closing stanza.

As Susan Rogers said, the sequencing of an album is essential. Her brilliance on *Around the World in a Day* is demonstrated most saliently on its final two songs. The gospel funk of "The Ladder" is followed by the hellish, funky heavy metal of "Temptation." At over eight minutes, the track opens with heavily saturated electric guitar riffs, ascending and descending, sounding like an animal gasping for air. They find resonance when the Linn-LM1 drums, the bass, and Eddie Mininfield's saxophone enter. The first two-thirds of the song is funk metal. But at around the five-minute mark, the song shifts. Much of the music falls away, with the space filled only by drum patterns, spoken words, riffs from Mininfield's sax, and piano chords that enter and exit.

Around the World in a Day was released on April 22, 1985, only fifteen days after the final *Purple Rain* tour date and just ten months after the release of the *Purple Rain* album. It was the second album credited to Prince and the Revolution. Because of the high of *Purple Rain*, *Around the World in a Day* entered the pop charts at number one and landed at four on the R&B chart.[23] Prince didn't want to release any of the songs as singles. But as album sales stalled, Warner Bros. stepped in and released "Raspberry Beret" with "She's Always in My Hair" on the B-side, "Pop Life" with "Hello" on the B-side, and "America" with an extended mix of "Hello" on the B-side.[24]

Around the World in a Day was Prince's most experimental album. And even though Warner Bros. didn't know how to respond to or market the post–*Purple Rain* project, the sounds it produced demonstrated that Prince was an innovative composer whose music was unlike any other in pop. The album sold 3 million units in the first week and knocked "We Are the World," the song written by Michael Jackson and Lionel Richie and produced by Quincy Jones with an all-star cast of singers, off the top spot on the Billboard pop chart.[25]

Despite the strong opening sales, *Around the World in a Day* didn't receive the high praise *Purple Rain*, 1999, or *Dirty Mind* had, although some critics did recognize its sonic innovations. Robert Palmer of the *New York Times* noted that although the album might not be a rock classic, the "collection of superb pop songs" is "an instrumental and stylistic tour de force."[26] Richard Harrington of the *Washington Post* called it "one of the most intriguing albums of the year." *Newsweek*'s Jim Miller said the "subtly textured music is playful, sensuous and straggly melancholy." Hometown critic Jon Bream didn't consider the album groundbreaking but found it "significant . . . in the boldness of its strategies," calling it the most personal and spiritual album of Prince's career.[27] But many saw it as a misstep. They felt the "neo-psychedelic" sound of *Around the World in a Day* was wrong for a funkster. Martin Keller of the *Twin Cities Reader* bluntly asked, "Where's the funk?" and, noting the record's maverick nature, concluded that "it won't be something he'll likely do again."[28]

One constant that ran through many album reviews was the perceived looming presence of the Beatles, particularly their album *Sgt. Pepper's Lonely Hearts Club Band*, in the psychedelic sounds Prince played with. Band members and those who worked closely with him have difficulty swallowing the pill. According to Wendy Melvoin, the Beatles did not significantly influence the album. Prince listened to them, Wendy said, but he found some of their music "too populist."[29] Lisa points to her brothers as a more significant influence on the album's sound.[30] In his first interview in three years, Prince told *Rolling Stone*, "The influence wasn't the Beatles. They were good for what they did, but I don't know how that would hang today."[31]

If the British band had an impact on him, it might have been in his touring. The Beatles famously stopped performing live as their music grew more complex, which made reproducing it onstage difficult, if not impossible. After *Purple Rain*, Prince decided to retire from live performance. On the final day of the *Purple Rain* tour on April 5, 1985, his manager, Steven Fargnoli, announced that he would withdraw from the stage "for an indefinite period of time."[32] The massive tour and catering to new, young, white fans who wanted to hear only a handful of songs got to Prince. But the music he'd created for his latest album, like the Beatles' late records, was challenging to translate to the stage. So, immersing himself in studio production and composing albums without worrying about stage translation made sense. But more than this, it also liberated him from the demands of the new fans who only wanted to hear "Little Red Corvette" and "Purple Rain."

A New Synthesis

Prince's decision to create an anti–*Purple Rain* album and pause performing created room for what many fans and scholars of Prince see as the most daring and creative period in his career. "You know how easy it would have been for me to open *Around the World in a Day* with a guitar solo on the end of 'Let's Go Crazy.' . . . I don't want to make an album like the earlier ones,"[33] Prince told *Rolling Stone*. His defense of the album and explanation of his creative drive also put fans and critics on notice. And over the next two years, he would make good on this promise not to make albums that sounded the same.

Between 1985 and 1987, Prince had one of the most productive periods in pop music history. He recorded six albums' worth of material, including two double albums. But much of the music stayed in his expanding vault of unreleased material. It wasn't until after he died in 2016 that fans could access *The Dream Factory*, the Camille Project, and *The Black Album*, one of the most bootlegged albums in history. Some of this material found its way onto *Sign o' the Times* in 1987 and *Crystal Ball*, released in the 1990s. The two albums that were released were done at breakneck speed.

Two of these albums were released during his lifetime. The first, *Parade*, was recorded just weeks after the *Purple Rain* tour ended and before *Around the World in a Day* hit the stores, after what was supposed to be an extended break from making music marked by a vacation at Copacabana Beach in Rio de Janeiro. The holiday only lasted a few days because Prince got bored by the beach. He ended the musical hiatus and decamped to Sunset Sound. For a few months, Prince poured out song after song. Soon, he'd amassed dozens that would become some of his best work.

Prince continued to collaborate with Wendy Melvoin and Lisa Coleman. They would build on the chord progressions he'd developed, adding rhythm and melody to the harmonies. As he'd done before, he'd send them a tape or play something he was working on and tell them to add to it. He also began working with arranger and composer Clare Fischer to expand his sound even more. Prince had first worked with Fischer years earlier on the Family's album. Susannah Melvoin most likely suggested they work together because her father, Mike, knew Fischer.[34] Like Prince, the Michigan-born pianist, composer, arranger, and bandleader formed his first band as a teenager. After graduating from Michigan State University, Fischer went on to play with Donald Byrd, Dizzy Gillespie, and Herbie Hancock, who saw his arrangements as indispensable. After successfully arranging Latin and bossa nova music in the late 1960s, in the 1970s, he began working in pop and R&B.[35]

Though Fischer and Prince had previously collaborated for a project by the Family, *Parade* marked their first collaboration for music that appeared on an album credited to "Prince." Prince would send Fischer tapes of nearly completed songs and Fischer and his son Brent would transcribe the pieces, add an orchestral arrangement to the transcribed music, record it, and return the tape to Prince. Prince liked his arrangements and used them on several *Parade* tracks. But the two never met in person. They were supposed to meet, but at the last minute, Prince canceled. According to Brent Fischer, Prince told them, "If I'd been there, I might have interfered. And I like what you all do so much that I will always stay away from the recording sessions." Prince remained true to his word.[36] He even refused to look at a photograph of Fischer because "I have the image of Clare Fischer in my head, and I don't want to change it."[37]

Working with Fischer allowed Prince to synthesize his growing fascination with classical music and jazz into pop. Prince began listening to classical at the suggestion of Lisa Coleman, who introduced him to English composer Ralph Vaughan Williams and German composer and music theorist Paul Hindemith. Given his love of jazz, especially the music of Miles Davis, Prince began to think about fusing the two idioms. Fischer's orchestral and jazz background was just what Prince needed to make it happen.

The first song Fischer worked on with Prince was "I Wonder U." Fischer crafted an orchestral arrangement, but just before the song was finished, Prince sent a note to the arranger saying he only wanted "a family of flutes." Fischer complied, and while he was recording, the engineer suggested playing both the flutes and the orchestration simultaneously. According to Brent Fischer, "They blended together beautifully." Prince used both arrangements in the final version of the song.[38]

Fischer also worked on "Christopher Tracy's Parade" (originally titled "Little Girl Wendy's Parade"), the piano instrumental "Venus de Milo," "Under the Cherry Moon," and "Do U Lie?" These arrangements gave the music an expansive classical feel. Wendy and Lisa's contributions are also important. They fed him chords he would have never encountered and suggested harmonies that greatly enriched *Parade*.

"The Whole Song in My Head"

While in Salzburg in 1771, Mozart wrote four divertimentos, several substantial works, eight symphonies, and a serenade. This music he didn't come from jam sessions with an orchestra but from inside his head. Because the only way to record it was to write it down in musical notation, Mozart only heard the pieces when an orchestra played them.

Prince's musical output during this mid-1980s period was equally astonishing. Within just a few weeks, he composed and recorded twenty-six songs. Rather than working on one piece at a time, he began recording several new songs during one lengthy session, each fully mapped out in his head with lyrics to guide him along as he played.[39] "By the time I pick up the instrument," he said, "I've got the whole song in my head. All I'm doing is committing it to music."[40] This translation of music in his mind to recorded composition is yet another illustration of Prince's musical genius and a direct parallel to Mozart's method.

With the music coming fast, Prince experimented with new ways to record. Because he could not write his compositions, he had to play them to hear them. Throughout his career, this meant piecing together the song by laying down a drum or rhythm track and then using overdubs to complete it. But the river of sounds flowing through him needed a new approach to capture them. According to Peggy McCreary, Prince told her to "put up a roll of tape, I'm gonna start playing the drums and when I stop, don't stop the tape. Just keep going, just let it roll." After playing the drum part for "Christopher Tracy's Parade," he went right into "New Position," then played the drums for "I Wonder U" and "Under the Cherry Moon" right after. In one session, Prince recorded "four drum tracks in a row, all first takes." After he finished, he told McCreary to put on a fresh tape, grabbed his bass guitar, and repeated the process.[41]

Prince's assembly-line approach to recording sped up the music-making process. Days-long recording sessions with little or no sleep also amplified musical output. This kept everyone working around the clock in a casino-like world where they didn't know whether it was day or night.[42] Prince's trusted recording engineers, Susan Rogers and McCreary, dealt with this in ways the other musicians, Wendy and Lisa aside, didn't. Because Prince didn't write his compositions in musical notation and recorded what was in his head, his engineers were, essentially, the pen and paper. Indeed, they were, as Rogers put it, "facilitators of his vision and his art."[43] However, as facilitators, they had to work when he did, resulting in only a few hours of sleep a night. For Susan Rogers, this lasted for years.[44] Susan was committed to playing this role and didn't trust anyone else to do it. Peggy, however, was "struggling." The rapid and unrelenting pace of recording Prince since 1981 burned her out. By the time *Parade* began, she was handing over most of the responsibilities to Rogers.[45]

The expanding synthesis in his sound also led Prince to incorporate new instruments. "The instruments I choose," he said, "depends on the song. . . . I'm always looking for new instruments, new sounds, and new rhythms."[46] One such instrument was the Fairlight CMI keyboard. This digital synthesizer and sampler could sample sounds and reproduce them. Lisa Coleman described it as the "coolest sampler keyboard monster ever." Her enthusiasm is well founded. The instrument "inspired a lot of unique ideas," said Coleman. The songs Prince used the Fairlight on, however, never made it onto the album. They became part of his growing collection of unreleased vault material.[47]

The collaborative spirit that expanded with *Purple Rain* exploded with *Parade*. Fischer's orchestral arrangements were on several songs. Wendy and Lisa's contributions were significant, too. Their musical training and deep sense of melody and rhythm profoundly enriched Prince's compositions. "More than mere accompaniments," these women were central to Prince's creative explosion.[48] Instead of seeing them as competition, Prince recognized that they represented a sonic direction for his music. Wendy and Lisa were more than studio musicians; they were writers, which allowed them to listen to something Prince was composing and offer their take on the music while remaining true to his original idea. Prince frequently sent them ideas for songs and gave them creative control—something he'd never done before and would never do after the Revolution disbanded. Like Susan Rogers and Peggy McCreary, Wendy and Lisa were central components in his process of composing music and recording it; they also lived in the studio along with Prince. According to saxophonist Eric Leeds, when working with Prince, they "didn't see the light of day."[49]

Washington Avenue Warehouse

Prince, always looking for ways to get his art into the world, began pondering another movie idea. He would call it *Under the Cherry Moon* after the *Parade* track. That album would come to serve as the movie's soundtrack. Prince set this one on the French Riviera. It would tell the story of a young American "gigolo" named Christopher Tracy. The film was modeled after the romantic comedies of the 1930s and 1940s but set in the present (the 1980s), which makes understanding its period difficult as the film's décor and costumes signaled the early twentieth century while the dialogue was contemporary. Christopher Tracy was a barroom pianist who moved to southern France to find a rich wife. Aided by his sidekick Tricky (played by former Time hype man Jerome Benton), Tracy pursues Mary Sharron (Kristin Scott Thomas), the daughter of a wealthy businessman. Sharron's father is not happy about Christopher wooing his upstanding British daughter. The culture, class, and racial clashes result in Christopher's death at the film's climax.

Like *Purple Rain*, the film was hastily put together. Managers Bob Cavallo and Steven Fragnoli secured $10 million from Warner Bros. for the movie, mainly based on the success of *Purple Rain*.[50] Eric Leeds and Fragnoli took Prince to Paris in June 1985 to see if shooting on location would work. While walking the streets of the City of Lights, Prince found a music store and bought so much equipment that he turned his hotel room into a makeshift studio. The trio traveled to the south of France, to the seaside city of Nice. Prince loved the location and decided to shoot the movie there.[51]

Prince and company returned to Minneapolis in late June after deciding on the location. The travel and equipment he bought in Paris stimulated his creative juices, and he threw himself into recording. He needed a new workplace because the warehouse had been demolished to create a more extensive recording and performance space that Prince would name after one of the songs on *Around the World in a Day*, "Paisley Park." The band moved into a location Prince rented for his side project, the Family, while the new facility was being built. Located in Edina, a suburb south of Minneapolis, it was the largest of the three warehouses Prince used. He recorded there from 1985 to 1987, the longest time he worked at any one place. Prince and the Revolution completed the music for *Parade* at the warehouse.[52]

By the end of the summer of 1985, Prince had assembled an album to serve as the soundtrack to a film yet to be made. *Parade* was the most collaborative work of his career, reflected in the album's sound and his changing band. The Revolution was no longer just Wendy, Lisa, Dr. Fink, Brown Mark, and Bobby Z; saxophonist Eric Leeds, the brother of Prince's tour manager Alan Leeds, and Sheila E. also joined the band. These additions created tensions that would boil over.

Becky Johnson, from New York, was hired to write *Under the Cherry Moon* despite having no screenwriting experience. Shooting began in September at Victorine Studios in Nice. Alan Leeds recalls the three months they spent shooting as "exciting times in the Prince camp."[53] But the wheels quickly started falling off. After sending his girlfriend Susannah Melvoin home, Prince began an affair with his lead actress, Kristin Scott Thomas. When Martin Scorsese turned down Prince's offer to direct the film, Prince hired music video director Mary Lambert, who directed some of Madonna's most popular videos. But Lambert and Prince clashed. Lambert quit, and Prince took control. Now he had to direct a movie, which he'd never done before, and work with a crew that spoke limited English. Prince quickly shot the rest of the film, often accepting first takes rather than reshoots. The film wrapped on November 21.[54]

The Flesh Sessions

Prince returned to Minneapolis shortly after completing *Under the Cherry Moon*. It was a busy time because he was moving into a new home he'd purchased on Galpin Boulevard in Chanhassen. Susannah Melvoin was decorating the sprawling three-story house with a basement for his new home studio. It was the first home Prince and Susannah lived in and his first attempt at domestic cohabitation.[55] His megacomplex, Paisley Park Studios, was being built a mile and a half away. The state-of-the-art home studio was put together by Susan Rogers and designed by Westlake Audio of Los Angeles.[56] Susannah Melvoin installed stained glass doors to the studio, giving it a churchlike feel when the light came through.[57] The home was a festive space where band members came for cookouts, movie nights, and game nights. Prince began recording there in early 1986 after completing *Parade*.

While Susan Rogers set up the home studio, Prince flew back to Los Angeles to record at Sunset Sound. While there, he had a one-on-one meeting with jazz legend Miles Davis. The meeting profoundly inspired him, so much so that he turned his attention to making jazz. Prince admired Davis's musical ability and that they both spoke the language of music first and foremost. According to Prince, "I learned a lot about space from Miles. Space is a sound, too, and it can be used very inventively."[58] After a four-day break for Christmas, Prince recorded "A Couple Miles" and "Can I Play With U?" These Davis-inspired jazz tracks were Prince's first foray into the genre. He called on Eric Leeds to play sax on them. Prince sent a tape of the songs to Davis, and the two worked on the track. Although they profoundly respected each other, their need for control over the recording process stalled the kind of collaboration Prince hoped for. Nevertheless, Miles recorded a trumpet part for "Can I Play With U?" The song sat for decades in Prince's vault until it was finally released on the super-deluxe version of *Sign o' the Times* in 2020.[59]

The time Prince spent with Miles had a lasting impact on his sound. Miles helped Prince feel comfortable playing jazz. Miles helped Prince to "stretch the scales, invert the chords, harmonically stretch something, screw with the rhythms and polyrhythms," says Wendy Melvoin. With the support of Eric Leeds, Prince developed his own "jazz philosophy" and felt more confident by the day.[60] Prince quickly gathered some musicians from his inner circle—Eric Leeds, Sheila E., Wendy, Lisa, Jonathan Melvoin, and Sheila E.'s new guitarist Levi Seacer Jr. on bass—to join him in the recording studio to try out his new jazz philosophy. In Studio 3 at Sunset Sound, the group played nonstop instrumental jams all night, filling up hours of tape. The jams, called the "Flesh Sessions," yielded what Eric Leeds called "some amazing music." Prince's jazz chops were snowballing. More seasoned musicians like Leeds and Seacer were impressed, and the long nights Susan Rogers captured on half-inch tape produced nearly seven-foot-tall stacks of music. Prince assembled the tapes into tracks. But they remain unreleased.[61]

Orchestral Minimalist Funk

Parade was released on March 31, just weeks after Prince returned to Minneapolis to play at First Avenue with his newly expanded Revolution.[62] The album opens with "Christopher Tracy's Parade," one of several tracks worked on by Clare Fischer. This funk/soul/orchestral mashup is a sonic cornucopia. With more than two dozen musicians and nearly an equal number of instruments, this two-minute-and-nine-second song sets the tone for what will come.[63] The alto vocals, backed by Wendy and Lisa, live under the heavy orchestral arrangements.

Prince kept this arrangement style on "New Position." This track is funk-heavy, expressed by the bass line and Prince's vocals, backed by Wendy and Lisa. The steel drums add a sparse, minimalist feel to this two-minute-and-twenty-one-second song.

If the instrumental arrangement is a dominant theme on *Parade*, then sparseness is another. Not since *Dirty Mind* had a Prince composition been so stripped down. "I Wonder U" demonstrates this saliently. Touched with Clare Fischer's understated arrangements, this one-minute-and-forty-second song, with taut guitar riffs, subtle bass, Linn-LM1 drums, reverbed synthesizer, and breathy vocals backed by the dynamic duo, save for the addition of a crowd laughing in the opening seconds, is a testament to minimalism. The song's lyrics were inspired by a woman in a club in Rio who propositioned Prince for sex by saying, "How . . . how do you say? I wonder U . . . I wonder U."[64]

"Under the Cherry Moon," like "Christopher Tracy's Parade," lists John Nelson, Prince's father, as cowriter. This piano-driven track, which Prince claims is built from a chord progression written by John, is also sonically sparse.[65] Filled with melancholy harmonies, spare orchestral arrangements, and alto vocals, this track comes in at just under three minutes but feels longer because of the space placed between the notes (a lesson from Miles Davis, no doubt).

The orchestral funk of *Parade* has a few high points. "Girls & Boys" is one of them. The song's sonic spine is the acoustic drum riff, string arrangement, alto vocals, and heavy bass line that open the track. It's accented with a perfectly timed sax line from Eric Leeds and well-sprinkled finger cymbals from Prince.

Built from an epic jam session, "Life Can Be so Nice" is the least sparse song on the album. Rehearsed and recorded over twenty-four hours in L.A.'s Sunset Sound, this track is built on the early version of the Minneapolis Sound. The song is driven by programmed drums, synthesizers, guitar riffs, subtle bass lines, and falsetto vocal arrangements backed by Wendy and Lisa. The elasticity of the Minneapolis Sound enables the polyrhythmic clash to melt together into a funky synthesis.

If "Life Can Be so Nice" was retro Minneapolis Sound, then "Venus de Milo" was a version of its future. Prince said this song was "so different for me, musically"—an understatement.[66] "Venus de Milo" was his first attempt at instrumental arrangements. Written for *Under the Cherry Moon*, this slow-tempo, melancholy, piano-driven score with string arrangements from Clare Fischer is one of the most beautiful pieces of music in the Prince catalog.

"Mountains" is the only track created by the Revolution. They worked on and recorded it between London and the Washington Avenue warehouse in Edina. While filming *Under the Cherry Moon* in Nice, Wendy and Lisa went to London to work on songs for the album and wrote "Mountains." This nearly four-minute song is more robust sonically than other tracks on the album. It's driven by synthesizer riffs courtesy of Lisa and Matt Fink, with Sheila E.'s guitarist Miko Weaver, Prince, and Wendy. Bright trumpet and saxophone by Matt "Atlanta Bliss" Blistan and Eric Leeds float over the rhythm, paced by Bobby Z's drums. Brown Mark's bass, layered with Prince's falsetto vocals, holds the track together.

"Do U Lie?" is a minute-and-forty-five-second interlude with string arrangements by Clare Fischer and heavy bass grooves. Falsetto vocal arrangements, with backing by Wendy and Lisa, deepen this jazz-inspired track.

The album's standout track is "Kiss." The sparse funk jam with a falsetto vocal arrangement is controversial because Prince took the song away from Brown Mark without crediting his work or that of David Rivkin. "Kiss" is pre-'84 Minneapolis Sound with its minimalist electronic funk, electric guitar riffs with acoustic accents, programmed drums, sizzling synthesizer, and absent bass (like "When Doves Cry"). The track's emptiness elevates all the instruments, especially Prince's vocals.

This funk continues on the next track. More sonically verbose than "Kiss," the penultimate song, "Anotherloverholeinyohead," is driven by funky slap bass licks mixed with percussive piano chords and riffs from the Roland G-707 synth guitar. This track is the high point of orchestral funk on the album.

In the aftermath of Prince's death in April 2016, no song has become more iconic and emotionally painful as "Sometimes It Snows in April." Written and performed by Wendy, Lisa, and Prince, this song is the peak of Prince's collaborative efforts and one of the most powerful in his corpus. Completed in just two hours at Sunset Sound, it is organized around Lisa's classically inflected piano arrangement, around which Wendy's acoustic guitar wraps like a warm coat.[67] Prince's almost tearful vocal arrangements evoke a longing and loss without peer in his canon. It's one of the most emotionally vulnerable songs the artist ever released.

Testing the Limits

Parade's experimental turn produced mixed reactions. John Milward of *USA Today* called it "sophisticated" and said Prince was one of the leading artists of the 1980s. Richard Harrington of the *Washington Post* called *Parade* a "mixed bag, with only a few truly memorable moments."[68] The *New York Times* pronounced the album "very good," singling out "Kiss" and "Anotherloverholeinyohead" as standouts.[69] *Los Angeles Times* critic Richard Cromelin contended that *Parade* "is more of a holding action; good enough in its strongest moments to keep your faith alive, but too dull and aimless everywhere to raise much passion."[70] Jon Bream of the *Minneapolis Star Tribune* said that the album had three epic songs that established Prince as the most prolific pop artist since the Beatles and reestablished his reign over contemporary funk.[71]

Minneapolis music critic Steve Perry lambasted it. While arguing that the album's "Kiss," "Anotherloverholeinyohead," "Girls & Boys," and "New Position" were some of Prince's best music, Perry said the rest of the album suffered from bloat and too many musical ideas. For Perry, Prince's attempt to synthesize jazz, funk, rock, and classical music made the album "cluttered and schizophrenic."[72] In a moment when much pop music could be safely situated in discernable categories, Prince's experimental music crashed into the brutal reality of genres. Perry understood the diversity of the Minneapolis Sound, but what Prince did with it, quipped Perry, made the music sometimes sound "silly as hell."[73]

But not only critics found *Parade* frustrating. Prince himself saw the album as a "disaster," saying that his "temptation to go right back into the studio and make a killer album," so soon after *Around the World in a Day*, was a mistake. "I just didn't have enough good material," he lamented.[74] *Parade* also suffered from its association with *Under the Cherry Moon*. The film was a flop. Critics derided its campy acting, confusing storylines, lousy dialogue, and amateurish directing. Not even the best tracks on *Parade*—especially "Kiss," which reached number one on the Billboard charts—could rescue this film from the chorus of bad reviews. The film was so terrible that it tied for top "honors" at the Golden Raspberry Awards, which recognizes the year's worst movies. Prince knew how bad the movie was.

Susannah Melvoin found him face down on the floor of their home, repeating, "I hate this movie."[75] The damage and embarrassment were so bad that Prince even cut short his Stateside tour, performing only a handful of shows in New York. However, the album was more enthusiastically received in Europe, and Prince and the Revolution toured the continent for most of August. Then he and the band played four shows in Japan in September.[76]

Parade was an experiment in fusing jazz, classical music, and funk. Prince was trying to innovate, continually pushing the Minneapolis Sound beyond the boundaries of race and genre. From the settler period to the years between and after the world wars, the Minneapolis Sound mapped the territories of sonic possibility. But as *Los Angeles Times* critic Richard Cromelin observed, *Parade* was more of a "holding action" than a breakthrough.[77] Susan Rogers agreed. *Parade*, she argued, "is not the ultimate Prince album." Its sonic innovations made it "a great record," she said, but added, "It's not as important as the record that followed it."[78]

Chapter 14

MASTERPIECE OF MINNEAPOLIS

It was really a song a day coming out of the studio. You'd show up and he'd be playing another new brilliant song. . . . And just about every creative aspect of Prince the musician was represented and updated on *Sign o' the Times*.

—Alan Leeds

***Sign o' the Times* had a portion of almost everything he had to offer in the past, but all delivered with a feeling of total self-assurance. . . . That is . . . what is . . . "black" about *Sign o' the Times*.**

—Dave Hill

By the summer of 1986, Prince was moving the Minneapolis Sound in a new direction, but not as he had been working since forming the Revolution. He wanted to work solo once again, and this decision led to the Minneapolis Sound's apex with *Sign o' the Times*. The album, released in 1987, distills sounds Prince had been working on in the various Near North and South Side locations where he created the rooms that held his early compositions in Minneapolis. On this album, Prince pivoted from his heterodox sound toward what biographer Dave Hill calls the "black" sounds of funk and R&B

of his earlier works. This was primarily achieved by disbanding the Revolution in September 1986 during a very productive recording period with his collaborators Wendy Melvoin and Lisa Coleman. Dissolving the band opened a space of "total self-assurance" where he was "at ease with himself" and could compose without the influence of Wendy and Lisa.[1] After disbanding the group, he shelved the music he'd been making with them, conceived as a three-album set called *Dream Factory* and then *Crystal Ball*, along with his alter ego project *Camille*. *Sign o' the Times* emerged in the wake.[2]

Sign o' the Times was the creative highpoint of Prince's career and fully articulated what the Minneapolis Sound was capable of. As Alan Leeds argued, every creative aspect of Prince during this period is harnessed on *Sign o' the Times*. This masterpiece encompasses all the sounds Prince experimented with in the music rooms, basements, and studios in North and South Minneapolis and worked with between *For You* and *Around the World in a Day*. The album demonstrated more than any other Prince project that the Minneapolis Sound was the sonic equivalent of water. No matter what shape it took, what colors and tones it was inflected with, it would still be the Minneapolis Sound. Flexibility and representing pop music's diversity were the cornerstones of Prince's music. And that flexibility rested on Blackness. The Minneapolis Sound's capaciousness came from Black musicians who merged Black and white music in the 1960s and 1970s. Before them, the Minneapolis Sound was trapped in racially segregated genres. Their mixing made the musical form elastic and transgressive. And Prince deepened the mix. *Sign o' the Times* made the Minneapolis Sound prophetic because it represented a range of possibilities for music and social organization.

Ending a Revolution

After receiving a $10 million advance for *Under the Cherry Moon*, Prince found himself in a financial hole from the construction costs of his new Paisley Park recording complex in Chanhassen. These constraints spurred him and the Revolution to hit the road for the first time since the *Purple Rain* tour. After a brief tune-up performance at First Avenue, the band began a US tour at the Warfield Theater in San Francisco on May 14, 1986—the series of shows ended in August with a two-night stand in New York at Madison Square Garden.

The US tour was cut short in response to the bad reviews for *Under the Cherry Moon*. Instead, Prince and the Revolution headed to Europe, where critics and fans praised the album. They performed sold-out shows in London, Copenhagen, Paris, Rotterdam, Stockholm, Frankfurt, Brussels, Hamburg, and Essen. While in London, Prince began his tradition of playing after-shows at local clubs for fans. "Prince enjoyed the intimacy and immediacy that small clubs provided," said Alan Leeds.[3] And the band also enjoyed the creative possibilities they offered. Critics and fans praised the shows as the band's best work. Members of the band felt the same. Wendy Melvoin remarked, "Musically, it was magical. We were playing better than ever, going to places we'd never visited."[4]

Despite the excellent music onstage, offstage, Prince and the Revolution were coming apart at the seams. Prince was angry, and things were not good socially. The original members were hurt and upset at Prince's changes to the band. Percussionist Sheila E., saxophonists Alan Leeds and Atlanta Bliss, guitarist Miko Weaver, bassist Levi Seacer Jr., and keyboardists Matt Fink and Boni Boyer had been added to the group, and former bodyguards Wally Safford and Greg Brooks became dancers.[5] The tight pop-rock-funk band had become a funk soul revue in the style of Parliament Funkadelic. This change might have been a response to the critics and fans who felt his sound had drifted too far into white pop. Prince wanted to recapture his Black fanbase.[6] Whatever the reason, the tensions came to a head on the tour's final dates in Japan.

The band flew to Japan for four shows at the beginning of September. It was Prince's first time in Asia. By the time they arrived, the band was "already falling apart." Wendy felt, "He's gonna fire us." She knew "something was wrong."[7] This set the tone for an ominous conclusion that happened at the final show on September 9 at the Yokohama Stadium. Prince performed a heartfelt rendition of "Sometimes It Snows in April," thanked Wendy and Lisa for their performances, then smashed the cloud guitar from *Purple Rain* and another guitar on the stage. He had dinner with Wendy and Lisa when the band returned to Los Angeles. He told them, "You guys can't go where I'm going next." When his longtime collaborators protested, he told them, "I've got to let you go."[8]

After their firing, Brown Mark quit to pursue a solo career. Bobby Z was eventually let go, too. When the dust settled, only Matt Fink remained. The end of the Revolution was the end of a period of profound musical creativity and collaboration for Prince, the members of the band, and the Minneapolis Sound. Neither Prince nor the sound he popularized would again experience the kind of collaboration and sonic expansion they did with the Revolution. Although Prince grew the Minneapolis Sound in new ways between *For You* and *Dirty Mind*, it was between *Purple Rain* and *Parade* that it experienced its most extraordinary growth.

Being fired profoundly hurt Lisa and Wendy. They valued the collaborative spirit and the music they had created and wanted to continue working with Prince. Their icy relationship lasted for decades, finally thawing when

Wendy performed with Prince on the *Tavis Smiley Show* in 2004. Two years later, Wendy and Lisa reunited with Prince for a performance at the Brit Awards. In 2007, they worked with him on tracks for his album *Planet Earth*.[9]

Five Records

When Prince fired Wendy and Lisa, the two musicians thought, "But we just finished five records' worth of material."[10] That material has been the obsession of Prince fans and scholars for decades. Much of it was recorded between the release of *Parade* in 1986 and *Sign o' the Times* in 1987. Prince recorded a song a day and created concepts for albums just as quickly during this period. Lisa and Wendy were creating alongside him. Much of that music was put in the vault and would not emerge until decades later. One of the albums made during this time was *The Black Album*, one of the most bootlegged albums in history.[11] The emotionally dark material on it, sparked by the end of his relationship with Susannah Melvoin, led him to tell people not to buy the album.

After *Parade*, Prince began working on *Dream Factory*. Several songs were recorded in Prince's new home studio on Galpin Boulevard in Chanhassen. Prince created some of his most innovative music during this period. According to Eric Leeds, the music made before the end of the Revolution, during the *Dream Factory* period, was "some of the most wonderful stuff we ever did."[12] It included "The Ballad of Dorothy Parker," which appeared on *Sign o' the Times*, and "Colors," a one-and-a-half-minute guitar piece by Wendy. The soulful "Witness 4 the Prosecution" and the symphonic, ten-minute-long "Dream Factory" stayed in the vault for over a decade.[13] The rapid pace of Prince's recording after *Parade* expanded the album. By July, *Crystal Ball* had become a triple-album project.

Prince was also working on a project called *Camille*, the name given to a female tormentor in his song "Shockadelica" (released as the B-side of the *Sign o' the Times* single "If I Was Your Girlfriend"). On this project, he employed a recording technique used on "Erotic City," where he sped up his recorded vocals, altering their pitch and lending them a gendered ambiguity. This technique allowed him to sing from different gendered positions on songs like "If I Was Your Girlfriend." *Camille* may have been inspired by a nineteenth-century intersex person, Herculine Barbin, who was assigned a female gender at birth and also went by the name Camille (most often a female name in French but also sometimes given to males). The French poststructuralist Michel Foucault brought Barbin to broader attention in his 1980 critical biography, *Herculine Barbin*.[14] Prince used this alter ego on several songs during the post-*Parade* period.[15]

Prince's embodying Camille fit within the gender-fluid performance that he crafted from the moment he entered the realm of popular music. Thigh-high stockings, bikini briefs worn under a trench coat, eyeliner, feathered hair, crop tops, and high heels were outward markers of this fluidity. How Prince navigated gender aligned with the sonic geographic force of his Minneapolis Sound. His blending of the city's contested musical landscape to create a new kind of sound also resonated in his performance of gender. Since music was how he made sense of the world, it stands to reason that the fluid sounds he produced would find expression in other parts of his life. *Sign o' the Times* marks the moment when Prince merged his gender-bending outward expression with the sonic force of his music through Camille. Although all the *Camille* tracks have appeared on other albums over the years, no album like the one Prince envisioned has ever been released.[16]

The music on *Sign o' the Times* represented a new transition in the Minneapolis Sound. During the Revolution period, the sonic colors Wendy Melvoin and Lisa Coleman brought to each song buttressed an experimental period that took his sound in new directions. During the Revolution era, Prince was involved in a musical family that incorporated new kinds of music from geographies beyond Minneapolis. Once it ended, Prince returned to the sounds of his city, which informed the music he made between *For You* and *Dirty Mind*. "We wanted to be Prince's muses," said Wendy Melvoin, "but he felt like he needed to take back the initial thing that got him to where he was at."[17] According to Bobby Z, "I was getting the sense that we had become such a huge part of his everyday life and I think he was kind of growing a little tired of it."[18] Indeed, after years of learning from the Revolution, he had everything he needed to move forward without them.

That would take some effort, however. Not only would he have to reconstruct his musical identity in their absence, but he would also have to reconstitute his sound. What would the Minneapolis Sound be without Wendy, Lisa, and the band? Recording without the Revolution was a radical change in the sonic direction of the Minneapolis Sound. The tones, colors, harmonies, chord progressions, instrumentation, tempo, vocals, everything about the music he'd made since 1999 moved in a new direction. This meant shelving the music he'd made with Wendy and Lisa during and after *Parade*. Once Prince put these projects aside, he reconceived his musical identity and sound on *Sign o' the Times*.

Motivations

Sign o' the Times was motivated by at least two developments. The first was Warner Bros.' refusal to put out his triple album, which was first titled *Dream*

Factory and then *Crystal Ball*.[19] He stopped work on it in July 1986 and, in November, finished sequencing the album.[20] He sent his managers to Warner Bros. with copies of the album on cassette. He believed that it was his magnum opus. Warner's head, Mo Ostin, told him that the company could not release a twenty-two-track triple album given that his record sales since *Purple Rain* had flattened and the disaster of *Under the Cherry Moon* was still fresh in the public's mind. Ostin told Prince, "I respect your vision, but it just won't fly." He insisted that Prince make *Crystal Ball* a double album instead.[21] Prince fought Warner Bros. for weeks, but in the end, he reluctantly acquiesced. Prince felt that the company had committed the cardinal sin: getting in the way of his art. This began a protracted tension between Prince and Warner Bros. that ultimately ended their relationship.[22]

The second development involved sound. Since the creation of the Revolution, the tones and colors of the Minneapolis Sound had expanded beyond the city. The punk funk of *Dirty Mind*, the rock funk of *Controversy*, the electro-pop of *1999*, the Black and white pop of *Purple Rain*, and the experimental psychedelic orchestral funk and jazz of *Around the World in a Day* and *Parade* all demonstrate the sound's growth during this period. However, the pop music he composed became the target of critics who argued that the funk, soul, and R&B that had been key to his sound had been lost in his music with the Revolution. Given Prince's desire to be the crossover king, this period represents a pivot toward pop music and a predominantly white audience. Indeed, since *1999*, the tidal wave of white fans at his shows continued through the final Revolution projects, not to mention his increased presence on pop radio stations, which he wanted. Although his sound remained heterodox, the ever-increasing influence of rock, new wave, and classical music enabled in large part by his band, all of which made him a better composer, also pushed the Black music forms that made up the cornerstone of the Minneapolis Sound to the background. Prince wanted to return Black music to the forefront of his compositions. Susan Rogers said he was "hurt that R&B and soul radio weren't playing him as much as they used to," which explains why he didn't think the Revolution could go where he was going.[23]

Sign o' the Times grew out of this tension. Over a few weeks, Prince took the bloated *Crystal Ball* project and slimmed it to a more coherent one that put Black musical styles at its core. He submitted the album to Warner Bros., and the label released it on April 7, 1987. The sixteen-track album was recorded between Sunset Sound and Paisley Park, his home recording studio in Chanhassen. It comprises eleven songs he recorded solo before dissolving the Revolution, four final collaborations with the Revolution, and two from his vault.[24]

The album opens with the eponymous track he wrote in response to the explosion of the space shuttle *Challenger* in 1986 and the expanding AIDS crisis. The sound of "Sign o' the Times" is produced almost entirely from the Fairlight computer and the Linn-LM1 electronic drums. With few embellishments, this sparse, five-minute track with alto and spoken vocals was a unique sound for Prince. Though he'd experimented with electronic music before, the computerized sound of "Sign o' the Times" was new territory, somber, even melancholy, but funky, too.

"Play in the Sunshine" returns to the pre-Revolution era in content and form. Up-tempo Linn-LM1 drum rhythms, subtle bass lines, expressive electric guitar riffs, prominent synthesizers, and bits of piano sprinkled in make this poppy track a sonic throwback. The final minute and a half transitions to a melodic groove with a different rhythm from the first three and a half minutes. However, the distinct sections don't sound incongruent; they are like two sides of the same coin.

"Housequake" introduces Prince's alter ego, Camille. It is a relentless return to the funk of Prince's youth. Recorded just one day after the dissolution of the Revolution, the "bewitching" rhythm of "Housequake," anchored by the Linn-LM1, is more James Brown than Minneapolis Sound.[25] This is demonstrated by the slightly heavier bass line and the horn arrangements by Eric Leeds and Atlanta Bliss. But Prince still makes the Minneapolis Sound present by using a synthesizer to fill in the spaces between the horns, bass, percussion, guitar riffs, and the Fairlight. The vocal arrangements are varied, with Prince rapping (for the first time), talking, and singing, all in the altered voice of Camille. The backing vocalist is his trusted engineer, Susan Rogers.[26]

"The Ballad of Dorothy Parker" demonstrated that Prince was "one of the most eclectic artists in all of pop music."[27] Recorded in just a few takes, the song has a funky but subtle groove anchored by the seductive, asymmetrical rhythms from the Linn-LM1, funky bass lines, riffing guitars, and unobtrusive synthesizer chords. Prince's vocals shift between his falsetto and alto range, with backing by Susannah Melvoin.

The subtle funk of "Dorothy Parker" becomes hard-hitting on "It." Recorded at Sunset Sound during a fifteen-hour session, "It" fuses the Linn-LM1 with synthesizers, electric guitar riffs, hand claps, and the Fairlight CMI. Prince's multitracked backing vocals in different registers create a choir-like sound that recalls *For You*. At about the four-minute mark, the song turns into a funk jam rich in sonic embellishments.

If there ever were questions about the range of the Minneapolis Sound, "Starfish and Coffee" should put them to rest. Inspired by a story about Susannah Melvoin's childhood friend Cynthia Rose, "Starfish and Coffee" is a sparkly and melodic pop song driven by piano chords. Using the piano pedals to stretch the chords gives this track a robust sound despite the sparse instrumentation.

"Slow Love" was cowritten with Carole R. Davis, a former model Prince met in 1984 during the casting call for *Purple Rain*. The two became friends, and she pitched him a few of her songs, including "Slow Love." Prince liked it so much that they recorded it in his Kiowa Trail home studio that year. When Prince began creating *Sign o' the Times*, he pulled the song from his vault and added new sounds and vocals. The track's sound spans the period from *Purple Rain* to *Parade*, with appearances by Wendy Melvoin and Lisa Coleman. With a Clare Fischer orchestral arrangement, the slow-tempo track is driven by the horns played by Eric Leeds and Atlanta Bliss. Wendy Melvoin's electric guitar, piano, synthesizer, drums, Prince's guitar, and his falsetto vocals, backed by Wendy and Lisa, make the song a classic R&B ballad.

The opposite of "Slow Love's" tone is "Hot Thing." This track is deep in the tradition of Minneapolis funk, with its pronounced synthesizers, a mix of acoustic and programmed drums, and electric guitar in the background. Like several other tracks on the album, the song becomes an extended funk groove, with Eric Leeds's saxophone out front. "Forever in My Life" fuses lyrical vulnerability and pulsating, foot-tapping rhythm. Recorded at the Galpin home studio while Susannah was sleeping just a few floors above, the arrangement marries arpeggiated guitar lines to a funky drum beat. Prince's bluesy alto vocal makes "Forever in My Life" one funky love song.

The second disc opens with "U Got the Look," a duet with Scottish pop star Sheena Easton, heavy on rock with funk undertones. There are distorted and layered electric guitar riffs, soloing not heard since "Let's Go Crazy," and the electronic sounds of the Fairlight CMI. But Sheila E.'s percussion is the most robust sound on the track, with a sonic punch that elevates Prince's guitar solo while pushing him to sing in a higher range close to his alter ego, Camille.[28]

The next track, "If I Was Your Girlfriend," is in Camille's voice, and the lyrics imagine what it would be like to be her girlfriend. The vocals fit well with the song's Kate Bush–inspired arrangement. Prince loved Bush's 1985 hit "Running Up That Hill." (The song reentered the pop charts in 2022 after being used on the Netflix series *Stranger Things*.)[29] Prince programmed his Linn-LM1 drums, backed by sparse synthesizers and bass, and blended sounds from his guitar pedal. This created the string-like percussion, which enters during the bridge. But the continuous drum rhythm and the precise hi-hat slap give the song that Kate Bush sound. During the final chorus, singing gives way to talking, and the synthesizer and bass disappear, leaving only the languid funk of the drum beat and high-pitched vocals.

"I Could Never Take the Place of Your Man" was a rediscovered track Prince found in his vault while writing *Lovesexy*, his tenth album. First written in 1979, Prince rebuilt the song by replacing the drums with Linn-LM1 sounds, bass, synthesizers, and guitars. They create a buoyant poppy sound. "The Cross" is the album's rawest cut. Repeated E and A guitar chords open the track; a steady drum beat and guitar riffs enter at the one-minute-and-twenty-second mark. Then the tempo quickens, the guitar becomes more percussive and forceful, and the drums speed up. What began as folky becomes rock.

"It's Gonna Be a Beautiful Night" is Prince and the Revolution's last statement. Recorded in Paris during the *Parade* tour, this is Prince's first live recording. He reworked it at Sunset Sound, adding new vocals, strings, horns, and rap from Sheila E. The song is an extended funk groove with a Black church–inspired call-and-response between Prince and the audience.

It's hard to imagine a more fitting end to Prince's magnum opus than the sacred soul-drenched slow jam "Adore." *Rolling Stone* called it one of the greatest songs of all time.[30] Music critic Mike Joseph said it was "the love song to end all love songs."[31] For Black culture critic Touré, it was the central song in Prince's canon.[32] Susan Rogers said that Prince wrote the song as a "conscious effort to write for black radio" and to counter claims that he'd left his core fanbase for white audiences.[33] It worked. The song, which was never released as a single but got ample airplay on Black radio nationwide, helped reestablish Prince as an R&B artist.

"Adore" is built around a blend of acoustic and Linn-LM1 drums, electric guitar, horns by Eric Leeds and Atlanta Bliss, and digital sounds from the Fairlight, Margie, and Prophet VS computer instruments, which created the harp and sitar sounds that give the track its gospel flavor.[34] The tempo moves at a languid pace over a deep bass groove. The horns evoke the soul music of Ray Charles and Al Green, but the vocals provide the strongest links to that style. Prince's falsetto vocals might be the best of his career. Moving up and down in the register, he makes a case for committed love, being on Black radio again, and for "Adore" to be considered a love song for the ages.

Roots

Sign o' the Times confidently distills the musical forms Prince had been working with—funk, rock, R&B, jazz, soul, new wave, and punk. Critics universally praised it, comparing it to masterworks like the Rolling Stones' *Exile on Main Street* and the Beatles' *White Album*.[35] "Clearly this man is a genius," said Ted Mico of *Melody Maker*.[36] Martin Keller of the *Twin Cities Reader* said the album was so full of good material "you could choke on its bounty."[37] Kurt

Loder of *Rolling Stone* wrote that half of the album was "brilliant" and the other half "was better than ninety percent of what's on the radio."[38] Charles E. Rogers of the *Amsterdam News* observed that there "are so many exceptional cuts on this album it's difficult to choose which is best."[39]

Sign o' the Times's return to the musical roots that launched Prince's career and the modern Minneapolis Sound makes it powerful for many. Biographer Dave Hill put it succinctly: *Sign o' the Times* was Prince's "culturally most Black album."[40] For Dennis Hunt of the *Los Angeles Times*, *Sign o' the Times* was Prince returning "to his senses" musically.[41] For Martin Keller, the album was the brilliant "inventory" of the music that shaped his earlier career.[42] Richard Harrington of the *Washington Post* made the most salient point about the album's Blackness when he said it was a return to funk. Harrington argued that "much of the record seemed like a payback to black radio," which the critic felt Prince had moved away from during his Revolution period.[43] Harrington thought the centering of Black sound made the album "better than Prince's last two efforts." Another critic, Ted Mico, heard "hints of the Temptations, slices of Isaac Hayes, traces of Sly Stone."[44] Kurt Loder of *Rolling Stone* declared that *Sign o' the Times* was Prince reasserting "his mastery of . . . black funk idioms."[45]

The Black in *Sign o' the Times* might seem like a contradiction from the artist who famously said, "Don't make me black, my idols come from everywhere." But by 1987, Prince and the Minneapolis Sound had come full circle. Prince's diverse musical interests, which were always part of his life, expanded rapidly in the 1980s. Prince's first two albums, *For You* and *Prince*, were based mainly in Black sound—funk, R&B, disco—with tinges of rock and punk. As his musical interests grew, the roominess of the Minneapolis Sound facilitated that growth. The city's music, by incorporating a range of geographies, genres, and styles while still being sonically coherent, enabled Prince to follow any sounds he heard or imagined. Between *Dirty Mind* and *Parade*, Prince tested the limits of the Minneapolis Sound by incorporating punk, hard rock, electronic music, psychedelic rock, and classical music into his sound. In doing so, he produced a slew of hit records, became one of the most prominent musicians of the decade, and made the Minneapolis Sound the center of pop music. Doing this also moved the Black sound he'd always been invested in to the periphery.

The fact that critics talked about Prince's engagement with Black music on *Sign o' the Times* references the gift and curse of the Minneapolis Sound. The gift was that he could expand his sound in any desired direction. However, in doing this, Black sound lost a clear place in his compositions. But the self-assured *Sign o' the Times* drew "upon white styles" while offering "a kind of mystery tour through popular black music history."[46] This balance gave the album a cohesion that many of his previous albums didn't have, not even *Purple Rain*. Other albums demonstrated the Minneapolis Sound's sonic range, but none synthesized sounds like *Sign* did. The album showed the Minneapolis Sound could do it all: the hard rock and psychedelia of "U Got the Look," "It," and "Starfish and Coffee"; the James Brown, Sly Stone, and Parliament funk of "Housequake" and "It's Gonna Be a Beautiful Night"; the soul-drenched balladeering of "Slow Love" and "Adore"; the R&B of "If I Was Your Girlfriend" and "Strange Relationship"; the rock gospel of "The Cross"; and the pop of "I Could Never Take the Place of Your Man." It could do all this while still centering Black music.

Despite critical praise, US sales of the album were tepid. *Sign o' the Times* reached number six on the pop charts.[47] And the four singles it produced—"Sign o' the Times," "U Got the Look," "If I Was Your Girlfriend," and "I Could Never Take the Place of Your Man"—landed at number three, two, sixty-seven, and ten, respectively.[48] The European market, however, devoured the album. It flew off the shelves in the United Kingdom, Sweden, Denmark, and Germany. Warner Bros. hoped the album's popularity in Europe and a two-month tour there would boost sales.

Prince and his new band—percussionist Sheila E., saxophonists Alan Leeds and Atlanta Bliss, guitarist Miko Weaver, bassist Levi Saucer Jr., keyboardists Matt Fink and Boni Boyer, and dancer Cat Glover—began rehearsing for the tour at the Washington Avenue warehouse in Chanhassen.[49] The new band brought a harder-edged sound than the smoother Southern California style represented by Wendy Melvoin and Lisa Coleman.[50] This harder edge worked well in the funk review that made up his live show, which he debuted on March 27, 1987, at his favorite hometown venue, First Avenue, just two days before the album hit stores. This new sound and stage presence was evident from this first show. Prince never picked up the guitar; instead, he orchestrated the band while performing several James Brown–esque microphone tilts and splits. The set opened with the frenetic funk of "Housequake" and continued with five more *Sign* tracks that included "Hot Thing," "Strange Relationship," and "It's Gonna Be a Beautiful Night" alongside older hits like "Girls & Boys" and "Kiss." The public rehearsal ended after just over an hour, but it was a landmark. It would be two decades before he graced that stage again.

Sign o' the Times revealed its mastery of the Minneapolis Sound through the seamless and deft synthesizing of popular music wrapped in self-assured Blackness. The album used the city's fraught physical and musical apartheid to create a vibrant sonic landscape. Prince turned the social and sonic walls into bridges—pathways for musical innovation. The native son achieved this by leaning to the capaciousness of his sound. Between 1977 and 1987, Prince and the Minneapolis Sound experienced astonishing experimentation and growth unequaled by any other pop star. Prince's expansive tastes and the flexibility of the Minneapolis Sound created the space for him to incorporate funk, punk, rock, soul, classical, R&B, and jazz. Each album during this period—and, in some cases, each song—covered the range of Western popular music, all the while creating a sound that was a composite of them.

Sign o' the Times was the apex of this period of creative endeavor. The album mapped the sonic and social range of possibilities that only Minneapolis's out-of-touch reality could foster. The album also demonstrated that Minneapolis Sound is Western pop music's most sonically flexible and expressive musical form, and Prince is its best composer. This sound developed over a century and a half, beginning with the arrival of white settlers, the displacement of Indigenous people, and the establishment of Minneapolis. This city welcomed European immigrants but subjected Black people to an apartheid system. Prince revolutionized Minneapolis's sound by synthesizing the tension of the city's apartheid and its musicality. He used this contradiction to transform the city's racially distinct musical traditions into an expansive and geographically distinct funky sound.

Chapter 15

MOVING THE MINNEAPOLIS SOUND

Prince's hiatus from First Avenue was precipitated by completing the mega recording and performance space he'd worked on for two years in Chanhassen—Paisley Park. More than ending his long-standing run of shows at the former bus station, the building of Paisley Park moved the epicenter of the Minneapolis Sound from its downtown core to a largely rural plot of land on the outskirts of the city. This was the most significant change to the city's musical geography since Black migration, when the creation of the city's Black music scene moved the city's epicenter of music to the Near North and South Sides in the years after the First World War. The impetus for the move had begun years before. Since the early 1980s, Prince had been slowly moving his recording and rehearsals away from the city. As Morris Day said, Prince liked to create on the city's edge rather than be right in the mix. The other reason was to create a third space, away from the coasts, for high-quality audio and video recording.

Minneapolis had some good places to record, like the Moon Studios and Hothouse Studio. However, the city needed more high-quality multitrack recording facilities like Sunset Sound in Los Angeles (where Prince did lots of recording) and Electric Ladyland in New York. Minneapolis and the entire Midwest needed more recording studios like those found on the coasts. As a result, Prince recorded in an array of spaces—basements, local and out-of-state commercial studios, home studios, warehouses, and one concert venue. Many of these locations were in and around Minneapolis. None gave Prince consistent, high-quality output, nor were they always available, something Prince's herculean work ethic couldn't tolerate.

That changed when Paisley Park was built. The landmark compound was designed by architect Bret Thoeny, owner and president of Venice, California–based Boto Design. Thoeny was twenty-three when he met Prince in 1981 or 1982. Prince's management team hired him to build a home studio in Prince's first house on Kiowa Trail in Chanhassen. Thoeny found land that would become Paisley Park.[1] The windowless compound was built from scratch, wrapped in white aluminum and metal panels to match the austere Chanhassen landscape. Funded by *Purple Rain* money, the $10 million compound was spread out over 55,000 square feet. The entrance to the compound sets the tone for the entire building. Its large square extends at an angle, and a large glass pyramid is on top. "He loved pyramids," said Thoeny. Smaller pyramid skylights were used on offices throughout the complex.[2]

Paisley Park has three large recording studios. At 1,500 square feet, Studio A had a forty-eight-track recording console and a granite isolation room. The walls and floors were adorned with six tons of hand-cut Italian marble and cherry wood wall paneling. Studio B was 1,000 square feet with a thirty-six-track recording console. Purple aesthetics dominated the space, including purple shag carpet and a purple mural of the man himself. While it didn't have the same high-end touches as Studio A, Thoeny designed them so both studios could be wired to record sound in other parts of the compound.[3]

Studio C had the fewest bells and whistles and was used for audio and video recording. It was nearly the same size as Studio B, with a twenty-four-track recording console, video and photography equipment, and a rehearsal space with a mirror-reflected wall.[4]

The compound's crown jewel was the 12,400-square-foot soundstage. The massive structure is the performance space version of Antoni Gaudí's skyscraper-tall Barcelona basilica, the Sagrada Familia. The soundstage is as big as a concert hall and has "the height of an arena," with the "acoustics and intimacy of a theater."[5] The space is ample enough for trade shows and the filming of music videos.

One of the first projects Prince did at Paisley Park was to shoot theatrical scenes for his third film in as many years—a *Sign o' the Times* concert movie. The film largely emerged because Prince didn't want to tour the United States. Except for a few hit-and-run dates in a handful of cities, the *Sign o' the Times* tour was exclusively European, much to the dismay of his band and management. Prince created a concert film to give US fans access to the tour. The film is a composite of a show at Rotterdam mixed with sound overdubs and rerecorded performances from the Paisley Park soundstage. It is narratively held together with theatrical scenes on a soundstage spliced with musical performances. The film received critical praise; Martin Keller of the *Twin Cities Reader* called it "sexy, funny, seriously funky, and seriously cinematic."[6] Despite critical praise, the film was a commercial flop. It wasn't until decades later, after its reissue, that its uniqueness would be appreciated.

The multipurpose soundstage lived up to the hopes Prince had for it. Over the years, Prince used it to give concerts, shoot music videos, and even make another film, *Graffiti Bridge*, a sequel to *Purple Rain* with The Kid and Morris Day returning. (In another example of the size and flexibility of Paisley Park, in 2023, I attended a gala for the George Floyd Global Memorial. During the auction, I won a thirty-six-hour stay in the iconic Paisley playground.)

In addition to recording and video production spaces, Paisley Park also had rooms for costume-making and clothing, offices, production spaces, a pre-stage area, a salon suite, a kitchen, a bay to load and unload trucks, and sleeping rooms. The total compound streamlined and housed all elements of recording and performing in one place. "Back then, this wasn't done," remarked Thoeny. "Artists weren't building their own compounds; only record labels were. But Prince, Prince had the vision to have everything under one roof."[7]

A New Epicenter

Paisley Park gave Minneapolis and the Midwest a world-class audio and visual recording facility. The vast complex also shifted the epicenter of the Minneapolis Sound. Since its beginning, the Minneapolis Sound, in all its iterations, was created and performed along the city's riverbanks (east and west) and then within its urban core. Indeed, from the daily bugle calls at Fort Snelling to the Hutchinson Singers at Woodman Hole to the Minneapolis Auditorium to King Solomon's Mines to First Avenue, the Minneapolis Sound, for much of its history, lived near Minneapolis's core. But Prince changed the city's music geography when he moved his base of operation to the suburbs. The move had a greater impact even than the work of music educator Thaddeus Giddings in the early and middle twentieth century and more than the racism of the middle and late century. Prince altered in a decade what took over a century and a half to build.

The Minneapolis Sound, born in Minneapolis's fraught geography, expanded its influence far beyond the city's borders, yet it remains a testament to the city's intricate history and social dynamics. Despite, if not because of, this contentious musical geography, the city's musical landscape, stretching back to the building of Fort Snelling, was the perfect setting to establish Prince's creative sanctuary, Paisley Park, not only because of its simultaneous isolation and proximity to the city, which Prince liked, but also because Minneapolis musically marches to its own beat. Paisley Park was the physical expression of this ethos. This colossal recording complex, a testament to Prince's vision and influence, revolutionized the region's recording capabilities and provided a haven for musicians. Famous ones like Madonna and Stevie Wonder as well as local ones recorded there. For Prince, it was a place where his boundless creativity could thrive, shielded from the outside world.

The inaugural show at this new epicenter happened on New Year's Eve, 1987. The thirty-four-song set, which lasted just over two hours, culminated many of the sounds and moves that had carried Prince and the Minneapolis Sound to that point. His new ten-piece band, anchored by Sheila E. on drums, was the expression of funk that *Sign o' the Times* gave him access to. The performance was sexy, funny, and funky. The soundstage was packed with fans. With his horn section and the rhythmic percussion of Sheila E., along with dancer Cat Glover, Prince proved the wisdom of his decision to disband the Revolution because the band couldn't go where he was going musically. Extended funk jams accompanied older hits like "Little Red Corvette," "Erotic City," and "Let's Pretend We're Married," as well as new hits like "I Could Never Take the Place of Your Man," "Hot Thing," and "If I Was Your Girlfriend." Prince's band had become the funk revue that Wendy Melvoin didn't want it to be. Prince had discovered a new sound by returning to the music he grew up with, the sounds that filled late-night radio shows, basements, backrooms, and school music rooms on the Near North and South Sides of Minneapolis.

ACKNOWLEDGMENTS

Prince's Minneapolis is indebted to the support of many people. The labor it took to write this book owes a great debt to the librarians at the Gale Family Library at the Minnesota Historical Society in Saint Paul and the Hennepin County Library in downtown Minneapolis. For years, they answered my questions, set aside materials they thought would be helpful (they were right every time), suggested collections to explore, and offered encouragement and support. Without them, *Prince's Minneapolis* would have remained an idea. Thank you all for helping to make it a reality.

During the gestation period of *Prince's Minneapolis*, many people—family, friends, and colleagues—offered their support and encouragement. I want to give them a shout-out: Maddie Adelman, Janelle Austin, Molly Brigzy, Scott Brooks, Craig Calhoun, Charla Carrano, Jillian Childress, Brittany Corrales, George De Stefano, Marisa Duarte, Terrance Fasion, Camila Fojas, Mary Margret Fonow, Danial Fountainberry, Miki Garcia, K. T. Gipson, Jennifer Goldberg, Rudy Guvera, Kathy Hanna, Barbara Howard, Ben Hurlbut, I-Dee, Stanily James, Nancy Jurik, David King, Wei Li, Vera Lopez, Aaron Mallory, Jacques McKissick, Michael McQuarry, Brandon Ogbunu, Ersula Orr, Tracy Perkins, Deirdre Pheiffer, H. T. L. Quan, Francis Richards, Trisha Robinson, David Sailor, Stephanie Seguenio, Alicia Stewart, Dwan Thomas, Olga Viso, Karen Wesley, Rodney Wesley, *Places Journal*, the Humanities Institute at Arizona State University, the Cultural Geography specialty group of the American Association of Geographers, the bartenders at Casey Moore's Oyster House in Tempe (especially you, Robin), and Hanny's in downtown Phoenix, all the staff at L'Accolade in New York City, and many more I know I'm forgetting. Thanks, everyone, for your support.

This is my second time working with Dawn Durante, editorial director at the University of North Carolina Press. Dawn was the acquisition editor for my first book, *Spatializing Blackness*. In the acknowledgments, I mentioned that working with her was so rewarding that I wanted to do it again. *Prince's Minneapolis* is the realization of that wish. Dawn's support, vision, guidance, and editorial suggestions have contributed significantly to completing this project. The first was memorable; the second is special. Thank you, Dawn.

The faculty, staff, and students from the School of Social Transformation and the School of Geographical Sciences and Urban Planning at ASU—where I am a faculty member and where *Prince's Minneapolis* came to life—provided me with valuable space to work on the project. I want to thank both units for their support. Additionally, the Center for Work and Democracy at ASU and the ASU Art Museum supported this project. Thank you all for breathing life into it.

I want to extend a special shout-out to Christina Leijonhufvud. Closing this project without your enthusiastic support, care, and generosity would have been unimaginable. Thank you for being there when it mattered most.

Lastly, I want to thank my children, Ellison and Simone. You all sat with me through every part of this book and listened to me talk about Minneapolis and Prince for many years. You two were my most important sounding boards; I could not have written it without you.

My colleague and chosen family member, Gray Cavender, passed away while I was writing this book. Gray showed my family and me so much love. I dedicate *Prince's Minneapolis* to his memory.

NOTES

Introduction

1. “Prince on American Bandstand 1980,” YouTube, accessed August 29, 2023, https://www.youtube.com/watch?v=krEXzOEsP9I.

2. Connell and Gibson, *Sound Tracks*, 192.

3. Karlen, *This Thing Called Life*, 36.

4. Karlen, *This Thing Called Life*, 36.

5. Karlen, *This Thing Called Life*, 37.

6. Touré, “Alone in a World That’s So Cold.”

7. Tudahl, *Prince and the Parade*, 1.

8. Tudahl, *Prince and the Parade*, 609.

9. See Leyshon, Matless, and Revill, *Place of Music*; Carney, “Music Geography”; Shabazz, “Prince & Place”; Wood, Duffy, and Smith, “The Art of Doing (Geographies of) Music”; Feisst, “Music as Place, Place as Music”; and Krims, *Music and Urban Geography*.

10. Connell and Gibson, *Sound Tracks*, 192.

11. Hill, *Prince*.

12. Bream, “Local Producers Shoot Stars to the Top of the Charts,” *Star Tribune*, December 2, 1984, https://startribune.newspapers.com/article/star-tribune-the-minneapolis-sound/114001091/.

13. Lipsitz, *Footsteps in the Dark*, vii.

14. Lipsitz, *Footsteps in the Dark*, vii.

15. Lipsitz, *Footsteps in the Dark*, vii.

16. Foucault, *Discipline and Punish*.

17. See Foucault, “Nietzche, Genealogy, History.”

18. Rogers and Ogas, *This Is What It Sounds Like*.

Chapter 1

1. "Successfully Opened," *Minneapolis Tribune*, June 11, 1884.

2. Hennepin, *Description of Louisiana*, 99.

3. Hennepin, *Description of Louisiana*, 119.

4. Goodman, "'But They Differ from Us in Sound.'"

5. Attali, *Noise*, 6.

6. Fridley, "Fort Snelling," 178.

7. Beck, "Military Music," 85.

8. Beck, "Military Music," 48–50.

9. Beck, "Military Music," 89.

10. Beck, "Military Music," 89.

11. Beck, "Military Music," 83.

12. "Proceedings at Mass Temperance Convention," *Weekly Minnesotian*, September 14, 1853.

13. Turino, *Music as Social Life*, 2.

14. Canova, "Music in French Geography"; Wood et al., "Art of Doing (Geographies of) Music"; Harrison, "Factory Music"; Cohen, "Sounding Out the City"; Connell and Gibson, *Sound Tracks*.

15. Attali, *Noise*, 6.

16. Day and Wick, *Nordeast Minneapolis*, 29.

17. Rosie et al., *Minneapolis Music History*, 6.

18. The minstrel shows are important foreshadows. Coming upriver from the Confederate South, minstrel shows were the early canaries of southern musical culture that would impact Minneapolis. In the early twentieth century, the Mississippi River would serve as the most important location for the city's musical evolution. Chapman, "First Fifty Years of Music in Minneapolis."

19. See Chapman, "First Fifty Years of Music in Minneapolis"; and Rosie et al., *Minneapolis Music History*.

20. Rosie et al., *Minneapolis Music History*, 9; "Gossip about Town," *Minneapolis Tribune*, September 6, 1878.

21. These music halls included Barber's (opened in 1854), Bibbins (1855), Summer Garden Verity Theater, Elfelt's, Fletcher's, Scandinavian, Nedderley's, Chambers, and Edwards (1856), the Universalist Church (1857), Woodsman's (1857), Stanchfiels (1858), and Hawe (1859). See Chapman, "First Fifty Years of Music in Minneapolis," 3–5.

22. Woods, "Playhouse for Pioneers," 169.

23. Harrison's Hall was erected in 1862, the same year as the battle at Antietam. Harmonica Hall, built in 1865, was the rehearsal and performance space for the German Harmonica Society, an opulent, 700-seat facility with a painted ceiling. A second Harmonica Hall was built during Reconstruction in 1884 on Second Avenue South and Third Street. See Rosie et al., *Minneapolis Music History*, 10–11.

24. Woods, "Playhouse for Pioneers," 171.

25. On the night of its dedication, William D. Washburn, who amassed his fortune from milling, called the Pence opera house "one of the largest and most commodious and tastefully decorated audience rooms west of Chicago." See Woods, "Playhouse for Pioneers," 178.

26. "October Announcements," *Minneapolis Tribune*, 1871.

27. Rosie et al., *Minneapolis Music History*, 12.

28. Chapman, "First Fifty Years of Music in Minneapolis."

29. Chapman, "First Fifty Years of Music in Minneapolis," 10.

30. Maxwell, "History of American Protest Music."

31. Northwestern National Life Insurance Company, "Early Music in Minnesota," 4.

32. The Norwegian violinist G. G. Rostad performed there as well. This period also saw the return of another Scandinavian violinist, Ole Bull, from Norway. See Chapman, "First Fifty Years of Music in Minneapolis," 14.

33. Sacks, "Turning About Jim Crow"; Johnson, *Burnt Cork*, 24.

34. Johnson, *Burnt Cork*, 5–7.

35. Lott, *Love and Theft*.

36. Chapman, "First Fifty Years of Music in Minneapolis," 4.

37. Lott, *Love and Theft*.

38. Chapman, "First Fifty Years of Music in Minneapolis."

39. "La Rue's Minstrels," *Minneapolis Daily Tribune*, July 23, 1870, https://startribune.newspapers.com/article/star-tribune-la-rues-minstrel-show-penc/55301133.

40. "Record of a Day," *Minneapolis Tribune*, February 24, 1884.

41. "The Musical Festival," *Minneapolis Tribune*, May 18, 1884.

42. "The Grand Musical Pyramid," *Minneapolis Tribune*, May 24, 1884.

43. "Successfully Opened," *Minneapolis Tribune*, June 11, 1884.

44. Rosie et al., *Minneapolis Music History*, 7–8.

45. "Harp of Nature," *Minneapolis Tribune*, August 28, 1892.

46. Northwestern National Life Insurance Company, "Early Music in Minnesota," 10.

47. Attali, *Noise*, 1.

Chapter 2

1. "Father Hennepin Statue Is Dedicated in All Day Program in His Honor," *Minneapolis Star*, October 13, 1930, https://startribune.newspapers.com/article/the-minneapolis-star-hennepin/60530909/.

2. Kane, *Waterfall That Built a City*.

3. Kane, *Waterfall That Built a City*.

4. "Minnesota Firsts," *Minneapolis Star*, April 22, 1978.

5. Anfinson, "12,000 Years at St. Anthony Falls."

6. Anfinson, "12,000 Years at St. Anthony Falls"; Day and Wick, *Nordeast Minneapolis*, 15.

7. See Kane, *Waterfall That Built a City*; Anfinson, "12,000 Years at St. Anthony Falls"; Day and Wick, *Nordeast Minneapolis*.

8. Day and Wick, *Nordeast Minneapolis*, 18.

9. Kendi, *Stamped from the Beginning*; Dunbar-Ortiz, *Indigenous Peoples' History*.

10. Wills, *Boosters, Hustlers, and Speculators*, 13.

11. "Minnesota Firsts."

12. Day and Wick, *Nordeast Minneapolis*, 22.

13. Day and Wick, *Nordeast Minneapolis*, 24.

14. Day and Wick, *Nordeast Minneapolis*, 22; Lass, *Minnesota*, 94–96.

15. Wills, *Boosters, Hustlers, and Speculators*, 17.

16. Kane, *Waterfall That Built a City*, 7.

17. Day and Wick, *Nordeast Minneapolis*, 25.

18. Day and Wick, *Nordeast Minneapolis*, 22.

19. The massive fort was completed in 1822. Wills, *Boosters, Hustlers, and Speculators*, 22.

20. Wills, *Boosters, Hustlers, and Speculators*, 26.

21. Walker, *American City*, 13.

22. Wills, *Boosters, Hustlers, and Speculators*; Day and Wick, *Nordeast Minneapolis*, 27, 35.

23. The Dakota War of 1862, which lasted six weeks, cemented the marginalization of Native Americans in Minnesota. In the aftermath, the Dakota Indians were pushed to the far reaches of the state; many were interned at Fort Snelling, and thirty-eight were hanged in the southern Minnesota town of Mankato. See "US-Dakota War of 1862," Gale Family Library, Minnesota Historical Society, http://www.mnhs.org/fortsnelling/learn/us-dakota-war; Petersen, *Minneapolis Madams*; and Day and Wick, *Nordeast Minneapolis*.

24. Petersen, *Minneapolis Madams*, 3.

25. Petersen, *Minneapolis Madams*, 4.

26. Holmquist, *They Chose Minnesota*, 223.

27. Holmquist, *They Chose Minnesota*, 248.

28. Holmquist, *They Chose Minnesota*, 248.

29. Taylor, *African Americans in Minnesota*, 3.

30. Lehmen, *Slavery's Reach*, 6.

31. Lehmen, *Slavery's Reach*; Curt Brown, "Southern Slave Owner Helped Revive U," *Star Tribune*, June 19, 2016, https://startribune.newspapers.com/article/star-tribune-slavery-in-minnesota/64456942/.

32. Lehmen, *Slavery's Reach*, 6.

33. Spangler, *Negro in Minnesota*, 20.

34. Spangler, *Negro in Minnesota*, 21.

35. Spangler, *Negro in Minnesota*; Curt Brown, "She Found Her Freedom in Minnesota," *Star Tribune*, July 5, 2015, https://startribune.newspapers.com/article/star-tribune-slavery-in-mslp/64461633/.

36. Spangler, *Negro in Minnesota*, 38.

37. Spangler, *Negro in Minnesota*, 22.
38. Taylor, *African Americans in Minnesota*, 8–9.
39. Schmid, *Social Saga of Two Cities*, 172.
40. Taylor, *African Americans in Minnesota*, 8.
41. US Census Bureau, United States Voter Return, Precinct No. 3, State of Georgia.
42. US Census Bureau, Twelfth Census of the Unites States; Haines, "Social Explorer Dataset (SE), Census 1900."
43. This information is compiled from census data, marriage certificates, and other public records.
44. Kane, *Waterfall That Built a City*, 177.
45. Haines, "Social Explorer Dataset (SE), Census 1900"; Haines, "Social Explorer Dataset (SE), Census 1850."

Chapter 3

1. Blanche R. MacDonald, "Fifty Thousand Minneapolis Children Are Studying Music," *Minneapolis Sunday Tribune*, May 2, 1915, https://startribune.newspapers.com/article/star-tribune-50000-children-studying-mu/55988832/.
2. MacDonald, "Fifty Thousand Minneapolis Children."
3. Data obtained from "Minnesota Digital Newspaper Hub," Gale Family Library, Minnesota Historical Society, accessed July 23, 2025, https://newspapers.mnhs.org/jsp/PsSearchResults.jsp.
4. "What the Public Library Contains for Music Lovers," *Minneapolis Tribune*, May 20, 1906, https://startribune.newspapers.com/article/star-tribune-minneapolis-musial-matters/89638818/.
5. "Music education" referenced in newspapers, https://newspapers.mnhs.org/jsp/PsSearchResults.jsp.
6. Kane, *Waterfall That Built a City*, 144.
7. Kane, *Waterfall That Built a City*, 145.
8. Maynard, *Thaddeus P. Giddings*, 4.
9. Maynard, *Thaddeus P. Giddings*, 46.
10. Maynard, *Thaddeus P. Giddings*, 48.
11. Maynard, *Thaddeus P. Giddings*, 84–91.
12. Giddings, *School Music Teaching*, 1.
13. Walker, *American City*, 5.
14. Maynard, *Thaddeus P. Giddings*, 97.
15. Maynard, *Thaddeus P. Giddings*, 95.
16. Maynard, *Thaddeus P. Giddings*, 95.
17. Maynard, *Thaddeus P. Giddings*, 93.
18. Maynard, *Thaddeus P. Giddings*, 106–7.
19. Giddings, *Course in Music*.
20. MacDonald, "Fifty Thousand Minneapolis Children."

21. MacDonald, "Fifty Thousand Minneapolis Children."

22. Caryl B. Storrs, "T .P. Giddins Outlines Plans for Public School Music, 1916–17," *Minneapolis Sunday Tribune*, September 10, 1917.

Chapter 4

1. "Harriet Negro Trouble Is Taken to Police," *Minneapolis Morning Tribune*, December 29, 1909.

2. "Negro Residents Not Wanted," *Minneapolis Morning Tribune*, December 6, 1912, https://www.newspapers.com/article/star-tribune-white-residents-protest-bla/91810981/.

3. "Unwelcome Negro Neighbor Says He'll Make Trouble: Thomas Green Declares He Won't Run from Whatever Comes His Way," *Minneapolis Morning Tribune*, June 3, 1912, https://www.newspapers.com/article/star-tribune-thomas-h-green/92077780.

4. "Negro Question Causes Protest: Residents of Thirteenth Ward Object to Members of Race as Neighbors," *Minneapolis Morning Tribune*, November 16, 1920, https://startribune.newspapers.com/article/star-tribune-whites-protest-black-reside/91830496/.

5. Governor's Interracial Commission, *Negro Worker in Minnesota*; Governor's Interracial Commission, *Negro and His Home in Minnesota*; Spangler, *Negro in Minnesota*.

6. Governor's Interracial Commission, *Negro Worker in Minnesota*, 6.

7. Governor's Interracial Commission, *Negro and His Home in Minnesota*, 4.

8. Du Bois, *Black Reconstruction in America*.

9. Governor's Interracial Commission, *Negro Worker in Minnesota*.

10. Wilkerson, *Warmth of Other Suns*.

11. Wilkerson, *Warmth of Other Suns*.

12. Zschomler, "National Register of Historic Places," 11.

13. Zschomler, "National Register of Historic Places," 10.

14. "Movement of Jews out of the North Side and into St. Louis Park." Religions in Minnesota. Carleton College, n.d. https://religionsmn.carleton.edu/exhibits/show/st-louis-park-eruv-jewish/history/1800s/movement-of-jews-out-of-the-no.

15. Taylor, *African Americans in Minnesota*, 32.

16. Taylor, *African Americans in Minnesota*, 32.

17. Zschomler, "National Register of Historic Places," 10.

18. Zschomler, "National Register of Historic Places," 10.

19. Zschomler, "National Register of Historic Places," 10.

20. Hahn and Tiebert, *Rise of Prince*, 52.

21. "Negro Family's Coming Arouses Neighborhood," *Minneapolis Morning Tribune*, June 1, 1912, https://startribune.newspapers.com/image/181090600/?clipping_id=91811278&fcfToken=eyJhbGciOiJIUzI1NiIsInR5cCI6IkpXVCJ9.eyJmcmVlLXZpZXctaWQiOjE4MTA5MDYwMCwiaWF0IjoxNjkxNDUzNzUzLCJleHAiOjE2OTE1NDAxNTN9.wi4GshQ9MeSYcjHuMowZniF1PQqRDeLdNN9pejFmX1c.

22. "Negro Family's Coming Arouses Neighborhood."

23. "Negro Family's Coming Arouses Neighborhood."

24. "Unwelcome Negro Neighbor."

25. "Harriet Negro Trouble Is Taken to Police."

26. "Negro Minister Is Under Exclusion Ban," *Minneapolis Morning Tribune*, December 28, 1909, https://startribune.newspapers.com/article/star-tribune-prospect-park-protest-black/92071002/.

27. "'Spite House' Embargo Nears Peaceful Ending," *Minneapolis Morning Tribune*, January 10, 1910, https://startribune.newspapers.com/article/star-tribune-elder-house/91904901/; "Malone May Get His Price," *Minneapolis Morning Tribune*, January 5, 1910, https://startribune.newspapers.com/article/star-tribune-elder-gets-money-to-move/91904773/.

28. "Negro Question Causes Protest."

29. "Home Stoned in Race Row," *Minneapolis Tribune*, July 15, 1931, https://www.newspapers.com/article/star-tribune-black-home-stoned-by-white/93242386/.

30. "Home Stoned in Race Row."

31. Mapping Prejudice, home page, https://mappingprejudice.umn.edu.

32. As of 2025, 42,000 covenants have been found by the diligent researchers at the Mapping Prejudice project, which is uncovering how racism shaped the city's geography. Since 2016, this team of geographers, historians, digital humanists, and community activists has been mapping Minneapolis's racist past with an eye to racially restrictive covenants. The project's research shows in vivid and often painful detail how covenants cut Blacks off from vast amounts of housing and pushed them North and South. See Mapping Prejudice, home page.

33. Bergin, *Jim Crow of the North.*

34. Bergin, *Jim Crow of the North.*

35. Bergin, *Jim Crow of the North.*

36. Mapping Prejudice, home page.

37. Curt Brown, "Pioneering Lawyer Faced Familiar Issues," *Star Tribune*, October 4, 2015, https://startribune.newspapers.com/image/250739053/?terms=Lena%20Smith&match=1.

38. Oral history interviews of the Minnesota Black History Project, 1970–1975 David Taylor, interview with Nellie Stone Johnson (transcript), July 15, 1975, Gale Family Library, Minnesota Historical Society.https://collections.mnhs.org/search/collections/record/72653725-1f59-4743-8ded-7fe44ed2360d?.

39. Davis, *Women, Race and Class.*

40. The Wheatley House was also a resource for Black male fraternal clubs like the Elks Club and the Masons. Black men were not in favor of having a woman-led organization offer services. But once these fraternal organizations bumped up against the reality of racism, which truncated their ability to rent rooms to hold meetings, they changed their minds about the Wheatley House. See Hase, "W. Gertrude Brown's Struggle."

41. Governor's Interracial Commission, *Negro and His Home in Minnesota*, 22–25.

42. Mapping Inequality, "Minneapolis."

43. Mapping Inequality, "Minneapolis."

44. Bergin, *Jim Crow of the North.*

45. Spangler, *Negro in Minnesota*, 107.

46. Governor's Interracial Commission, *Negro Worker in Minnesota*, 21.

47. Governor's Interracial Commission, *Negro Worker in Minnesota*.

48. Governor's Interracial Commission, *Negro Worker in Minnesota*, 33.

49. Zschomler, "National Register of Historic Places," 10.

50. Zschomler, "National Register of Historic Places," 10; Sirdar and Kronick, "Tilsenbilt Homes Historic District."

51. This and the previous two subheadings are from the Langston Hughes poem "Harlem." Hughes, *Collected Poems of Langston Hughes*, 426.

52. Frank Murray, "Home Owners Urge Changes in Freeway," *Minneapolis Star*, March 14, 1957, https://startribune.newspapers.com/image/178825992/.

53. Frank Murray, "Expert OKs City Freeway Plans, Urges Few Changes," *Minneapolis Star*, February 18, 1957, https://www.newspapers.com/article/the-minneapolis-star-i-35/94206497/; Pike, "Old Southside Minneapolis."

54. Pike, "Old Southside Minneapolis."

55. Zschomler, "National Register of Historic Places," 12.

56. Tillman Durdin, Clayton Knowles, Milton Bracker, and A. H. Raskin, "Negro Equality in 'Unsegregated' North Still Long Way Off," *Minneapolis Sunday Tribune*, May 13, 1956, https://www.newspapers.com/article/star-tribune-black-life-and-housing-stor/93235283/.

57. Sirdar and Kronick, "Tilsenbilt Homes Historic District."

58. Sirdar and Kronick, "Tilsenbilt Homes Historic District."

59. Zschomler, "National Register of Historic Places," 12.

60. Piepenbring, *Prince*, 79.

61. Zschomler, "National Register of Historic Places," 14.

62. Spangler, *Negro in Minnesota*, 143.

63. Piepenbring, *Prince*, 85.

64. Piepenbring, *Prince*, 85.

65. Piepenbring, *Prince*, 92.

66. Richard P. Kleeman, "School Segregation No Stranger in City," *Minneapolis Sunday Tribune*, June 23, 1963, https://startribune.newspapers.com/article/star-tribune-school-segregation/96261529/.

67. Kleeman, "School Segregation No Stranger in City."

68. Zschomler, "National Register of Historic Places," 17.

69. Thorne, *Prince*, 1.

70. Shabazz, "Minneapolis's 'Long, Hot Summer' of '67."

71. Shabazz, "Minneapolis's 'Long, Hot Summer' of '67."

Chapter 5

1. Brothers, *Louis Armstrong's New Orleans*, 272.

2. St. Paul was Minnesota's first jazz city. The music took hold there before moving west to Minneapolis in large part because St. Paul had a more robust port and was the state capital. Goetting, *Joined at the Hip*, 5.

3. "City News: Phinney's Band Concert," *Minneapolis Journal*," July 7, 1899, https://startribune.newspapers.com/article/the-minneapolis-journal-ragtime-on-a-ste/97323940/.

4. Brothers, *Louis Armstrong's New Orleans*.

5. Goetting, *Joined at the Hip*, 5–6; Brothers, *Louis Armstrong's New Orleans*, 272.

6. Goetting, *Joined at the Hip*, 9.

7. Goetting, *Joined at the Hip*, 7–8.

8. Gelly, *Being Prez*, 1.

9. Gelly, *Being Prez*, 4–6.

10. Gelly, *Being Prez*, 13, 19, 34, 140.

11. Goetting, *Joined at the Hip*, 9–10.

12. Burns, *Jazz*.

13. Battle, ":Music During the Great Depression," 5.

14. Stahl, *Five Star Minstrel Book*.

15. Cruz, "Blackface Minstrelsy in Minnesota."

16. See Morrison, *Blacksound*.

17. See Crutcher, *Tremé*; Horn, *Jazz and Justice*.

18. Shiffer, *King of Skid Row*; Goetting, *Joined at the Hip*, 18; Rosie et al., *Minneapolis Music History*, 8.

19. Goetting, *Joined at the Hip*, 61; Bob Murphy, "Dizzy Gillespie Orpheum," *Minneapolis Sunday Tribune*, November 22, 1953, https://startribune.newspapers.com/article/star-tribune-dizzy-gillespie-orpheum/98573528/.

20. Goetting, *Joined at the Hip*.

21. Goetting, *Joined at the Hip*, 61–64.

22. Goetting, *Joined at the Hip*, 58; *Minneapolis Tribune*, "One More Arrest Made in Prospect in Gambling Drive," December 3, 1938.

23. Goetting, *Joined at the Hip*.

24. Goetting, *Joined at the Hip*, 20.

25. Rosie et al., *Minneapolis Music History*; Goetting, *Joined at the Hip*.

26. Rosie et al., *Minneapolis Music History*, 57.

27. Fisher, "Caucasian Storms Harlem," 393.

28. Daniels, "North Side Jazz," 104.

29. Earl Wingard, "Kid Cann Says: I've Sold Out and Am Leaving Town," *Minneapolis Sunday Tribune*, January 27, 1952, https://startribune.newspapers.com/article/star-tribune-kid-cann/100657613/.

30. Daniels, "North Side Jazz," 98.

31. "Gateway Vainly Awaits Sleuths," *Minnesota Daily Star*, August 17, 1921, https://startribune.newspapers.com/article/the-minneapolis-star-north-side-black-an/100137976/.

32. "New Charges Name Wilson," *Minneapolis Journal*, January 13, 1932, https://startribune.newspapers.com/article/the-minneapolis-journal-ben-wilson-nort/100138789/; "U.S. Court to Try North Side Mayor," *Minneapolis Tribune*, February 21, 1932, https://startribune.newspapers.com/article/star-tribune-ben-wilson-arrested/100139141/; "North Side 'Mayor' Draws 90 Day Term," *Minneapolis*

Star, July 12, 1932, https://startribune.newspapers.com/article/the-minneapolis-star-ben-wilson-sentence/100139230/; Wingard, "Kid Cann Says."

33. "Mayor Revokes Dance License," *Minneapolis Star*, January 13, 1932, https://startribune.newspapers.com/article/the-minneapolis-star-club-dance-license/100138945/.

34. "Mayor Revokes Dance License."

35. Don Morrison, "Wreckers Write Finis to Clef Club: Dust of Jazz Era Rises from Ancient Building," *Minneapolis Sunday Tribune*, November 10, 1957, https://startribune.newspapers.com/article/star-tribune-clef-club-part-1/98710339/.

36. Don Morrison, "Clef Club Jam Sessions Wound Up at Dawn," *Star Tribune*, November 10, 1957.

37. Morrison, "Clef Club Jam Sessions."

38. "89 Arrested in Clef Club Morals Raid," *Minneapolis Star Journal*, January 15, 1942, https://startribune.newspapers.com/article/the-minneapolis-star-clef-club-raid-2/98713873/.

39. Rosie et al., *Minneapolis Music History*, 27.

40. Rosie et al., *Minneapolis Music History*, 22–23.

41. Hase, "W. Gertrude Brown's Struggle," 130.

42. Rosie et al., *Minneapolis Music History*, 23.

43. Twin Cities Music Highlights, "Labor Temple."

44. Twin Cities Music Highlights, "Labor Temple."

45. Rosie et al., *Minneapolis Music History*.

46. Twin Cities Music Highlights, "Nacirema Club."

Chapter 6

1. Day and Ritz, *On Time*, 35.

2. Rosie et al., *Minneapolis Music History*, 37–41.

3. Hahn and Tiebert, *Rise of Prince*, 59.

4. Alan Leeds, former tour manager of James Brown and Prince's manager during the 1980s, said that his understanding of John was that of a "frustrated jazz man." See Touré, "Alone in a World That's So Cold."

5. Karlen, *This Thing Called Life*, 68.

6. Day and Ritz, *On Time*, 28; Karlen, *This Thing Called Life*, 67.

7. Karlen, *This Thing Called Life*, 66.

8. Honeywell is a Minneapolis-based company technology and manufacturing company. During the Vietnam War, John was among several employees who worked on the "Honeywell Project," a military contract under which the company made the deadly chemical weapon napalm. According to Prince, when he was in sixth grade his inebriated father told him, "I make hell, boy, I make it rain orange hell." Karlen, *This Thing Called Life*, 70.

9. Hahn and Tiebert, *Rise of Prince*, 59; *Purple Rain*.

10. Karlen, *This Thing Called Life*, 68.

11. Karlen, *This Thing Called Life*, 68–70.

12. Hahn and Tiebert, *Rise of Prince*, 58–59; Morton, *Prince*, 19; Karlen, *This Thing Called Life*, 58–59. In what seems like another personal episode replayed in the movie *Purple Rain*, Prince recounts, "One night [I] remember hearing them arguing & it got physical. At some point my mother crashed in 2 my bedroom and grabbed me. She was crying but managed to smile & said, 'tell Ur father 2 b nice 2 me.' She held me up as a buffer so that he wouldn't fight with her anymore." Piepenbring, *Prince*, 97.

13. Hahn and Tiebert, *Rise of Prince*, 59.

14. Piepenbring, *Prince*; Hahn and Tiebert, *Rise of Prince*; Thorne, *Prince*.

15. Thorne, *Prince*; Hahn and Tiebert, *Rise of Prince*, 53; Touré, "Alone in a World That's So Cold."

16. Day and Ritz, *On Time*, 28.

17. Touré, "Alone in a World That's So Cold."

18. According to Karlen, Prince may have felt obligated to give John credit: "It's not my fault that the biggest accomplishment, besides thieving credits from me for songs he didn't write, was to be the only Negro at Honeywell." Karlen, *This Thing Called Life*, 75.

19. Prince resented the association of his name with the family dog. "Any-one call me 'Prince' growing up," he told Karlen, "I punched hard fast and dirty because I had to. Nobody calls me a dog's name." Karlen, *This Thing Called Life*, 74. Also see Hahn and Tiebert, *Rise of Prince*, 53.

20. Hahn and Tiebert, *Rise of Prince*, 56.

21. Hahn and Tiebert, *Rise of Prince*, 53.

22. In a 1991 interview on the newsmagazine television show *A Current Affair*, John L. Nelson explained his reason for giving Prince his name: "I wanted him to do everything that I really intended to do." *A Current Affair*, "Interview with John L. Nelson," https://www.youtube.com/watch?v=Byr-TaMiogA&t=82s.

23. Swensson, *Got to Be Something Here*, 1–3.

24. Ripani, *New Blue Music*, 17.

25. McCourt, "Bright Lights, Big City," 1.

26. Goosman, *Group Harmony*, 11; Ripani, *New Blue Music*, 17–19; McCourt, "Bright Lights, Big City," 2–3.

27. Goosman, *Group Harmony*.

28. Lydon, *Ray Charles*, 13–16.

29. Lydon, *Ray Charles*.

30. Lydon, *Ray Charles*.

31. Ripani, *New Blue Music*, 67.

32. Rosie et al., *Minneapolis Music History*, 37; Swensson, *Got to Be Something Here*, 3; Hill, *Prince*.

33. Swensson, *Got to Be Something Here*, 1–3.

34. Swensson, *Got to Be Something Here*, 3, 95.

35. Swensson, *Got to Be Something Here*, 8.

36. Swensson, *Got to Be Something Here*, 8.

37. Piepenbring, *Prince*, 98.

38. "Rock 'DJ' Purs on KDWB Radio All Night," *Minneapolis Star*, May 6, 1969; Twin City Music Highlights, "Brief History of Radio"; Billboard, "Billboard Hot 100."

39. Will Jones, "Food for Jazz Buffs," *Star Tribune*, December 10, 1964.

40. Jones, "Food for Jazz Buffs."

41. "Weekend Girlwatching Tip," *Star Tribune*, July 30, 1965.

42. Swensson, *Got to Be Something Here*, 58.

43. Swensson, *Got to Be Something Here*, 58–61.

44. Swensson, *Got to Be Something Here*, 26–27.

45. Swensson, *Got to Be Something Here*, 70.

46. Swensson, *Got to Be Something Here*, 70.

47. Swensson, *Got to Be Something Here*, 72.

48. Swensson, *Got to Be Something Here*, 71–73; David Nimmer, "Proposal: Suspend License of Bar," *Minneapolis Star*, November 7, 1968, https://startribune.newspapers.com/article/the-minneapolis-star-king-solomons-mine/104225479/; "Woman Faced with Marijuana Charge," *Minneapolis Star*, October 18, 1968. Twenty-year-old Janice Brantly, a Black woman who lived along Plymouth Avenue, was charged with unlawful possession and held on $2,500 bail. This kind of heavy-handed response to simple weed possession demonstrates that Minneapolis was using its state power to disrupt King Solomon's Mines and punish its patrons for any and all infractions.

49. Nimmer, "Proposal."

50. Swensson, *Got to Be Something Here*, 76.

51. "What's Doing," *Minneapolis Tribune*, February 9, 1969, https://startribune.newspapers.com/article/star-tribune-king-solons-mines-closed-an/104225986.

52. "Here's what the white club owners are worried about. See, more black men are going with white women. In fact, there are white women who go to a club and try to be chosen by a black man in the band. But the ordinary Joe who comes from Bemidji or Rochester and sees a black man with a white woman gets upset. . . . I know what the police say when a club gets closed for some reason or another. There's always a reason. They just say we just can't have trouble spots." Allan Holbert, "Black Bands Abound, but Not in Downtown Night Clubs," *Minneapolis Tribune*, November 9, 1969.

53. While the Regal was popular, it also had lots of fights. The bar was also known as "The Bucket of Blood," presumably from the blood spilled during altercations. See Gilbert, Foss, and Sigelman, "Twin Cities Funk & Soul," 29.

54. Allan Holbert, "Clubs: A Study in Black and White," *Minneapolis Tribune*, August 18, 1968, https://startribune.newspapers.com/article/star-tribune-black-night-clubs-case-stud/105476320/; Gilbert, Foss, and Sigelman, "Twin Cities Funk & Soul."

55. Gilbert, Foss, and Sigelman, "Twin Cities Funk & Soul," 30.

56. Rosie et al., *Minneapolis Music History*, 41; Swensson, *Got to Be Something Here*, 7.

57. Petry, "Sights, Sounds, and Soul."

58. McBride, *Kill 'Em and Leave*, 7.

59. Ripani, *New Blue Music*, 80.

60. Hahn and Tiebert, *Rise of Prince*, 63; Gilbert, Foss, and Sigelman, "Twin Cities Funk & Soul."

61. Shabazz, "Minneapolis's 'Long, Hot Summer' of '67."

62. Zschomler, "National Register of Historic Places," 17.

63. According to reviews of the show, Brown dealt with numerous interruptions, including audience members roaming around, unreliable microphone connections, and erratic spotlight functionality. See Peggy J. Murrell, "Shows Sizzle, Fizzle," *Minneapolis Star*, December 1, 1969. For Prince dancing onstage, see Hahn and Tiebert, *Rise of Prince*, 63.

64. Ripani, *New Blue Music*.

65. As much as Prince loved Sly, he also found Stone's life to be a "cautionary tale" about the impact of drugs on making music. "I'm not going to be like Sly," he told bandmates. Ripani, *New Blue Music*, 9.

66. Zschomler, "National Register of Historic Places," 18.

67. Piepenbring, *Prince*, 99.

68. Zschomler, "National Register of Historic Places," 18.

Chapter 7

1. Mills, "Read Prince's First Inverview."

2. "Today's Personality," *Minneapolis Morning Tribune*, October 19, 1940, https://startribune.newspapers.com/image/?clipping_id=105602899&fcfToken=eyJhbGciOiJIUzI1NiIsInR5cCI6IkpXVCJ9.eyJmcmVlLXZpZXctaWQiOjE4MjY4NDE2NCwiaWF0IjoxNjU3OTEyODkwLCJleHAiOjE2NTc5OTkyOTB9.CMz_5b_PndbKZVFY4pLaNTg41_z9nCY5omXWURmNoC4.

3. "Slap at 'Soft Teaching' Wins Giddings a Rebuke," *Minneapolis Morning Tribune*, May 13, 1942, https://startribune.newspapers.com/article/star-tribune-giddings-on-soft-teaching/105602410.

4. Giddings, *School Music Teaching*, 3.

5. Zellie, "Minneapolis Public Schools Historic Context Study," 2.

6. Zellie, "Minneapolis Public Schools Historic Context Study," 2.

7. Zellie, "Minneapolis Public Schools Historic Context Study," 3.

8. Zellie, "Minneapolis Public Schools Historic Context Study," 2.

9. Zellie, "Minneapolis Public Schools Historic Context Study," 4.

10. Zellie, "Minneapolis Public Schools Historic Context Study," 2–3.

11. Prince and Andre may have originally met when they were "seven or eight" at a Seventh-Day Adventist Church. See Karlen, *This Thing Called Life*, 94. They also may have met as children when their dads performed at another neighborhood church. See Swensson, *Got to Be Something Here*, 151.

12. Swensson, *Got to Be Something Here*, 149–50.

13. Hahn and Tiebert, *Rise of Prince*, 68.

14. Hahn and Tiebert, *Rise of Prince*, 68.

15. Swensson, *Got to Be Something Here*, 148–51.

16. Zschomler, "National Register of Historic Places," 20.

17. Swensson, *Got to Be Something Here*, 148–51; Hill, *Prince*, 17; Zschomler, "National Register of Historic Places," 20.

18. Zschomler, "National Register of Historic Places," 20.

19. Swensson, *Got to Be Something Here*, 157.

20. Minneapolis Public School Board, "Lincoln Junior High."

21. Minneapolis Public School Board, "Lincoln Junior High."

22. Amsterdam Academy of Architecture, *Music, Space and Architecture*, 31.

23. No records have been found that give insight into the classes Prince took and the time he spent in those rooms. We do know that he had one of the following music teachers: Don H. Brinkman (whom he had in high school), Thomas W. Doggett, Franklin Gaymond, or Margaret J. Noring. The classes most likely took place in the third-floor music room. No evidence has been found that Prince was in the orchestra or school band.

24. Zschomler, "National Register of Historic Places," 15.

25. Hahn and Tiebert, *Rise of Prince*, 71.

26. Karlen, *This Thing Called Life*, 109.

27. Karlen, *This Thing Called Life*, 110.

28. Hahn and Tiebert, *Rise of Prince*, 71.

29. Minutaglio, "Prince's First Music Teacher."

30. Minutaglio, "Prince's First Music Teacher"; Hahn and Tiebert, *Rise of Prince*, 71.

31. Minneapolis Public School Board, "Bryant Junior High School."

32. Touré, "Honey, I'm Rich on Personality."

33. Touré, "Alone in a World That's So Cold."

34. Childhood friend Morris Day, who lived near Prince, was there the night John kicked him out. According to Day, Prince "snuck a girl up to his room . . . and John found out about it. He told Prince, 'Put your key on the table.'" Touré, "Alone in a World That's So Cold." Also see Hahn and Tiebert, *Rise of Prince*, 68–69.

35. Zschomler, "National Register of Historic Places," 18; Piepenbring, *Prince*, 109.

36. "When I was in Andre's basement. I found out about myself then. The only reason I stayed was because of Andre's mother." Lizie, *Prince on Prince*. Also see Touré, "Alone in a World That's So Cold."

37. Swensson, *Got to Be Something Here*, 158.

38. Hahn and Tiebert, *Rise of Prince*; Zschomler, "National Register of Historic Places," 18.

39. Touré, "Alone in a World That's So Cold"; Touré, "Honey, I'm Rich on Personality."

40. Karlen, *This Thing Called Life*, 117; Dan Freeborn, "Composer's Key Instrument Is Her Computer Keyboard," *Star Tribune*, September 24, 1992, https://startribune.newspapers.com/article/star-tribune-katherine-doepke/106504991/.

41. Karlen, *This Thing Called Life*, 118.

42. Zellie, "Minneapolis Public Schools Historic Context Study," 3–4; Minneapolis Public School System, "Central Senior High School," 329.

43. Wilkins, *Aesthetics of Equity*.

Chapter 8

1. Matrix Basement System, "An Insight into the History of Basements."
2. Hahn and Tiebert, *Rise of Prince*, 69.
3. Hahn and Tiebert, *Rise of Prince*, 70.
4. Swensson, *Got to Be Something Here*, 165.
5. Swensson, *Got to Be Something Here*, 178.
6. Day and Ritz, *On Time*, 18–19.
7. Day and Ritz, *On Time*, 27.
8. Day and Ritz, *On Time*, 18.
9. Day and Ritz, *On Time*, 18.
10. Day and Ritz, *On Time*, 18.
11. Day and Ritz, *On Time*, 20–21.
12. Andy Sturdevant, "Out of the Basement: North Minneapolis Bands of the '70s," *MINNPOST*, February 8, 2017, https://www.minnpost.com/stroll/2017/02/out-basement-north-minneapolis-bands-70s/.
13. Hahn and Tiebert, *Rise of Prince*, 175–76.
14. Swensson, *Got to Be Something Here*, 175–76.
15. Sturdevant, "Out of the Basement"; Swensson, *Got to Be Something Here*, 178.
16. Swensson, *Got to Be Something Here*, 145.
17. Swensson, *Got to Be Something Here*, 145.
18. Paulsen, "Black Power," 9–11.
19. "No More Sixth Avenue North," *Minneapolis Spokesman*, September 10, 1937.
20. "Mayor Naftalin Defends Action on Disorder," *Minneapolis Spokesman*, August 11, 1966.
21. Paulsen, "Black Power," 1.
22. Swensson, *Got to Be Something Here*, 135.
23. Swensson, *Got to Be Something Here*, 135.
24. Swensson, *Got to Be Something Here*, 134–35.
25. Swensson, *Got to Be Something Here*, 136.
26. Swensson, *Got to Be Something Here*, 136.
27. Swensson, *Got to Be Something Here*, 141.
28. Swensson, *Got to Be Something Here*, 141.
29. Swensson, *Got to Be Something Here*, 144.
30. Willie, *If You See Me*.
31. Willie, *If You See Me*, 126–27.
32. Willie, *If You See Me*, 125–26.
33. Willie, *If You See Me*, 129.

34. Willie, *If You See Me*, 130.

35. Years later, Wendell and Dale would play in Prince's jazz-fusion side project, Madhouse. See Willie, *If You See Me*, 128; and Thorne, *Prince*, 19.

36. Willie, *If You See Me*, 138.

37. Thorne, *Prince*, 19.

38. Willie, *If You See Me*, 128.

39. Willie, *If You See Me*, 134.

40. Willie, *If You See Me*, 141.

41. Campbell, "ASI Records."

42. Zschomler, "National Register of Historic Places," 25.

43. Thorne, *Prince*, 24.

44. Hill, *Prince*, 29.

45. Moon, "History of Moon Sound Studios"; Hill, *Prince*, 29.

46. Thorne, *Prince*, 22.

47. Thorne, *Prince*, 22.

48. Thorne, *Prince*, 23.

49. According to Moon, Daughtry wasn't happy with this deal and neither were the other members of the band. Thorne, *Prince*, 23.

50. Day and Ritz, *On Time*, 30.

51. Day and Ritz, *On Time*, 30–35.

52. Hill, *Prince*, 31; Thorne, *Prince*, 30.

53. Hill, *Prince*, 31.

54. Hill, *Prince*, 33.

55. Hahn and Tiebert, *Rise of Prince*, 95; Zschomler, "National Register of Historic Places," 28; Hill, *Prince*, 39.

56. Zschomler, "National Register of Historic Places," 29.

57. Hill, *Prince*, 39.

58. Willie, *If You See Me*, 143–44.

59. Day and Ritz, *On Time*, 33.

60. Hahn and Tiebert, *Rise of Prince*, 97.

61. Hill, *Prince*, 40.

62. Hahn and Tiebert, *Rise of Prince*, 99; Willie, *If You See Me*, 146.

63. Hahn and Tiebert, *Rise of Prince*, 99.

64. Hahn and Tiebert, *Rise of Prince*, 100–101.

65. Zschomler, "National Register of Historic Places," 30.

Chapter 9

1. Collins, "Complicated Fun."

2. Atkins, "At Home in the Heart of the City," 287.

3. Atkins, "At Home in the Heart of the City," 287–91.

4. Atkins, "At Home in the Heart of the City," 295.

5. Martin and Goddard, *Impact of Urban Renewal*, 13.

6. Millett, "Ghost of the Gateway," 114.

7. Martin and Goddard, *Impact of Urban Renewal*, 1; Carmona, *Haussmann*.

8. Martin and Goddard, *Impact of Urban Renewal*, 1.

9. Millett, "Ghost of the Gateway," 113.

10. Atkins, "At Home in the Heart of the City," 302–3.

11. Atkins, "At Home in the Heart of the City."

12. "Spenders Prefer Suburbs to Downtown," *Minneapolis Star*, March 31, 1970, https://startribune.newspapers.com/article/the-minneapolis-star-shopper-prefer-subu/108681172/.

13. Dick Gordon, "Vike Fan Planned Survey on City Stadium," *Minneapolis Star*, January 11, 1972, https://startribune.newspapers.com/image/190028978; "An Open Letter to Other Taxpayers in Minneapolis About the Proposed Domed Stadium," *Minneapolis Tribune*, January 14, 1973, https://www.newspapers.com/article/star-tribune-open-letter-about-the-metro/108680869.

14. "An Open Letter to Other Taxpayers."

15. Rosie et al., *Minneapolis Music History*.

16. Rosie et al., *Minneapolis Music History*, 62.

17. Rosie et al., *Minneapolis Music History*, 64.

18. Riemenschnieider, *First Avenue*, 14.

19. Riemenschnieider, *First Avenue*.

20. Marshall Fine, "Depot Planning Bad, Show Good," *Minneapolis Star*, April 6, 1970, https://startribune.newspapers.com/article/the-minneapolis-star-opening-night-at-th/109074174/.

21. Riemenschnieider, *First Avenue*, 31.

22. Riemenschnieider, *First Avenue*, 32.

23. Riemenschnieider, *First Avenue*, 40–41.

24. Collins, "Complicated Fun," 44.

25. Riemenschnieider, *First Avenue*, 52–53.

26. Collins, "Complicated Fun," 23.

27. Collins, "Complicated Fun," 23.

28. Collins, "Complicated Fun," 123.

29. Collins, "Complicated Fun," 123.

30. Collins, "Complicated Fun," 123; Jon Bream, "Street-Wise DeVille Making Local Debut," *Minneapolis Star*, July 29, 1977; Jon Bream, "Lang's Humor Accents His Guitar," *Minneapolis Star*, October 21, 1977.

31. Collins, "Complicated Fun," 132.

32. Riemenschnieider, *First Avenue*, 61.

33. Riemenschnieider, *First Avenue*, 62–63.

34. Riemenschnieider, *First Avenue*, 64.

35. Riemenschnieider, *First Avenue*, 68.

36. Riemenschnieider, *First Avenue*, 70.

37. Alam, "First Avenue & 7th Street Entry."

38. Riemenschnieider, *First Avenue*, 88.

39. Jon Bream, "Prince Gives City Claim to a Star," *Minneapolis Star Journal*, March 10, 1981, https://startribune.newspapers.com/article/the-minneapolis-star-princes-first-show/110830240/.

40. Shabazz, "Prince & Place."

Chapter 10

1. Tim Carr, "Prince: A One-Man Band and a Whole Chorus, Too," *Minneapolis Tribune*, April 30, 1978, https://startribune.newspapers.com/article/star-tribune-prince-on-learning-music/107793334/.
2. Carr, "Prince."
3. Lizie, *Prince FAQ*, 17.
4. Hill, *Prince*, 49.
5. Day and Ritz, *On Time*, 51.
6. Piepenbring, *Prince*, 154–55; Thorne, *Prince*, 30.
7. Day and Ritz, *On Time*, 36.
8. Clerc, *Prince: All the Songs*, 26.
9. Clerc, *Prince: All the Songs*, 27.
10. Miller, *Segregating Sound*.
11. Lizie, *Prince FAQ*, 18; Piepenbring, *Prince*, 164–65.
12. Thorne, *Prince*, 44; Willie, *If You See Me*, 163.
13. Hahn and Tiebert, *Rise of Prince*, 113; Thorne, *Prince*, 41.
14. Willie, *If You See Me*, 164.
15. Hill, *Prince*, 55.
16. Hahn and Tiebert, *Rise of Prince*, 115.
17. Huw, *Prince: A Purple Reign*.
18. Hahn and Tiebert, *Rise of Prince*, 115.
19. Willie, *If You See Me*, 166.
20. Thorne, *Prince*, 44; Hahn and Tiebert, *Rise of Prince*, 115.
21. Hahn and Tiebert, *Rise of Prince*, 115.
22. Morton, *Prince*, 37.
23. Willie, *If You See Me*, 176.
24. Willie, *If You See Me*, 176.
25. Willie, *If You See Me*, 171–78.
26. Piepenbring, *Prince*, 170.
27. Willie, *If You See Me*, 183.
28. Lizie, *Prince FAQ*, 18.
29. Lizie, *Prince FAQ*, 18.
30. Hahn and Tiebert, *Rise of Prince*, 129.
31. Hahn and Tiebert, *Rise of Prince*.
32. Hahn and Tiebert, *Rise of Prince*.
33. Connie Johnson, "Prince: A Regal Pop Mixture," *Los Angeles Times*, February 17, 1980.

34. Michael Wells, "Count, Uke, Arl—Move over! Here's Prince!" *Amsterdam News* (New York), March 29, 1980.

35. Morton, *Prince*, 58.

36. Morton, *Prince*, 58.

37. Hill, *Prince*, 76.

38. Piepenbring, *Prince*.

39. Clerc, *Prince: All the Songs*, 42.

40. Laura Fissinger, "Princely Pleasures and Passions," *Twin Cities Reader*, March 19, 1981, https://startribune.newspapers.com/article/twin-cities-reader-prince-at-sams/115792701/.

41. Adler, "Will the Little Girls Understand?"

42. Thorne, *Prince*, 61.

43. Lizie, *Prince FAQ*, 20.

44. Lizie, *Prince FAQ*, 20–21.

45. Thorne, *Prince*, 57.

46. Thorne, *Prince*, 59–60.

47. Lizie, *Prince FAQ*, 30; Swensson, "Prince: The Story of 1999."

48. Hill, *Prince*.

49. Britt Robson, "New Jack Cities," *City Pages*, May 8, 1991.

50. John Bream, "Local Producers Shoot Stars to the Top of the Charts," *Star Tribune*, December 2, 1984, https://startribune.newspapers.com/article/star-tribune-the-minneapolis-sound/114001091/; Hill, *Prince*; Shabazz, "How Prince Introduced Us to the 'Minneapolis Sound'"; Swensson, *Got to Be Something Here*, xiii; Chris Riemenschnieider, "The Sound of Genius," *Star Tribune*, May 1, 2026; Martin Keller, "What's in a Sound?," *Twin Cities Reader*, September 4, 1985, https://startribune.newspapers.com/article/twin-cities-reader-the-minneapolis-sound/114000579/; Jack Spencer, "Seeing Purple: Minneapolis R&B and Funk's Formative Years Celebrated in New Compilation," *City Pages*, December 4, 2013, https://startribune.newspapers.com/article/city-pages-purple-snow/114916884/.

51. Huw, *Prince: A Purple Reign*; Randy Anderson, "Pop du Jour '81," *City Pages*, January 14, 1982.

52. The punk funk of *Dirty Mind* has been a subject of inquiry for many Prince biographers and scholars. Many have argued that bandmates Dez Dickerson and Bobby Z influenced the sounds that made up *Dirty Mind*. It's without question that bandmates were feeding Prince new music, like that of the Cars. Rather than dispute this argument, I want to suggest that this influence came from more than just bandmates. Bobby Z and Dez were indeed putting records on his turntable that helped him develop *Dirty Mind*. But Prince was also a student of the Minneapolis music scene. He was going to clubs and listening to local talent. See Hahn and Tiebert, *Rise of Prince*.

53. Bream, "Local Producers."

54. Spencer, "Seeing Purple."

55. Clerc, *Prince: All the Songs*, 46.

56. Hill, *Prince*, 93.

57. Holden, "Rock: Prince at Palladium," *New York Times*, December 4, 1981.

58. Gene Gillis, "Prince's 'Dirty Mind' Delights Palladium Crowd," *Amsterdam News* (New York), December 12, 1981.

59. Gene Gillis, "Prince: Tomorrow's Black Superstar!," *Amsterdam News*, January 24, 1981.

60. Gillis, "Prince's 'Dirty Mind.'"

61. Karlen, *This Thing Called Life*.

62. Robert Palmer, "Is Prince Leading Music to a True Biracism?," *New York Times*, December 2, 1981.

63. Palmer, "Is Prince Leading Music to a True Biracism?"

64. Adler, "Will the Little Girls Understand?"

65. Adler, "Will the Little Girls Understand?"

66. Tucker, "Dirty Mind."

Chapter 11

1. Riemenschnieider, *First Avenue*, 87.

2. Riemenschnieider, *First Avenue*, 87.

3. Riemenschnieider, *First Avenue*, 87.

4. Riemenschnieider, *First Avenue*, 87.

5. Riemenschnieider, *First Avenue*, 88.

6. Riemenschnieider, *First Avenue*, 88.

7. Lizie, *Prince FAQ*, 23.

8. Day and Ritz, *On Time*, 46.

9. Day and Ritz, *On Time*, 56.

10. Day and Ritz, *On Time*, 56.

11. Day and Ritz, *On Time*, 57.

12. Day and Ritz, *On Time*, 57.

13. Day and Ritz, *On Time*, 59; Tudahl, *Prince and the Purple Rain Era Studio Sessions*.

14. Lizie, *Prince FAQ*, 56.

15. Day and Ritz, *On Time*, 57.

16. Riemenschnieider, *First Avenue*, 88.

17. Lizie, *Prince FAQ*, 22.

18. Randy Anderson, "Pop du Jour '81," *City Pages*, January 14, 1982.

19. Michael Anthony, "Prince: Developing Strengths, Exploiting Weaknesses," *Minneapolis Tribune*, November 20, 1981, https://startribune.newspapers.com/article/star-tribune-controversy/115276246/.

20. Holden, "Controversy."

21. Hill, *Prince*, 98.

22. Hill, *Prince*, 98.

23. Lizie, *Prince FAQ*, 20; Thorne, *Prince*, 70.

24. Hahn and Tiebert, *Rise of Prince*, 174.

25. Riemenschnieider, *First Avenue*, 98.

26. Hahn and Tiebert, *Rise of Prince*, 161–62.
27. Riemenschnieider, *First Avenue*, 94–95.
28. Thorne, *Prince*, 67.
29. Light, *Let's Go Crazy*, 42–43; Swensson, "Prince: The Story of 1999."
30. Swensson, "Prince: The Story of 1999."
31. Day and Ritz, *On Time*, 73–74.
32. Day and Ritz, *On Time*, 76–77.
33. Hahn and Tiebert, *Rise of Prince*, 189.
34. Hill, *Prince*, 115.
35. Swensson, "Prince: The Story of 1999."
36. Swensson, "Prince: The Story of 1999"; Lizie, *Prince FAQ*, 21, 48.
37. Swensson, "Prince: The Story of 1999."
38. Lizie, *Prince FAQ*, 49, 108.
39. Clerc, *Prince: All the Songs*, 76, 77, 80, 81.
40. Clerc, *Prince: All the Songs*, 68.
41. Lizie, *Prince FAQ*, 55.
42. Christensen, "What Is New Wave Music?"
43. A dance created by actor Alfonso Ribiero that he performed as his character, Carlton, on the Will Smith television series *Fresh Prince of Bel-Air*.
44. Jon Bream, "Prince's New Album Motivates Body, Middles Brain," *Minneapolis Tribune*, November 28, 1982, https://www.newspapers.com/article/star-tribune-prince-1999/116114761/.
45. Tudahl, *Prince and the Purple Rain Era Studio Sessions*, 1.
46. Tudahl, *Prince and the Purple Rain Era Studio Sessions*, 5–7.
47. Tudahl, *Prince and the Purple Rain Era Studio Sessions*, 10.
48. Tudahl, *Prince and the Purple Rain Era Studio Sessions*, 11.
49. Tudahl, *Prince and the Purple Rain Era Studio Sessions*, 11.
50. Tudahl, *Prince and the Purple Rain Era Studio Sessions*, 21.
51. Tudahl, *Prince and the Purple Rain Era Studio Sessions*, 22.
52. Tudahl, *Prince and the Purple Rain Era Studio Sessions*, 23.
53. Tudahl, *Prince and the Purple Rain Era Studio Sessions*, 23.
54. During their time as bandmates in the Revolution, Prince was not particularly interested in Wendy and Lisa's sexuality; instead, he focused on their musical talents. His unwavering dedication to music and the desire to be understood solely through it made Wendy and Lisa's sexuality seem unimportant. He insisted that the only aspect of his life he wanted others to grasp was his music, allowing Wendy and Lisa the same freedom. While he alluded to their sexuality in the opening lines of "Computer Blue," Prince prioritized their musicianship. Throughout their time together, he never acknowledged the sexual orientation publicly. The only instance of Prince referencing their sexuality occurred when he became a Jehovah's Witness in the early 2000s. When Wendy and Lisa approached him during this period to revive the Revolution and tour, according to Melvoin, Prince "declined because of my homosexuality and the fact I'm half-Jewish." However, he changed his stance just a few years later. He performed with Melvoin at the Brit Awards and

on the *Tavis Smiley Show* and collaborated with them on *The Rainbow Children* album. Prince's change of heart might suggest that despite his religious beliefs, music still took precedence. See Hoffman, "Prince's Life as a Jehovah's Witness."

55. Tudahl, *Prince and the Purple Rain Era Studio Sessions*, 23.
56. Thorne, *Prince*, 66.
57. Light, *Let's Go Crazy*; Thorne, *Prince*.
58. Light, *Let's Go Crazy*, 64.
59. Tudahl, *Prince and the Purple Rain Era Studio Sessions*, 80.
60. Tudahl, *Prince and the Purple Rain Era Studio Sessions*, 35.
61. Tudahl, *Prince and the Purple Rain Era Studio Sessions*, 29.
62. Tudahl, *Prince and the Purple Rain Era Studio Sessions*, 39.
63. Day and Ritz, *On Time*.
64. Hahn and Tiebert, *Rise of Prince*.
65. Light, *Let's Go Crazy*.

Chapter 12

1. Light, *Let's Go Crazy*, 193.
2. Light, *Let's Go Crazy*, 193.
3. Light, *Let's Go Crazy*, 193.
4. Light, *Let's Go Crazy*, 51.
5. Light, *Let's Go Crazy*, 54.
6. Light, *Let's Go Crazy*, 55.
7. Light, *Let's Go Crazy*, 55.
8. Light, *Let's Go Crazy*, 58.
9. Light, *Let's Go Crazy*, 52, 58.
10. Piepenbring, *Prince*, 218–21.
11. Light, *Let's Go Crazy*, 68.
12. Tudahl, *Prince and the Purple Rain Studio Era Sessions*, 100–101.
13. Light, *Let's Go Crazy*.
14. Light, *Let's Go Crazy*, 111–12.
15. Light, *Let's Go Crazy*, 74.
16. "6651 Highway 7," St. Louis Park (MN) Historical Society, accessed July 23, 2025, https://slphistory.org/hwy76651/.
17. Wendy pushed the Minneapolis Sound away from the electronic dance music that dominated *Dirty Mind*, *Controversy*, and *1999*, and toward more complex chord progressions and suspended notes. See Tudahl, *Prince and the Purple Rain Studio Era Sessions*; and Light, *Let's Go Crazy*.
18. Tudahl, *Prince and the Purple Rain Studio Era Sessions*, 105.
19. Tudahl, *Prince and the Purple Rain Studio Era Sessions*, 104.
20. Tudahl, *Prince and the Purple Rain Studio Era Sessions*, 105.
21. Tudahl, *Prince and the Purple Rain Studio Era Sessions*, 105.
22. Tudahl, *Prince and the Purple Rain Studio Era Sessions*, 105.

23. During the summer of 1983, the warehouse was a multipurpose space where Prince collaborated with band members, recorded songs, took acting lessons, and began laying the foundation for his new Minneapolis Sound. It was also where he and the Revolution rehearsed for a benefit concert at First Avenue. The Minnesota Dance Theater was strapped for cash, and its future was hanging in the balance. Even more immediately for the band, executives from Warner Bros. were in the audience. They wanted to hear the music for the movie they'd given seed money. If the songs slapped, funding was guaranteed. If they fell flat, hope for the movie would be all but extinguished.

24. Tudahl, *Prince and the Purple Rain Studio Era Sessions*, 106.

25. Tudahl, *Prince and the Purple Rain Studio Era Sessions*, 105.

26. Tudahl, *Prince and the Purple Rain Studio Era Sessions*, 125.

27. Tudahl, *Prince and the Purple Rain Studio Era Sessions*, 128–29.

28. Day and Ritz, *On Time*, 87.

29. Jon Bream, "Prince Gives City Claim to a Star," *Minneapolis Star Journal*, March 10, 1981, https://startribune.newspapers.com/article/the-minneapolis-star-princes-first-show/110830240/.

30. After *Purple Rain* was released in 1984, First Avenue honored its hometown hero. In the 1990s, it was painted over with a grunge-inspired mural. In 2000, the stars returned and were again updated in 2010. There are 425 stars on the facade; most are musicians who played at the venue (Outkast, Babies in Toyland, Har Mar Superstar), and some are political figures like John Lewis and George Floyd. See Marsh, "First Avenue's Star Wall."

31. Riemenschnieider, *First Avenue*, 88.

32. Riemenschnieider, *First Avenue*, 88.

33. Light, *Let's Go Crazy*, 1.

34. Light, *Let's Go Crazy*, 2.

35. Tudahl, *Prince and the Purple Rain Studio Era Sessions*, 122.

36. Tudahl, *Prince and the Purple Rain Studio Era Sessions*, 121–22.

37. Light, *Let's Go Crazy*, 108.

38. Day and Ritz, *On Time*, 85.

39. Light, *Let's Go Crazy*, 108.

40. "Purple Rain" was recorded live at the August 3 event with overdubs, and some editing done at Sunset Sound with Peggy McCreary and David Leonard. And at Sunset Sound, Susan Rogers recorded "Take Me with You," "The Beautiful Ones," and "When Doves Cry." "I Would Die 4 U," "Baby I'm a Star," and "Purple Rain" were recorded live at the August 3 show at First Avenue by sound engineers David Leonard, David Rivkin, David Hewitt, and Kooster McAllister.

41. Light, *Let's Go Crazy*, 147.

42. Tudahl, *Prince and the Purple Rain Studio Era Sessions*, 283.

43. Tudahl, *Prince and the Purple Rain Studio Era Sessions*, 283.

44. Tudahl, *Prince and the Purple Rain Studio Era Sessions*, 287.

45. Tudahl, *Prince and the Purple Rain Studio Era Sessions*, 287.

46. Light, *Let's Go Crazy*, 148.

47. Light, *Let's Go Crazy*, 148.

48. Tudahl, *Prince and the Purple Rain Era Studio Sessions*, 322–23.

49. Tate, "Stagolee Versus the Proper Negro."

50. Light, *Let's Go Crazy*, 152.

51. Lizie, *Prince FAQ*, 59.

52. Lizie, *Prince FAQ*, 57–59; Light, *Let's Go Crazy*, 171.

53. Light, *Let's Go Crazy*, 146.

54. The only other time Prince had a colead in vocals were Lisa Colman's and Dez Dickerson's vocals on "1999."

55. Tudahl, *Prince and the Purple Rain Studio Era Sessions*, 243.

56. Clerc, *Prince: All the Songs*, 96.

57. Tudahl, *Prince and the Purple Rain Studio Era Sessions*, 246.

58. Clerc, *Prince: All the Songs*, 100.

59. Clerc, *Prince: All the Songs*, 100.

60. Tudahl, *Prince and the Purple Rain Studio Era Sessions*, 164.

61. Tudahl, *Prince and the Purple Rain Studio Era Sessions*, 164.

62. Palmer, "Prince Creates a Winner with 'Purple Rain,'" *New York Times*, July 22, 1984.

63. Loder, "Purple Rain (Soundtrack)."

64. Jon Bream, "Prince's Soundtrack Album Pelts Listener, but Seems Tame," *Minneapolis Star Tribune*, July 8, 1984, https://startribune.newspapers.com/article/star-tribune-purple-rain-album-review/119551585/.

65. Day and Ritz, *On Time*.

66. Light, *Let's Go Crazy*, 173.

67. Light, *Let's Go Crazy*, 173.

68. Light, *Let's Go Crazy*, 181.

69. Light, *Let's Go Crazy*, 182.

70. Shelia Benson, "Prince's Poignant, Hot *Purple Rain*," *Los Angeles Times*, July 27, 1984.

71. Charles E. Rogers, "Prince's 'Purple' Reign Supreme," *Amsterdam News* (New York), July 28, 1984.

72. Light, *Let's Go Crazy*, 176.

73. Rogers, "Prince's 'Purple' Reign Supreme."

74. Jon Bream, "City, Too, Is Star of 'Purple Rain,'" *Minneapolis Star Tribune*, July 27, 1984, https://www.newspapers.com/article/star-tribune-purple-rain-and-minneapolis/119555658/.

75. Light, *Let's Go Crazy*, 171.

76. Tate, "Stagolee Versus the Proper Negro."

Chapter 13

1. Tudahl, *Prince and the Parade*, 343.

2. Charles E. Rogers, "Prince's 'Purple' Reign Supreme," *Amsterdam News* (New York), July 28, 1984.

3. Tudahl, *Prince and the Parade*, 3.
4. Tudahl, *Prince and the Purple Rain Studio Era Sessions*, 476.
5. Tudahl, *Prince and the Parade*, 79.
6. Jensen, "Weird, Wonderful, World of Prince."
7. Thorne, *Prince*, 118.
8. Tudahl, *Prince and the Purple Rain Studio Era Sessions*, 471.
9. Tudahl, *Prince and the Purple Rain Studio Era Sessions*, 364.
10. Tudahl, *Prince and the Parade*, 29.
11. Thorne, *Prince*, 126.
12. Tudahl, *Prince and the Purple Rain Studio Era Sessions*, 379.
13. Hahn and Tiebert, *Rise of Prince*, 234.
14. Thorne, *Prince*, 118.
15. Hahn and Tiebert, *Rise of Prince*, 234.
16. Thorne, *Prince*, 119.
17. Tudahl, *Prince and the Purple Rain Studio Era Sessions*, 403.
18. Tudahl, *Prince and the Purple Rain Studio Era Sessions*, 417.
19. Tudahl, *Prince and the Purple Rain Studio Era Sessions*, 315.
20. Tudahl, *Prince and the Purple Rain Studio Era Sessions*, 365, 384.
21. Tudahl, *Prince and the Parade*, 55.
22. Tudahl, *Prince and the Purple Rain Studio Era Sessions*, 384–85.
23. Lizie, *Prince FAQ*, 60.
24. Lizie, *Prince FAQ*, 60.
25. Draper, *Prince*.
26. Martin Keller, "What's in a Sound?," *Twin Cities Reader*, September 4, 1985, https://startribune.newspapers.com/article/twin-cities-reader-the-minneapolis-sound/114000579/.
27. Harrington, "Prince, Back on Track."
28. Martin Keller, "Riding in Prince's Time Machine: A Passage to Paisley Park," *Twin Cities Reader*, April 24, 1985.
29. Tudahl, *Prince and the Parade*, 271.
30. Tudahl, *Prince and the Parade*, 272.
31. Draper, *Prince*, 64.
32. Cox News Service, "Prince Says He'll Quit Stage after Concert in Orange Bowl," *Minneapolis Star Tribune*, April 4, 1985, https://startribune.newspapers.com/article/star-tribune-prince-pausing-stage-perfor/122640160/.
33. Draper, *Prince*, 64.
34. Thorne, *Prince*, 132.
35. Zan Stewart, "He Arranges, Composes, Performs Fischer: A Renaissance Man of Music," *Los Angeles Times*, May 14, 1987.
36. Thorne, *Prince*, 133.
37. Thorne, *Prince*, 134.
38. Thorne, *Prince*, 135.
39. Hahn and Tiebert, *Rise of Prince*, 254.
40. Tudahl, *Prince and the Parade*, 129.
41. Tudahl, *Prince and the Parade*, 127.

42. Tudahl, *Prince and the Parade*, 127.
43. Tudahl, *Prince and the Parade*, 144.
44. Tudahl, *Prince and the Parade*, 177.
45. Tudahl, *Prince and the Parade*, 90.
46. Tudahl, *Prince and the Parade*, 92.
47. Tudahl, *Prince and the Parade*, 92.
48. Tudahl, *Prince and the Parade*, 166.
49. Tudahl, *Prince and the Parade*, 166.
50. Draper, *Prince*, 65.
51. Draper, *Prince*, 66.
52. *Parade* was recorded between Sunset in L.A. and the Washington Avenue warehouse. Prince and the Revolution cut much of it in L.A. over marathon sessions. By early May, Prince had most of the tracks completed. They included "Wendy's Parade," "New Position," "I Wonder U," "Under the Cherry Moon," "Sometimes It Snows in April," and a song he'd given away to Browmark's new band, Maserati, called "Kiss." He would reclaim the song after David Rivkin and Maserati worked on it, arguing, "It's too good for you all." Tudahl, *Prince and the Parade*, 112.
53. Draper, *Prince*, 67.
54. Draper, *Prince*, 67.
55. Swensson, "Story of *Sign o' the Times*, Episode 2."
56. Hahn and Tiebert, *Rise of Prince*, 270–71.
57. Swensson, "Story of *Sign o' the Times*, Episode 2."
58. Tudahl, *Prince and the Parade*, 261.
59. Tudahl, *Prince and the Parade*, 260–63.
60. Tudahl, *Prince and the Parade*, 263.
61. Tudahl, *Prince and the Parade*, 264–65.
62. Clerc, *Prince: All the Songs*, 121; Tudahl, *Prince and the Parade*, 321.
63. Clerc, *Prince: All the Songs*, 137.
64. Clerc, *Prince: All the Songs*, 137.
65. Clerc, *Prince: All the Songs*, 137.
66. Clerc, *Prince: All the Songs*, 132.
67. Clerc, *Prince: All the Songs*, 132.
68. Quoted in Jon Bream, "Jagger, Richards Feud; Stones Tour This Year Unlikely," *Minneapolis Star Tribune*, April 4, 1986, https://www.newspapers.com/article/star-tribune-bream-review-parade/123973643/.
69. Tudahl, *Prince and the Parade*, 344.
70. Richard Cromelin, "Prince & the Revolution: *Parade*: Music from the Motion Picture *Under the Cherry Moon* (Paisley Park)," *Los Angeles Times*, March 30, 1986.
71. Jon Bream, "'Parade' Is Marketing Savvy Test," *Minneapolis Star Tribune*, March 31, 1986, https://www.newspapers.com/article/star-tribune-parade-review/123973854/.
72. Steve Perry, "Prin's Phab Phunk," *City Pages*, April 9, 1986.
73. Perry, "Prin's Phab Phunk."
74. Tudahl, *Prince and the Parade*, 343.

75. Tudahl, *Prince and the Parade*, 347.
76. Clerc, *Prince: All the Songs*, 126.
77. Cromelin, "Prince & the Revolution."
78. Tudahl, *Prince and the Parade*, 345.

Chapter 14

1. Hill, *Prince*, 195.
2. See Sharpe, *In the Wake*.
3. Draper, *Prince*, 77.
4. Tudahl, *Prince and the Parade*, 452, 473.
5. Draper, *Prince*, 77.
6. Draper, *Prince*, 77.
7. Tudahl, *Prince and the Parade*, 473.
8. Thorne, *Prince*, 152; Swensson, "Story of *Sign o' the Times*, Episode 6."
9. Draper, *Prince*, 80.
10. Thorne, *Prince*, 152.
11. Thorne, *Prince*, 152–53.
12. Tudahl, *Prince and the Parade*, 429.
13. Swensson, "Story of *Sign o' the Times*, Episode 2"; Tudahl, *Prince and the Parade*, 400.
14. Foucault, *Herculine Barbin*.
15. Thorne, *Prince*, 173–76.
16. This could change. Rock musician Jack White is reported to be releasing the shelved project on his Third Man label. See Maloney and Masterson, "Artist Formerly Known as Camille."
17. Tudahl, *Prince and the Parade*, 477.
18. Tudahl, *Prince and the Parade*, 478.
19. Tudahl, *Prince and the Parade*, 442.
20. Tudahl, *Prince and the Parade*, 576.
21. Hahn and Tiebert, *Rise of Prince*, 293.
22. Draper, *Prince*, 83; Hahn and Tiebert, *Rise of Prince*, 293.
23. Tudahl, *Prince and the Parade*, 561.
24. Tudahl, *Prince and the Parade*, 478–79.
25. Clerc, *Prince: All the Songs*, 147.
26. Clerc, *Prince: All the Songs*, 147.
27. Tudahl, *Prince and the Parade*, 354.
28. Clerc, *Prince: All the Songs*, 150.
29. Tudahl, *Prince and the Parade*, 542–43.
30. *Rolling Stone*, "Sign o' the Times."
31. Joseph, "'Adore' Is the Love Song to End All Love Songs."
32. Touré, "Prince's Holy Lust," *New York Times*, April 22, 2016, https://www.nytimes.com/2016/04/24/opinion/sunday/princes-holy-lust.html.
33. Tudahl, *Prince and the Parade*, 561.

34. Tudahl, *Prince and the Parade*, 561–62.

35. Hahn and Tiebert, *Rise of Prince*, 297.

36. Ted Mico, "Prince: *Sign O' The Times* (WEA)," *Melody Maker*, April 4, 1987. Available online at Rock's Backpages, accessed November 5, 2025, http://www.rocksbackpages.com/Library/Article/prince-isign-o-the-timesi-wea.

37. Martin Keller, "Land of 1000 Voices: Sign o' the Times," *Twin Cities Reader*, April 8, 1987.

38. Loder, "Sign o' the Times."

39. Charles E. Rogers, "Different Stages: Prince Captures 'Sign o' the Times,'" *Amsterdam News* (New York), May 24, 1987.

40. Hunt, "Prince: Back To His Senses."

41. Keller, "Sign o' The Times."

42. Hill, *Prince*, 196.

43. Richard Harrington, "Prince, Back on Track," *Washington Post*, May 2, 1987.

44. Hahn and Tiebert, *Rise of Prince*, 297.

45. Loder, "Sign o' the Times."

46. Hill, *Prince*, 205.

47. Lizie, *Prince FAQ*, 91.

48. Clerc, *Prince: All the Songs*, 146–51.

49. Thorne, *Prince*, 197.

50. Tudahl, *Prince and the Parade*, 523.

Chapter 15

1. Martin Keller, "Smash Palace," *Twin Cities Reader*, September 2, 1987; Karsen, "Inside Story on Designing Prince's Paisley Park."

2. Karsen, "Inside Story on Designing Prince's Paisley Park."

3. Keller, "Smash Palace."

4. Keller, "Smash Palace."

5. Keller, "Smash Palace."

6. Martin Keller, "Reel Life in the Dream Factory," *Twin Cities Reader*, November 18, 1987.

7. Karsen, "Inside Story on Designing Prince's Paisley Park."

BIBLIOGRAPHY

Primary Sources

NEWSPAPERS

City Pages (Minneapolis)
Los Angeles Times
Minneapolis Journal
Minneapolis Morning Tribune
Minneapolis Spokesman
Minneapolis Star
Minneapolis Star and Tribune
Minneapolis Star Journal
Minneapolis Sunday Tribune
Minneapolis Tribune
Minnesota Daily Star
MINNPOST
New York Amsterdam News
New York Times
Star Tribune (Minneapolis)
Twin Cities Reader
Washington Post
Weekly Minnesotian (St. Paul)

Secondary Sources

Adler, Bill. "Will the Little Girls Understand?" *Rolling Stone*, February 19, 1981.

Alam, Ehsan. "First Avenue & 7th Street Entry." MNopedia (Minnesota Historical Society), 2017. https://www.mnopedia.org/place/first-avenue-7th-street-entry.

Amsterdam Academy of Architecture. *Music, Space and Architecture*. Architecture & Natura, 2012.

Anfinson, John. O. "12,000 Years at St. Anthony Falls." *Minnesota History* 58, no. 5–6 (2003). https://storage.googleapis.com/mnhs-org-support/mn_history_articles/58/v58i05-06p252-269.pdf.

Atkins, Annette. "At Home in the Heart of the City." *Minnesota History* 58, no. 5–6 (2003): 287–304.

Attali, Jacques. *Noise: The Political Economy of Music*. University of Minnesota Press, 2017.

Battle, Willa Lee Grant. "Music During the Great Depression—Vocal and Piano, 1929–1937, Oral Interview with Mrs. Nettie Hayes Sherman, 76 Years Old, 1976." Gale Family Library, Minnesota Historical Society.

Beck, Roger Lawrence. "Military Music at Fort Snelling, Minnesota, from 1819 to 1858." PhD diss., University of Minnesota, 1987. Gale Family Library, Minnesota Historical Society.

Bergin, Daniel Pierce, dir. *Jim Crow of the North*. PBS Video, 2019.

Billboard. "Billboard Hot 100." June 26, 1965. https://www.billboard.com/charts/hot-100/1965-06-26/.

Brothers, Thomas David. *Louis Armstrong's New Orleans*. W.W. Norton, 2006.

Burns, Ken, dir. *Jazz*. PBS Video, 2000.

Campbell, Thomas R. "ASI Records—Wes Hayne." Minniepaulmusic.com, 2011. https://www.minniepaulmusic.com/artists/group1/asi-records-wes-hayne/.

Canova, Nicolas. "Music in French Geography as Space Marker and Place Maker." *Social and Cultural Geography* 14, no. 8 (2013): 861–67.

Carmona, Michel. *Haussmann: His Life and Times, and the Making of Modern Paris*. Ivan R. Dee, 2000.

Carney, George. "Music Geography." *Journal of Cultural Geography* 18, no. 1 (2011): 1–10.

Chapman, Louis. "The First Fifty Years of Music in Minneapolis: A Chronology of Musical Events from 1850 to 1900. Compiled from Newspaper Sources by Louise Chapman."1944. Gale Family Library, Minnesota Historical Society.

Christensen, Tricia. "What Is New Wave Music?" Musical Expert.org, December 19, 2022. https://www.musicalexpert.org/what-is-new-wave-music.htm.

Clerc, Benoit. *Prince: All the Songs—The Story Behind Every Track*. Mitchell Beazley, 2022.

Cohen, Sara. "Sounding Out the City: Music and the Sensuous Production of Place." *Transactions of the Institute of British Geographers* 20, no. 4 (1995): 434–46.

Collins, Cyn. "Complicated Fun: The Birth of Minneapolis Punk and Indie Rock, 1974–1984— An Oral History." Minnesota Historical Society Press, 2017.

Connell, John, and Chris Gibson. *Sound Tracks: Popular Music, Identity and Place*. Routledge, 2002.

Crutcher, Michael E. *Tremé: Race and Place in a New Orleans Neighborhood*. University of Georgia Press, 2010.

Cruz, Luis Ramirez. "Blackface Minstrelsy in Minnesota." MNopedia (Minnesota Historical Society), January 23, 2024. http://www.mnopedia.org/thing/blackface-minstrelsy-minnesota.

Daniels, Douglas Henry. "North Side Jazz: Lester 'Pres' Young in Minneapolis, the Formative Years." *Minnesota History* 59, no. 3 (2004): 97–109.

Davis, Angela Y. *Women, Race and Class*. Random House, 1981.

Day, Holly, and Sherman Wick. *Nordeast Minneapolis: A History*. History Press, 2015.

Day, Morris, and David Ritz. *On Time: A Princely Life in Funk*. Da Capo, 2019.

Draper, Jason. *Prince: Chaos, Disorder, and Revolution*. Backbeat, 2011.

Du Bois, W. E. B. *Black Reconstruction in America*. Atheneum, 1935.

Dunbar-Ortiz, Roxanne. *An Indigenous Peoples' History of the United States*. Beacon Press, 2015.

Feisst, Sabine. "Music as Place, Place as Music: The Sonic Geography of John Luther Adams." In *The Farthest Place: The Music of John Luther Adams*, edited by Bernd Herzogenrath. University Press of New England, 2012.

Fisher, Rudolph. "The Caucasian Storms Harlem." *American Mercury*, 1927.

Foucault, Michel. *Discipline and Punish: The Birth of the Prison*. Vintage, 1976.

Foucault, Michel. *Herculine Barbin (Being the Recently Discovered Memoirs of a Nineteenth-Century French Hermaphrodite)*. Vintage, 1980.

Foucault, Michel. "Nietzche, Genealogy, History." In *The Essential Foucault*, ed. Paul Rabinow. New Press, 1994.

Fridley, Russell W. "Fort Snelling: From Military Post to Historic Site." *Minnesota History*, December 1956, 178–92.

Gelly, Dave. *Being Prez: The Life and Music of Lester Young*. Equinox, 2007.

Giddings, Thaddeus Philander. *Course in Music*, 1915.

Giddings, Thaddeus Philander. *In a Major Key: Music in Minneapolis Schools: Why It Is Taught, How It Is Taught and What the Results Are*. Minneapolis School Board, 1916.

Giddings, Thaddeus Philander. *School Music Teaching*. C.H. Congdon, 1909.

Gilbert, Will, Eric Foss, and Danny Sigelman. "Twin Cities Funk & Soul." *Secret Stash*, September 25, 2012.

Goetting, Jay. *Joined at the Hip: A History of Jazz in the Twin Cities*. St. Paul: Minnesota Historical Society Press, 2011.

Goodman, Glenda. "'But They Differ from Us in Sound': Indian Psalmody and the Soundscape of Colonialism, 1651–75." *William and Mary Quarterly* 69, no. 4 (2012).

Goosman, Stuart L. *Group Harmony: The Black Urban Roots of Rhythm and Blues*. University of Pennsylvania Press, 2005.

Governor's Interracial Commission. *The Negro and His Home in Minnesota: A Report to Governor Luther W. Youngdahl of Minnesota*. June 1, 1947. https://www.lrl.mn.gov/docs/pre2003/other/I540.pdf.

Governor's Interracial Commission. *The Negro Worker in Minnesota: A Report to Governor Edward J. Thye of Minnesota by the Governor's Interracial Commission*. March 10, 1945. https://www.lrl.mn.gov/docs/pre2003/other/I537.pdf.

Hahn, Alex, and Laura Tiebert. *The Rise of Prince: 1958–1988*. Mad Cat, 2017.

Haines, Michael. "Social Explorer Dataset (SE), Census 1850." Digitally transcribed by Inter-University Consortium for Political and Social Research. Edited and verified by Michael Haines. Compiled, Edited and Verified by Social Explorer. https://pearson.socialexplorer.com/data/Census1850/metadata/.

Haines, Michael. "Social Explorer Dataset (SE), Census 1900." Digitally transcribed by Inter-University Consortium for Political and Social Research. Edited and verified by Michael Haines; compiled, edited, and verified by Social Explorer. https://www.socialexplorer.com/data/Census1900/metadata/.

Harrison, Leigh Michael. "Factory Music: How the Industrial Geography and Working-Class Environment of Postwar Birmingham Fostered the Birth of Heavy Metal." *Journal of Social History* 44, no. 1 (2010): 145–58.

Hase, Michiko. "W. Gertrude Brown's Struggle for Racial Justice: Female Leadership and Community in Black Minneapolis, 1920–1940." PhD diss., University of Minnesota, 1994.

Hennepin, Louis. *A Description of Louisiana*. Readex Microprint, 1966.
Hill, Dave. *Prince: A Pop Life*. Faber and Faber, 1989.
Hoffman, Claire. "Prince's Life as a Jehovah's Witness: His Complicated and Ever-Evolving Faith." *Hollywood Reporter*, April 28, 2016. https://www.hollywoodreporter.com/news/music-news/princes-life-as-a-jehovahs-888584/.
Holden, Stephen. "Controversy." *Rolling Stone*, January 21, 1982.
Holmquist, June Drenning. *They Chose Minnesota: A Survey of the State's Ethnic Groups*. Minnesota Historical Society Press, 1981.
Horn, Gerald. *Jazz and Justice: Racism and the Political Economy of the Music*. Monthly Review Press, 2019.
Hughes, Langston. *The Collected Poems of Langston Hughes*. Edited by Arnold Rampersad and David Roessel. Vintage, 1994.
Huw, Rhodri, dir. *Prince: A Purple Reign*. The Orchard, 2011.
Jensen, Jeff. "The Weird, Wonderful, World of Prince." *Entertainment Weekly*, April 23, 2004. Prince Interview Archive. https://sites.google.com/site/prninterviews/home/entertainment-weekly-761–23-april-2004?pli=1.
Johnson, Stephen, ed. *Burnt Cork: Traditions and Legacies of Blackface Minstrelsy*. University of Massachusetts Press, 2012.
Joseph, Mike. "'Adore' Is the Love Song to End All Love Songs: 365 Prince Songs in a Year." *Diffuser*, February 23, 2018. https://diffuser.fm/prince-adore/.
Kane, Lucile M. *The Waterfall That Built a City*. Minnesota Historical Society Press, 1966.
Karlen, Neal. *This Thing Called Life: Prince's Odyssey on + off the Record*. St. Martin's, 2020.
Karsen, Shira. "The Inside Story on Designing Prince's Paisley Park: Exclusive." April 22, 2016. https://www.billboard.com/music/music-news/prince-paisley-park-architect-design-7341629/.
Kendi, Ibram X. *Stamped from the Beginning: A History of Racist Ideas*. Nation Books, 2016.
Krims, Adam. *Music and Urban Geography*. Routledge, 2007.
Lass, William E. *Minnesota: A History*. 2nd ed. W. W. Norton, 1998.
Lehmen, Christopher P. *Slavery's Reach: Southern Slaveholders in the North Star State*. Minnesota Historical Society Press, 2019.
Leyshon, Andrew, David Matless, and George Revill, eds. *The Place of Music*. Guilford, 1998.
Light, Alan. *Let's Go Crazy: Prince and the Making of Purple Rain*. Atria, 2014.
Lipps Inc. "Funkytown." On Mouth to Mouth. Casablanca Records, 1980.
Lipsitz, George. *Footsteps in the Dark: The Hidden Histories of Popular Music*. University of Minnesota Press, 2007.
Lizie, Arthur. *Prince FAQ: All That's Left to Know About the Purple Reign*. Backbeat, 2020.
Lizie, Arthur. *Prince on Prince*. Chicago Review Press, 2023.
Loder, Kurt. "Purple Rain (Soundtrack)." *Rolling Stone*, 1984. https://www.rollingstone.com/music/music-album-reviews/purple-rain-soundtrack-99312/.
Loder, Kurt. "Sign o' the Times." *Rolling Stone*, 1987.

Lott, Eric. *Love and Theft: Blackface Minstrelsy and the American Working Class*. Oxford University Press, 2013.

Lydon, Michael. *Ray Charles: Man and Music*. Taylor & Francis Group, 2004.

Maloney, Liam, and Alice Masterson. "The Artist Formerly Known as Camille: Prince's Lost Album 'Comes Out.'" *The Conversation*, January 31, 2023. https://theconversation.com/the-artist-formerly-known-as-camille-princes-lost-album-comes-out-189486.

Mapping Inequality: Redlining in New Deal America. "Minneapolis, Minnesota, Area D3." n.d. https://dsl.richmond.edu/panorama/redlining/#loc=11/44.973/-93.411&city=minneapolis-mn&area=D3.

Marsh, Steve. "First Avenue's Star Wall." *Mpls. St. Paul Magazine*, May 13, 2019. http://mspmag.com/api/content/6147952c-7283–11e9-bd6a-12f1225286c6/.

Martin, Judith A., and Anthony Goddard. *The Impact of Urban Renewal on the Twin Cities*. Center for Urban and Regional Affairs, Hubert H. Humphrey Center, 1989.

Matrix Basement System. "An Insight into the History of Basements." 2016. https://www.mymatrixbasement.com/blog/p.161205044/an-insight-into-the-history-of-basements/.

Maxwell, Tom. "A History of American Protest Music: How the Hutchinson Family Singers Achieved Pop Stardom with an Anti-Slavery Anthem." Longreads, March 7, 2017. http://longreads.com/2017/03/07/a-history-of-american-protest-music-how-the-hutchinson-family-singers-achieved-pop-stardom-with-an-anti-slavery-anthem/.

Maynard, Charles. *Thaddeus P. Giddings: A Biography*. University of Michigan Press, 1967.

McBride, James. *Kill 'Em and Leave: Searching for James Brown and the American Soul*. Spiegel & Grau, 2016.

McCourt, Tom. "Bright Lights, Big City: A Brief History of Rhythm and Blues, 1945–1957." *Popular Music & Society* 9, no. 2 (2008): 1–18.

Millett, Larry. "Ghost of the Gateway: The Metropolitan Building, Minneapolis." *Minnesota History*, 53, no. 3 (1992): 112–15. https://storage.googleapis.com/mnhs-org-support/mn_history_articles/53/v53i03p112-115.pdf.

Mills, Ted. "Read Prince's First Interview, Printed in His High School Newspaper (1976)." *Open Culture*, January 26, 2017. https://www.openculture.com/2017/01/read-princes-first-interview-in-his-high-school-paper-in-1976.html.

Minneapolis Public School Board. "Bryant Junior High School." 1962. https://mpshistory.mpls.k12.mn.us/uploads/pff-1963-bryant.pdf.

Minneapolis Public School Board. "Lincoln Junior High." Minneapolis, 1962. Archives of the Hennepin County Library, Minneapolis.

Minneapolis Public School System. "Central Senior High School." Minneapolis, 1967. Archives of the Hennepin County Library, Minneapolis.

Minutaglio, Rose. "Prince's First Music Teacher: 'He Was at the Band Room Door at 8 a.m. Sharp Every Day Waiting to Be Let In.'" *People*, April 26, 2016. https://people.com/celebrity/princes-first-music-teacher-opens-up-about-singer-as-a-student/.

Moon, Chris. "History of Moon Sound Studios." n.d. https://moonsoundstudios.com/index.php/about/.

Morrison, Matthew D. *Blacksound: Making Race and Popular Music in the United States*. University of California Press, 2024.

Morton, Brian. *Prince: A Thief in the Temple*. Canongate, 2007.

Northwestern National Life Insurance Company. "Early Music in Minnesota." 1948.

O'Boyle, Maureen. "Interview With John L. Nelson." *A Current Affair*, 1991. https://www.youtube.com/watch?v=Byr-TaMiogA&t=82s.

Paulsen, Sarah Jayne. "Black Power and Neighborhood Organizing in Minneapolis, Minnesota: The Way Community Center, 1966–1971." University of South Carolina, 2018.

Petersen, P. A. 2013. *Minneapolis Madams: The Lost History of Prostitution on the Riverfront*. University of Minnesota Press, 2013.

Petry, Ben. "Sights, Sounds, and Soul: Twin Cities through the Lens of Charles Chamblis." *Minnesota History*, no. Spring (2014): 18–33. https://www.jstor.org/stable/43492656.

Piepenbring, Dan, ed. *Prince: The Beautiful Ones*. Spiegel & Grau, 2019.

Pike, Denise. "Old Southside Minneapolis and the 35W Dividing Line." A Public History of 35W, April 29, 2020. https://humantoll35w.org/essays/old-southside-minneapolis-and-the-35w-dividing-line/. Accessed August 7, 2023. Site discontinued.

Prince. "Paisley Park." On *Around the World in a Day*. Sunset Sound, Warner Bros., 1985.

Purple Rain. Warner Bros., 1984.

Riemenschnieider, Chris. *First Avenue: Minnesota's Mainroom*. Minnesota Historical Society Press, 2017.

Ripani, Richard J. *New Blue Music: Changes in Rhythm & Blues, 1950–1999*. University of Mississippi Press, 2006.

Rogers, Susan, and Ogi Ogas. *This Is What It Sounds Like: What the Music You Love Says About You*. W. W. Norton, 2022.

Rolling Stone. "Sign o' the Times." October 8, 2002. https://www.rollingstone.com/music/music-album-reviews/sign-o-the-times-190234/.

Rosie, Charlene, Elizabeth Gales, Kristin Koehlinger, Katheryn Goetz, and Kristen Zschomler. *Minneapolis Music History, 1850–2000: A Context*. Report prepared for the City of Minneapolis, 2018.

Sacks, Howard L. "Turning About Jim Crow." Review of *Raising Cain: Blackface Performance from Jim Crow to Hip Hop*, by W. T. Lhamon Jr., *American Quarterly* 51, no. 1 (1999): 187–94.

Schmid, Calvin Fisher. *Social Saga of Two Cities: An Ecological and Statistical Study of Social Trends in Minneapolis and St. Paul*. Bureau of Social Research, Minneapolis Council of Social Agencies, 1937.

Shabazz, Rashad. "How Prince Introduced Us to the 'Minneapolis Sound.'" *What It Means to Be American*, September 7, 2017. https://www.whatitmeanstobeamerican.org/places/how-prince-introduced-us-to-the-minneapolis-sound/.

Shabazz, Rashad. "Minneapolis's 'Long, Hot Summer' of '67—and the Parallels to Today's Protests over Police Brutality." *The Conversation*, June 5, 2020. https://theconversation.com/minneapolis-long-hot-summer-of-67-and-the-parallels-to-todays-protests-over-police-brutality-139814.

Shabazz, Rashad. "Prince & Place: A Primer on the Geography of Music." *Places*, November 2021. https://placesjournal.org/article/prince-minneapolis-geography-of-music/.

Sharpe, Christina. *In the Wake: On Blackness and Being*. Duke University Press, 2016.

Shiffer, James Eli. *The King of Skid Row: John Bacich and the Twilight Years of Old Minneapolis*. University of Minnesota Press, 2016.

Sirdar, Deebaa, and Richard L. Kronick. "Tilsenbilt Homes Historic District." Minneapolis Historical Society. https://minneapolishistorical.org/items/show/174. Accessed March 2, 2022. Site discontined.

Spangler, Earl. *The Negro in Minnesota*. T. S. Denison, 1961.

Stahl, Le Roy. *Five Star Minstrel Book*. Northwestern University Press, n.d.

Swensson, Andrea. *Got to Be Something Here: The Rise of the Minneapolis Sound*. University of Minnesota Press, 2017.

Swensson, Andrea. "Prince: The Story of 1999, Episode 3, The Idolmaker." *Prince: Official Podcast*, December 3, 2019. https://podcasts.apple.com/us/podcast/prince-the-story-of-1999-episode-3-the-idolmaker/id1488187430?i=1000526528937.

Swensson, Andrea. "The Story of *Sign o' the Times*, Episode 2: The Dream Factory." *Prince: Official Podcast*, September 3, 2020. https://podcasts.apple.com/us/podcast/the-story-of-sign-o-the-times-episode-2-the-dream-factory/id1488187430?i=1000526528995.

Swensson, Andrea. "The Story of *Sign o' the Times*, Episode 6: Pop Goes the Music." *Prince: Official Podcast*, October 1, 2020. https://podcasts.apple.com/us/podcast/the-story-of-sign-o-the-times-episode-6-pop-goes-the-music/id1488187430?i=1000526528849.

Tate, Greg. "Stagolee Versus the Proper Negro: The Treacherous Three Cross Over—Prince, Wynton Marsalis, and Eddie Murphy." In *Flyboy in the Buttermilk*. Simon and Schuster, 1992.

Taylor, David V. *African Americans in Minnesota*. Minnesota Historical Society Press, 2002.

Thorne, Matt. *Prince*. Faber and Faber, 2012.

Touré. "Alone in a World That's So Cold." *Who Was Prince?*, podcast, July 5, 2021. https://podcasts.apple.com/us/podcast/alone-in-a-world-thats-so-cold/id1508759059?i=1000527846383.

Touré. "Honey, I'm Rich on Personality." *Who Was Prince?*, podcast, June 19, 2021. https://podcasts.apple.com/us/podcast/honey-im-rich-on-personality/id1508759059?i=1000526088768.

Tucker, Ken. "Dirty Mind." *Rolling Stone*, February 19, 1981.

Tudahl, Duane. *Prince and the Parade & Sign o' the Times Era Studio Sessions, 1985 and 1986*. Roman & Littlefield, 2021.

Tudahl, Duane. *Prince and the Purple Rain Studio Era Sessions, 1983 and 1984*. Expanded ed. Roman & Littlefield, 2018.

Turino, Thomas. *Music as Social Life: The Politics of Participation*. University of Chicago Press, 2008.

Twin Cities Music Highlights. "Labor Temple." n.d. http://twincitiesmusichighlights.net/venues/labor-temple/.

Twin Cities Music Highlights. "Nacirema Club." n.d. http://twincitiesmusichighlights.net/venues/nacirema-club/.

Twin Cities Music Highlights. "A Brief History of Radio," n.d. https://twincitiesmusichighlights.net/radio/a-brief-history-of-radio/.

US Census Bureau. Fourteenth Census of the United States—Population (1920). National Archives, Washington, DC.

US Census Bureau. Twelfth Census of the Unites States—Population (1900). National Archives, Washington, DC.

US Census Bureau. United States Voter Return, Precinct No. 3, State of Georgia, Board of Elections, 1870. Twelfth Census of the Unites States—Population (1900). National Archives, Washington, DC.

Walker, Charles Rumford. *American City: A Rank and File History of Minneapolis*. University of Minnesota Press, 2005. Originally published in 1937 by Farrar and Rinehart.

Wilkerson, Isabel. *The Warmth of Other Suns: The Epic Story of America's Great Migration*. Vintage, 2011.

Wilkins, Craig L. *The Aesthetics of Equity: Notes on Race, Space, Architecture, and Music*. University of Minnesota Press, 2007.

Willie, Pepé, with Tony Kiene. *If You See Me: My Six-Decade Journey in Rock and Roll*. Minnesota Historical Society Press, 2020.

Wills, Jocelyn. *Boosters, Hustlers, and Speculators: Entrepreneurial Culture and the Rise of Minneapolis and St. Paul, 1849–1883*. Minnesota Historical Society Press, 2004.

Wood, Nichola, Michelle Duffy, and Susan J. Smith. "The Art of Doing (Geographies of) Music." *Environment and Planning D: Society and Space* 25 (2007): 867–89.

Woods, Donald Zacher. "Playhouse for Pioneers: The Story of the Pence Opera House." *Minnesota History* 33, no. 4 (1952); 169–78.

Zellie, Carole. "Minneapolis Public Schools Historic Context Study." Landscape Research, 2005.

Zschomler, Kristen. "National Register of Historic Places Multiple Property Documentation Form." US Department of the Interior, National Park Service, 2020.

INDEX